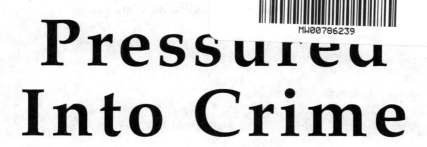

Pressured Into Crime

An Overview of General Strain Theory

Robert Agnew
Emory University

Roxbury Publishing Company
Los Angeles, California

Library of Congress Cataloging-in-Publication Data
Agnew, Robert, 1953–
Pressured into crime: an overview of general strain theory / Robert
Agnew.—1st ed.
    p. cm.
Includes bibliographical references.
ISBN 1-933220-25-2 (alk. paper)
1. Criminology. 2. Crime. 3. Criminal behavior. I. Title.

HV6018.A35 2006
364.3—dc22   2005019857

Publisher: Claude Teweles
Managing Editor: Dawn VanDercreek
Production Editor: Sacha A. Howells
Production Assistant: Nina M. Hickey
Typography: SDS Design, info@sds-design.com
Cover Design: Marnie Kenney

Printed on acid-free paper in the United States of America. This book
meets the standards for recycling of the Environmental Protection Agency.

ISBN 1-933220-25-2

ROXBURY PUBLISHING COMPANY
P. O. Box 491044
Los Angeles, California 90049-9044
Voice: (310) 473-3312 • Fax: (310) 473-4490
Email: roxbury@roxbury.net
Website: www.roxbury.net

Acknowledgments

This book is dedicated to Mary, Willie, and Jenny Agnew. I would also like to thank the following people for their helpful comments and suggestions on earlier versions of this book: Katherine Bennett, Armstrong Atlantic State University; George Capowichi, Loyola University of New Orleans; Keith E. Clement, University of West Florida; Ellen Cohn, Florida International University; Gregory J. DeLone, University of Nebraska at Omaha; Richard G. Hogan, University of Tennessee–Chattanooga; Sung Joon Jang, Louisiana State University; Kent Kerley, Mississippi State University; Alex Piquero, University of Florida; Pam Preston, Pennsylvania State University; Callie Rennison, University of Missouri–St. Louis; Steven Stack, Wayne State University; Michael Turner, University of North Carolina–Charlotte; and Judy Van Wyk, University of Rhode Island. And special thanks to Claude Teweles, Sacha A. Howells, and Scott Carter for their help in preparing the book for publication. ✦

Contents

Chapter 1

Why Do Individuals Engage in Crime?

Why do individuals engage in crime? Below are several explanations for individual offending. All are quotes from criminals who were asked why they engaged in crime or were thinking about doing so.

> [The idea of committing an armed robbery] comes into your mind when your pockets are low; it speaks very loudly when you need things and you are not able to get what you need. (Quote from an armed robber [Wright and Decker, 1997:33])

> My stepfather . . . used to sexually assault me a lot. And uh, I got fed up with it, and once I turned 13, I started running away. (Quote from a runaway living on the street [Hagan and McCarthy, 1997:29])

> I worked as a busboy for a week once. It was like being a pig in everyone else's slop. Why should I put up with that shit? . . . Doing crime is a lot more fun and pays a lot better. (Quote from a criminal [Fleming, 2003:101])

> I get depressed. Things start to pile up and I start shoplifting. Sometimes it's at finals [final exams] or when I have a fight with my boyfriend. One time when I thought I was pregnant. Who knows why. It's like I take out my feelings on them [the stores]. (Quote from a shoplifter [Cromwell, Parker, and Parker, 2003:117])

1

It was my way of getting even. You know, teachers were saying and doing all this nasty shit, and I wasn't going to put up
with that anymore. . . . I guess I was trying to protect my dig-
nity. . . . To them I was like shit. Just because you're Puerto
Rican or Latino, they treat you like dirt. (Quote from a delinquent describing why he misbehaved at school [Padilla,
2003:245])

That night I was really pissed off about a lot of things. . . . I
had been looking for a job, and that was not going well.
Money was tight, and I was getting hassled over the bills. I
was just mad at everything in general, nothing seemed to be
going my way. And then, out in the bar, I saw this girl who
seemed to have it all together, who seemed to have a lot. I
decided right then and there I was going to show her before
the night was over what it was like to lose something . . .
what it felt like to hurt. (Quote from a rapist [Hale, 2004:58])

We were at the White Castle one day and one of my partners
stepped on this guy's foot. . . . He punched my partner in the
face and we just got to fighting. (Quote from a gang member
[Decker and Van Winkle, 1996:177])

One of the guys said that he had fucked this guy's sister and
he heard it and they got to fighting. . . . He was just defending his sister's name. (Quote from another gang member
[Decker and Van Winkle, 1996:178])

I was faced with the choice of all of a sudden, and I mean
now, closing the doors or doing something else to keep that
business open. . . . You're sitting there with a dying patient.
You are going to try to keep him alive. (Quote from an
offender who passed "bad" checks [Benson, 2004:177])

These quotes illustrate the central ideas behind general strain
theory (GST), one of the leading theories of crime. *According to GST,
people engage in crime because they experience strains or stressors.* For example, they are in desperate need of money or they believe they are
being mistreated by family members, teachers, peers, employers, or
others. *They become upset, experiencing a range of negative emotions, including anger, frustration, and depression. And they cope with their
strains and negative emotions through crime. Crime may be a way to re-*

duce or escape from strains. For example, individuals engage in theft to obtain the money they desperately need or they run away from home to escape their abusive parents. *Crime may be a way for individuals to seek revenge against those who have wronged them.* For example, individuals assault those who have mistreated them. *And crime may be a way to alleviate the negative emotions that result from strains.* For example, individuals use drugs to make themselves feel better.

Not all individuals respond to strains with crime. If someone steps on your foot, for example, you are probably unlikely to respond by punching the person. *Some people are more likely than others to cope with strains through crime. Criminal coping is more likely when people lack the ability to cope in a legal manner.* For example, crime is more likely when people do not have the verbal skills to negotiate with those who mistreat them or do not have others they can turn to for help. *Criminal coping is more likely when the costs of crime are low.* For example, crime is more likely when people are in environments where the likelihood of being sanctioned for crime is low. *And criminal coping is more likely when people are disposed to crime.* For example, assault is more likely when people believe that violence is an appropriate response to being treated in a disrespectful manner.

I briefly elaborate on these arguments in this chapter. First, I describe what I mean by *strains* or *stressors*. Next, I describe why strains increase the likelihood of crime. I then discuss why some people are more likely than others to respond to strains with crime. I conclude by discussing how GST differs from other major theories of crime. GST is just one of several theories of crime, but it is distinguished from other theories by its argument that individuals are *pressured into crime by the strains they experience.*

Chapters 2 through 4 of this book provide a fuller description of GST. Chapter 2 explores in detail the reasons why strains lead to crime. Chapter 3 discusses the types of strains most likely to lead to crime. And Chapter 4 examines why some individuals are more likely than others to respond to strains with crime. Chapters 5 through 7 then use GST to explain many of the basic facts about crime, including why crime is higher among adolescents, males, lower-class individuals, members of certain racial and ethnic groups, residents of disadvantaged communities, and members of certain societies. Chapter 8 draws on GST to recommend several strategies for controlling crime. And Chapter 9 summarizes the key points made in this book and discusses the future of GST, including efforts to combine GST with other theories of crime. This book, then, provides an overview of one of the leading theories of crime.

What Are Strains?

Strains refer to events or conditions that are disliked by individuals. There are three major types of strains. *Individuals may lose something they value (lose something good).* Perhaps their money or property is stolen, a close friend or family member dies, or a romantic partner breaks up with them. *Individuals may be treated in an aversive or negative manner by others (receive something bad).* Perhaps they are sexually or physically abused by a family member, their peers insult or ridicule them, or their employer treats them in a disrespectful manner. Finally, *individuals may be unable to achieve their goals (fail to get something they want).* Perhaps they have less money, status, or autonomy than they want.

I sometimes ask the students in my juvenile delinquency and criminology classes to list the strains or stressors they have recently experienced. The strains they list are generally less severe than those listed at the start of this chapter, but they nevertheless illustrate the three major types of strains. A few examples follow:

I lost the paper that I was working on on my computer. I was almost done.

My roommate took my ethernet card with him to New Jersey without asking.

I got into a huge fight with my best friend and completely terminated our relationship.

My cheating ex is now engaged to the person he cheated with.

My roommate yelled at me for no good reason.

When I left for college this fall, I got into a fight with my dad right before leaving.

I was yelled at from a moving vehicle for biking in the near empty street, which I thought was legal.

When my light turned green, the intersection was blocked with cars running the red light. . . . Another car proceeded to clog the intersection. . . . I honked and pointed to his red light and he flipped me off.

I recently received a poor grade on a test that I had studied a fair amount for.

I didn't have enough time to finish my Sex and Gender class exam, even though I knew the answers.

To give you a more complete idea of the types of strains examined by GST, Table 1.1 lists the strains examined by a few researchers who have tested GST. Two of the tests were conducted on samples of adolescents, while the third was conducted on a sample of college undergraduates. Each test found that individuals who experienced some or all of the indicated strains were more likely to engage in crime. When examining this list of strains, ask yourself whether you can think of any additional strains that were *not* examined. Also, ask yourself whether some types of strains may be more likely to lead to crime than others (see Chapter 3). For example, which type of strain do you think is most likely to lead to crime, experiencing health problems or being criminally victimized?

Table 1.1 The Types of Strains Examined in Several Tests of General Strain Theory (GST)

A. From Paternoster and Mazerolle's (1994) Test of GST (with a sample of adolescents).

- Negative life events: Respondents report that they have experienced a number of stressful life events in the last year, such as the divorce/separation of parents, death or serious injury to a family member, parental unemployment, or changing schools.

- Neighborhood problems: Respondents report that they live in neighborhoods where vandalism, winos and junkies, traffic, abandoned houses, burglaries and thefts, and assaults and muggings are serious problems.

**Table 1.1   The Types of Strain Examined in Several Tests of
General Strain Theory (GST)—*continued***

- Negative relations with adults: Respondents report that they have poor relations with their parents and teachers. They state, for example, that their parents and teachers think they are "bad kids," that teachers do not call on them, and that they feel like outsiders within their families.

- School/peer hassles: Respondents state that they feel lonely and rejected by peers.

- Goal blockage: Respondents state that there is little chance they will be able to get a college degree or the type of job they would like.

B. From Mazerolle and Piquero's (1998) Test of GST (with a sample of college undergraduates).

- Failure to achieve positively valued goals: Respondents state that getting a college degree is important, but their chances for getting a degree are not high. Also, respondents state that during the last year they have received a lower grade than they deserved or a grade that was "unfair compared to the grade received by others in the course."

- Presentation of noxious stimuli: Respondents state that vandalism, winos and junkies, abandoned houses, burglaries and thefts, run-down and poorly kept buildings, and assaults and muggings are serious problems in their neighborhoods. Also, respondents state that the following events occurred in their homes in the past year: divorce, separation, or "father move in/out."

- Removal of positive stimuli: Respondents state that in the last year a "significant other" such as a boyfriend or girlfriend has broken up with them and that a "friend has broken off their friendship with [them]."

Table 1.1 The Types of Strain Examined in Several Tests of General Strain Theory (GST)—*continued*

C. From Aseltine et al.'s (2000) Test of GST (with an adolescent sample).

- Life stresses: Respondents report that they have experienced a number of stressful life events in the last year, including school problems, money problems, job difficulties, rape or criminal victimization, pregnancy, leaving home, health problems, parent or sibling health problems, parent or sibling legal problems, parental separation or remarriage, relationship problems between parents, parent job difficulties, or parental death.

- Family conflict: Respondents report that they frequently argue with their mothers and fathers and family members frequently argue with one another.

- Peer conflict: Respondents report that their peers criticize them, make too many demands on them, and "create tensions or arguments" while they are around them.

The Strains Examined in Other Versions of Strain Theory

General strain theory was not created "out of thin air." GST draws quite heavily on the work of others, especially the work of other strain theorists. If you are taking a criminology course, you may have examined other versions of strain theory. Each of these versions focuses on one or a few strains, with these strains usually involving the inability of individuals to achieve their goals.

Robert Merton (1938), Albert Cohen (1955), and Richard Cloward and Lloyd Ohlin (1960) pioneered the development of strain theory in criminology. They focus on that type of strain involving the inability to achieve the goal of monetary success or, in the case of Cohen, the somewhat broader goal of middle-class status. They argue that everyone in the United States—poor as well as rich—is encouraged to pursue the goal of monetary success or middle-class status. They are encouraged by family members, teachers, friends, politicians, the mass media, and others. But at the same time, significant segments of the population are prevented from achieving those goals through legal channels, like getting a good education and then a good job. This is especially true of the lower class. Lower-class families are often unable to provide their children with the skills and resources necessary to do well in school. Such families also lack the money and connections to set their children up in business. And lower-class individuals often live in communities with poor schools and a lack of decent jobs. As a consequence, lower-class individuals often find that they are unable to achieve monetary success or middle-class status through legal channels. Some of these individuals respond with crime; for example, they attempt to achieve their monetary goals through theft, prostitution, or drug selling.

Greenberg (1977) focuses on the inability of some adolescents to (a) get the money they need to finance their social activities, and (b) achieve the freedom or autonomy they desire, especially from school authorities (also see Moffitt, 1993; Tittle, 1995). Such adolescents may cope with these strains by committing income-generating crimes like theft, and by skipping school, flouting school rules, and vandalizing school property. Elliott and Voss (1974), Quicker (1974), and Agnew (1984) argue that adolescents often pursue a broad range of goals, including academic achievement, popularity with peers, athletic success, and getting along with parents. Some adolescents, however, have trouble achieving these goals through legitimate channels and may turn to crime as a result.

Messerschmidt (1993) and others focus on the inability of some males to "accomplish masculinity," or act in a "manly manner" in particular settings. Different groups have somewhat different views about what it means to be a "man," but most such views emphasize characteristics like "work in the paid-labor market, the subordination of women, heterosexism, control, competitive individualism, independence, and aggressiveness" (Messerschmidt, 1993:82). When males have trouble "acting manly" in a particular setting, they may attempt to "accomplish masculinity" through crime. So, for example, they may respond to subordination experienced at school by engaging in a range of disruptive behaviors like vandalism and fighting—behaviors designed to demonstrate masculine traits like independence and control (also see Anderson, 1999; Billson, 1996; Greenberg, 1977; Mullins et al., 2004).

Finally, Colvin (2000) focuses on that type of strain involving co-ercion, where people are compelled to act in a certain way through force or the threat of unpleasant consequences. Those types of coercion that are related to crime include harsh, excessive, and erratic discipline by parents; demeaning treatment by teachers; physical and verbal abuse by peers; and abusive treatment at work, including threats of dismissal. Such coercion may lead to crime for several reasons, including the anger it provokes.

General strain theory examines all of these types of strain and more. Furthermore, GST draws heavily on stress research in psychology and sociology (see Thoits, 1995 for an overview). While most strain theorists focus on that type of strain involving the inability to achieve your goals, stress researchers focus on the loss of those things we value and negative or aversive treatment by others. The fact that GST examines such a broad range of strains is the primary reason for the term *general* in general strain theory.

Objective and Subjective Strains

Some events and conditions are disliked by *most* people, or at least by most people in a given group. For example, most people dislike being physically assaulted or deprived of adequate food and shelter. And it has been argued that most males dislike having their masculine status called into question (Messerschmidt, 1993). I refer to these events and conditions as *objective strains,* because they are generally disliked. It is possible to measure the objective strains for a group of people in several ways (see Agnew, 2001). Perhaps the best method is to interview a carefully selected sample of group members or people familiar with the group. We can ask these people how much they (or the group members) would dislike a range of events and conditions (see Turner, Wheaton, and Lloyd 1995).

It is important to keep in mind, however, that people sometimes differ in their subjective evaluation of the same events and conditions—even those events and conditions classified as objective strains. So a given objective strain, like a death in the family, may be strongly disliked by one person, but only mildly disliked by another. This is because the subjective evaluation of objective strains is influenced by a range of factors, including people's personality traits, goals and values, and prior experiences (see Dohrenwend, 1998; Kaplan, 1996; Lazarus, 1999). Wheaton (1990), for example, found that there was some variation in how people evaluated their divorces. Among other things, the quality of their prior marriages strongly influenced their evaluations, with people in bad marriages evaluating their divorces in positive terms. I therefore make a distinction between objective and *subjective strains*. While an objective strain refers to an event or condition that is disliked by most people or most people in a given group, a subjective strain refers to an event or condition that is disliked by the particular person or persons being examined (see Agnew, 2001). As just suggested, there is only partial overlap between objective and subjective strains.

Most of the research on strain theory focuses on objective strains. Researchers ask respondents whether they have experienced events and conditions that are assumed to be disliked. For example, they ask respondents whether they have received failing grades at school. No attempt is made to measure the respondents' subjective evaluation of these events and conditions (although see Agnew and White, 1992; Landau, 1997; Sharp et al., 2001). This may cause researchers to underestimate the effect of strains on crime, because objective strains are *not* always disliked by the individuals being examined. Some people, for example, may not be particularly bothered by the fact that they have received failing grades. It is therefore desirable for criminologists to measure *both* the individual's exposure to objective strains and the individual's *subjective evaluation* of those strains (e.g., ask individuals whether they have received failing grades *and*, if so, how much they dislike such grades).[1]

Experienced, Vicarious, and Anticipated Strains

Strain theory focuses on individuals' *personal experiences with strains;* that is, did they personally experience disliked events or conditions? For example, were they physically assaulted? Personal experiences with strains should bear the strongest relationship to crime. However, it is sometimes important to consider the individual's vicarious and anticipated experiences with strains as well (see Agnew, 2002; Eitle and Turner, 2003).

Vicarious strains refer to the strains experienced by others around individuals, especially close others like family members and friends. For example, were any of their family members or friends physically assaulted? Vicarious strains can also upset individuals and lead to criminal coping. Agnew (2002), for example, found that individuals were more likely to engage in crime if they reported that their family members and friends had been victims of serious assaults (also see Eitle and Turner, 2002; Maxwell, 2001; Mullins et al., 2004). This held true even after Agnew took into account other factors, like individuals' own victimization experiences and prior criminal history. Agnew argued that vicarious strains may have increased the likelihood of crime for several reasons. For example, perhaps individuals were seeking revenge against those who had victimized their families and friends, or perhaps they were seeking to prevent the perpetrators from causing further harm.

Two examples of the effect of vicarious strains on crime are reported below.

> If a [gang] member becomes a victim, revenge [by the other gang members] is necessary. And this revenge is schismogenic, resulting in an increasing cycle of retaliation and revenge. (From Decker and Van Winkle's [1996:179–80] study of gangs)

> John understood full well the risks of venturing into the enemy territory that was Audrey's neighborhood. He had been involved with her for about six months. At that point Audrey was being harassed by some of the boys and girls in her neighborhood. For several days they had been bothering her, sitting and standing outside her house, teasing her and calling her names. This had been happening repeatedly over the past months, at times for no apparent reason. Upset, she would call John and complain, and he would feel, as a man, compelled to respond. [John ends up fighting with the young men in Audrey's neighborhood on several occasions, and on one occasion is arrested for carrying a gun.] (From Anderson's [1999:239] account of life in a poor inner-city community)

Not all vicarious strains are likely to cause crime. For example, consider the following two cases. In the first, a distant relative in another city has a minor illness that is successfully treated. In the second, a fellow gang member is deliberately shot by members of a rival gang. The second type of vicarious strain is much more likely to lead to crime, for several reasons. The second strain is more serious, it involves someone that the individual cares about and has assumed responsibility for protecting, it poses a threat to the individual—who may be subject to similar violence—and it involves unjust treatment by another person, which angers the individual (see Agnew, 2002 for a fuller discussion).

It is also sometimes important to consider anticipated experiences with strains. *Anticipated strains* refer to individuals' expectations that their current strains will continue into the future or that new strains will be experienced. For example, individuals may anticipate that they will be the victims of physical assault. Like vicarious strains, anticipated strains may upset individuals and lead to criminal coping. Individuals may engage in crime to prevent anticipated strains from occurring, to seek revenge against those who might inflict such strains, or to alleviate negative emotions. To illustrate, many adolescents, particularly in high-crime communities, anticipate that they will be the victims of violence. They often (illegally) carry weapons as a result, and may even engage in violence against others in an effort to reduce their own likelihood of victimization. In this area, Anderson (1999) argues that the young men in very poor, high-crime communities often try to reduce the likelihood they will be victimized by adopting a tough demeanor and responding to even minor shows of disrespect with violence. As Anderson (1999:92) states, they do this to "discourage strangers from even thinking about testing their manhood. . . . [One] builds a reputation that works to prevent future challenges" (also see Baron et al., 2001).

To give an example of the research in this area, Agnew (2002) examined a sample of adolescents from a nationwide study of high school sophomores and juniors. A small percentage of these adolescents stated that it was likely that they would be "shot with a gun," "stabbed with a knife," or "no longer be alive" by the time they were 25 years old. These individuals, then, anticipated that they would be the victims of serious violence. And they were somewhat more likely to engage in crime, even after taking account of a range of other factors, such as their prior victimization experiences and prior crime. It is important to note, however, that not all anticipated strains result in crime. Among other things, anticipated strains are most likely to result in crime when individuals believe they have a high probability of occurring in the near future, they are serious in nature, and they involve unjust treatment by others (see Agnew, 2002).

Summary

Strains involve events and conditions that are disliked by individuals. Individuals may lose something they value, be treated in a negative or aversive manner by others, or be unable to achieve their goals. It is important to distinguish between objective strains, which are disliked by most people in a given group, and subjective strains, which are disliked by the individuals being examined. And while the personal experience of strains is most likely to result in crime, vicarious and anticipated experiences with strains may sometimes result in crime as well.

Why Do Strains Increase the Likelihood of Crime?

Strains, by definition, are disliked events and conditions. Not surprisingly, then, the experience of strains often makes people *feel bad*. That is, strains contribute to one or more negative emotions, like anger, frustration, depression, or hopelessness. These negative emotions create pressure for corrective action. Individuals feel bad and they want to do something about it. As indicated above, *crime is one way to cope with strains.*

Crime May Allow Individuals to Reduce or Escape From Their Strains, at Least Temporarily

In particular, crime may allow individuals to protect or retrieve those things that they value. For example, individuals may assault those who try to take their possessions, or they may threaten romantic partners in an effort to prevent them from leaving. Crime may allow individuals to reduce or escape from negative treatment. For example, individuals may assault the peers who harass them or run away from the parents who abuse them. Crime may also allow individuals to achieve their goals. For example, individuals may engage in theft, drug-selling, or prostitution to achieve monetary goals. Crime is not always a successful strategy for reducing strains, and some evidence suggests that crime may create more problems than it solves *in the long run* (see Agnew, 2005b:90–93). For example, crime often leads to poor relations with parents and teachers, rejection by conventional peers, and problems with employers. But many individuals, especially those prone to crime, do not consider the long-term consequences of their behavior. They are merely looking for some way to alleviate their strain, even if only temporarily. A heroin-addicted offender illustrates this point when he explains why he committed a carjacking:

> I didn't have no money and I was sick and due some heroin so I knew I had to do something. . . . I just had to kill this sickness. . . . One way or another, I was going to get me some money to take me off this sickness. I just seen him and I got it [the car]. (Topalli and Wright, 2004:74)

Crime Allows Individuals to Obtain Revenge Against Those Who Have Wronged Them or, if This Is Not Possible, Against More Vulnerable Targets

Individuals may believe that certain of their strains are the result of accidents or "bad luck" (e.g., losing a paycheck, place of employment going out of business). They may believe that they are to blame for other of their strains (e.g., receiving a low grade as a result of failing to study, being punished for misbehavior). But they often believe that some of their strains are the result of unjust treatment by others. For example, they may believe that someone has insulted or assaulted them for no good reason. This unjust treatment usually makes them angry and creates a desire for revenge. They want to right the wrong that has been done to them, even if doing so does little or nothing to reduce their strains (see Carey, 2004; Mullins et al., 2004; Neergaard, 2004). And crime is often a good vehicle for revenge. Individuals can do such things as directly threaten or assault the person who wronged them, damage the person's property or related targets, or steal from the person.

A particularly horrendous instance of revenge is described in Miller's (2001) study of gangs. A female who was dating the member of one gang provided information to a rival gang; as a result, a member of the first gang was attacked and severely beaten. Members from the first gang later saw the female walking down the street. They kidnapped her and took her to a house used by the gang. The female was then badly beaten by several other females and gang raped by the male gang members:

> They really hurt her . . . grab her by the hair, stickin' their dick in her mouth, makin' her suck their dick, makin' her, punchin her . . . she's screamin . . . me and a group of us had already done beat her up, we had already beat her up so she was all beat up plus they were beatin' on her, callin' her

names . . . fuckin' her every which way. . . . Then we just drug her out, put her in a trunk and dropped her off [at a local park]. (Miller, 2001:139–140)

Angered individuals, however, may sometimes be reluctant to seek revenge against the source of their strain. This source may be a powerful person who can punish them. A student who is mistreated by a teacher, for example, may be afraid to retaliate directly. The same may be true of an employee who is mistreated by an employer. In such cases, studies suggest that angered individuals may behave aggressively against other, more vulnerable targets (De Coster and Kort-Butler, 2004). Mistreated employees, for example, may sometimes "take out" their anger on their spouses and children.

Crime May Allow Individuals to Alleviate Their Negative Emotions

Individuals may not be able to reduce or escape from their strains, and they may not be able to obtain revenge against those who have wronged them. But they may still be able to reduce the negative emotions that result from their strains. One way to do this is through crime, especially illegal alcohol and drug use. Individuals often drink excessively and use illegal drugs in an effort to seek relief from the strains they are experiencing (e.g., Aseltine and Gore, 2000; Cerbone and Larison, 2000; Hoffmann, 2000; Hoffmann et al., 2000). This point is illustrated in the following quote from a drug abuser:

I would get the same crap from every fucking teacher. "What's wrong with you?" "Don't you care about your future?" "Why don't you study?" "Why don't you listen— are you high on something?" Maybe getting high is what I should do, I said to myself. And when I did get high, the fucking teachers still gave me the same crap over and over again, but at least bein' high they didn't bother me. (Inciardi et al., 1993:147)

Is General Strain Theory Able to Explain All Types of Crime?

Most of the examples presented above refer to what are called "street crimes." Such crimes include homicide, assault, rape, robbery, burglary, larceny-theft, vandalism, and drug use. Certain of these examples also deal with "status offenses," or acts which are illegal for juveniles but not adults. Status offenses include running away from home, drinking alcohol, and truancy. The research on GST has focused on street crimes and status offenses, as has the research on most other theories of crime. GST, however, has the potential to help explain a wide range of crimes, including organized crime, white-collar crime, and terrorism (Bryant, 2001; Miethe and McCorkle, 2001).

GST can help explain any act which is condemned by most others in the society or that carries more than a trivial risk of punishment—including but not limited to punishment by the state. Almost all crimes meet these criteria. Most individuals refrain from engaging in such crimes unless they are under some pressure to do so. Strains provide the pressure to engage in these crimes, with the crimes providing some relief from the strains or negative emotions associated with the strains. GST, then, can help explain a broad range of criminal acts. Take, for example, a white-collar crime like embezzlement, where employees steal from their employers. This crime is often committed by employees who have serious financial problems that cannot be resolved through legal channels (Weisburd and Waring, 2001). So embezzlement is often used to cope with monetary strains. To give another example, terrorist acts are frequently used to cope with strains—as reflected in this journalistic account about the violence in Iraq:

> Moneer Munthir is ready to kill Americans. For months he has been struggling to control an explosion of miserable feelings: humiliation, fear, anger, depression. "But in the last two weeks these feelings blow up inside me," said Munthir, a 35-year-old laborer. "The Americans are attacking Shiite and Sunni at the same time. They have crossed a line. I had to get a gun." (Gettleman, 2004:A14)

Saying that a wide range of crimes are committed in response to strains is not, of course, to justify or excuse such crimes. Rather, it is an effort to better understand the causes of such crimes in the hope that we can prevent them. Future research should attempt to broaden the scope of GST by applying it to crimes such as terrorist acts and white-collar crime. Among other things, researchers should examine whether particular types of strains are especially relevant to these types of crimes (for further discussion, see Agnew, 2004; Langton and Piquero, 2004).

Summary

Strains, then, make people feel bad and create pressure for corrective action, and crime is one way in which people cope with strains. Crime may be a way of reducing or escaping from strains; obtaining revenge against those believed responsible for the strains or other, more vulnerable targets; and/or alleviating the negative emotions associated with strains. But not all people cope with strains through crime. Most people, in fact, cope in a legal manner. For example, they negotiate with the people who irritate or harass them, they file complaints against the people who wrong them, or they alleviate their negative emotions by exercising or listening to music. This raises a major question for strain theory, a question addressed in the next section.

Why Are Some People More Likely Than Others to Cope With Strains Through Crime?

A number of factors influence how individuals cope with the strains and negative emotions they experience. Criminal coping is most likely under the following conditions.

Individuals Lack the Ability to Cope With Strains in a Legal Manner

Some individuals are less able to cope with strains in a legal manner than others. Their ability to cope in a legal manner is partly a function of their individual traits, like their intelligence, social and problem-solving skills, and personality traits. It is partly a function of the resources they possess, including financial resources. And it is partly a function of their level of conventional social support. Are there conventional others, such as parents and friends, to whom they can turn to for aid and comfort? As an illustration, consider the following individual, who is high in monetary strain but unable to get money in a legal manner.

> A few months ago, the landlord was going to put us out, rent due, you know. Ask family and friends, you might try a few other ways of getting money, and as a last resort, I know I can go get some money [by committing an armed robbery]. (Wright and Decker, 1997:43)

The Costs of Criminal Coping Are Low

Many individuals avoid criminal coping because the costs of crime are high for them. There is a good chance that they will be sanctioned by others if they engage in crime, with such others including family members, friends, school officials, neighbors, and the criminal justice system. They also have a lot to lose if they engage in crime; they might get expelled from school, lose their jobs, or jeopardize relationships with people they care about. And engaging in crime will make them feel guilty, because they believe that crime is wrong—something they have been taught for much of their lives. For other individuals, however, the costs of criminal coping are low. They are in environments where the likelihood of sanction for crime is small. Perhaps they are poorly supervised by their parents, their friends do not care if they engage in crime, neighborhood residents seldom report crimes to the police, they do not have jobs to lose or close relationships with others that might be jeopardized by crime, or they do not believe that crime is wrong. Such individuals, then, are more likely to cope with strains through crime.

Individuals Are Disposed to Crime

Some individuals are more disposed than others to respond to strains with crime. They may possess personality traits which increase their inclination to crime. Some individuals, for example, are easily upset, become very angry when upset, and have aggressive tendencies. Also, some individuals may believe that crime is an appropriate response to certain strains, like disrespectful treatment by others. Further, some individuals have been reinforced for crime in the past, which increases their disposition to respond with crime in the present.

In sum, individuals are most likely to cope with strains in a criminal manner when they lack the ability to engage in legal coping, their costs of crime are low, and they are disposed to crime.

The Major Arguments of General Strain Theory

I have now presented the major arguments of general strain theory (GST). Individuals who experience strains become upset, and they may try to cope with their strains and negative emotions through crime. Crime may allow them to reduce or escape from their strains, seek revenge against those who have mistreated them, or alleviate their negative emotions (through illegal drug use). Some individuals, however, are more likely to cope with strains through crime than others.

Figure 1.1 illustrates the central propositions of GST presented up to this point. This figure, in particular, shows the three major types of strain; shows that strains affect crime primarily by increasing negative emotions; and shows that the effect of strains and negative emotions on crime is influenced by the individual's ability to cope in a legal manner, the costs of criminal coping, and the disposition for criminal coping.

Figure 1.1 The Central Propositions of General Strain Theory

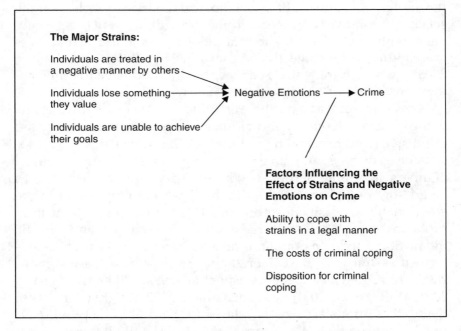

How Does General Strain Theory Differ From Other Major Theories of Crime?

GST is one of the leading theories of crime, but it is far from the only theory. There are literally scores of theories focusing on the causes of crime (see Cullen and Agnew, 2003, for an overview). Some of the other leading theories include biopsychological theories, social control theory, and social learning theory. I present brief overviews of these theories in this section and describe how they differ from and are related to GST (see Agnew, 1995b for a fuller discussion). I discuss the relationship between GST and still other theories of crime later in the book.

Biopsychological Theories

GST is a sociological theory. That is, it focuses on the effect of the social environment on crime. In particular, most of the events and conditions examined by GST involve relationships with others: other people take individuals' valued possessions, treat them in an aversive manner, or prevent them from achieving their goals through legal channels. Biopsychological theories focus less on the social environment and more on the individuals' traits, especially personality traits. Such theories argue that certain individual traits are conducive to crime (see Agnew, 2005a; Cullen and Agnew, 2003). Two such traits that seem especially conducive to crime are low constraint and negative emotionality.

Low constraint and negative emotionality are major dimensions of the human personality. Individuals who are low in constraint are impulsive (tend to act without thinking), like to take risks, reject social norms or rules, and have little concern for the feelings or rights of others. In popular terms, such individuals might be described as "wild" or "out of control." Individuals who are high in negative emotionality are easily upset and quick to anger, tend to blame their problems on others, and have an aggressive or antagonistic interactional style. In popular terms, such individuals might be described as "mean," "nasty," or "having a short fuse" (see Agnew, 2005a, b; Agnew et al., 2002; Caspi et al., 1994; Miller and Lynam, 2001; Moffitt et al., 2001; Pratt and Cullen, 2000; Wright et al., 1999). (Note: these traits are closely related to the trait of "low self-control," described by Gottfredson and Hirschi [1990].) It is easy to understand how the traits of low constraint and negative emotionality may increase the likelihood of crime. Individuals with these traits care little about others; give little thought to the costs of crime; are attracted to the exciting, risky nature of crime; and are easily provoked by others. Biopsychological theories, then, differ from GST in that they focus on individual traits rather than the social environment.

Biopsychological theories also ask why some individuals possess traits like low constraint and negative emotionality. Such traits are said to be influenced by a range of biological factors. They are partly inherited from one's parents (that is, genetically transmitted), and they are partly the result of experiencing certain "biological harms," such as head injuries, birth complications, and exposure to toxic substances like lead. Several excellent sources discuss how genetic inheritance and biological harms may contribute to those traits conducive to crime (e.g., Fishbein, 2001; Raine, 1993, 2002; Rowe, 2002; Walsh, 2002). These traits, however, are also influenced by the social environment, especially the early family environment. Among other things, some evidence suggests that the experience of certain strains, like parental rejection and harsh parental discipline, may contribute to these traits (e.g., Agnew et al., 2002; Bernard, 1990; Colvin, 2000; Mazerolle et al., 2003). In particular, individuals who are subject to strains on an ongoing basis may eventually develop a low tolerance for strains and an aggressive disposition (negative emotionality). So while biopsychological theories and GST differ in important ways, they are also related. Strains may be one source of those traits conducive to crime.

Conversely, traits such as low constraint and negative emotionality may contribute to strains and the negative emotions associated with strains. Individuals with these traits are more likely to dislike certain events and conditions and experience intense emotional reactions to them. Individuals low in constraint, for example, are more likely to dislike the rules and regulations imposed by family members, schools, and employers. Further, individuals with these traits often antagonize and provoke negative reactions from others, both in specific situations and over the long term. For example, they often frustrate and overwhelm their parents, who sometimes respond with harsh discipline and rejection. Finally, individuals with these traits often select themselves into environments where they are treated badly. For example, they are rejected by conventional peers and end up associating with delinquent peers—who tend to mistreat one another. They do poorly in school and end up unemployed or in low-paying jobs with poor working conditions. Individuals with these traits, then, are more likely to experience strains and the negative emotions associated with strains (see Agnew et al., 2002; Caspi, 1998; Mazerolle et al., 2000; Piquero et al., 2004; Rutter et al., 1998; Walsh, 2000).

In addition, the traits of low constraint and negative emotionality increase the likelihood that individuals will respond to strains and negative emotions with crime. There are several reasons for this. Individuals with these traits are less able to cope with strains in a legal manner: they tend to act without thinking, are easily upset, and do not have good interpersonal skills. Further, the actual and perceived costs of crime are lower for such individuals. They have little concern for conventional norms and the feelings and rights of others, and they give little thought to the consequences of their behavior. Finally, such individuals are disposed toward aggressive behavior. Agnew et al. (2002) found some support for these arguments. Using data from a national sample of children aged 12 to 16, they found that children high in negative emotionality and low in constraint were more likely to respond to strains with crime.

In sum, biopsychological theories and general strain theory (GST) are very different from one another: biopsychological theories focus on those individual traits that produce crime, while GST focuses on the effect of the social environment on crime. But despite this fundamental difference, the theories are related to one another in important ways. Strains contribute to the development of traits like low constraint and negative emotionality. These traits, in turn, increase the likelihood that individuals will experience strains and react to such strains with crime.

Social Control Theories

Social control theories do focus on the effect of the social environment on crime (see Agnew, 2005a; Cullen and Agnew, 2003; Hirschi, 1969; Sampson and Laub, 1993). Such theories, however, are distinguished from GST in two ways. First, *GST focuses on negative relationships with others:* relationships in which others take individuals' valued possessions, treat them in an aversive manner, or prevent them from achieving their goals. *Social control theories, by contrast, focus on the absence of positive relationships with conventional others and institutions.* In particular, crime is said to be more likely when *conventional others fail to exercise direct control* over individuals; that is, they fail to prohibit crime, monitor the individuals' behavior, and consistently sanction rule violations. Crime is more likely when *individuals have weak emotional bonds to conventional others,* such as family members and teachers. It is easier to engage in crime when bonds are weak, as the individuals do not have to worry about hurting close others or jeopardizing relationships with them. Crime is also more likely when individuals have *little investment in conventional institutions;* that is, they are doing poorly at school, are unemployed or employed in "bad" jobs, and have little hope for the future. Individuals in such circumstances have little to lose through crime. And crime is more likely when individuals *have not been taught to condemn crime.*

Second, GST argues that people are *pressured into crime* by the negative emotions that result from strains. They feel bad and these bad feelings create some pressure to act, with crime being one possible response. Social control theories, by contrast, do not argue that people are pressured into crime. Rather, control theories argue that the absence of positive relationships with conventional others and institutions *frees people to engage in crime.* Individuals who are low in social control are free to satisfy their needs and desires in the most expedient way possible, which is often crime. So if they see something they want, they are free to steal it. If someone annoys them, they are free to assault him or her. Since they are low in social control, there is little chance that their crime will be sanctioned by others, will jeopardize their ties to conventional others or institutions, or will provoke feelings of guilt. So they are free to do what they want; nothing is holding them back from crime.

Social control theory and GST, then, differ from one another in terms of (a) their description of the *type* of environmental factors that lead to crime, and (b) their explanation of *why* environmental factors lead to crime. GST focuses on negative relationships with others, while social control theory focuses on the absence of positive relationships with conventional others. GST argues that individuals are pressured to engage in crime, while social control theory argues that they are freed to engage in crime. But despite these differences, the theories are related to one another in important ways. As will be argued later, there is reason to believe that strains may reduce one's level of social control. For example, parental abuse may reduce one's emotional bond to parents. Likewise, low social control may lead to strains. For example, parents who do not care about their children are more likely to mistreat them. Finally, individuals who are low in social control are more likely to respond to strains with crime, because the costs of crime are lower for them.

Social Learning Theory

Social learning theory also focuses on the effect of the social environment on crime. However, while GST focuses on negative relationships with others, social learning theory tends to focus on *positive relationships with deviant others.* These others, most often friends, teach individuals to engage in crime. In particular, they reinforce individuals' crime, often with social approval. They model crime for individuals, which the individuals then imitate. And they teach individuals values and beliefs that are favorable to crime (e.g. Agnew, 2005a; Cullen and Agnew, 2003; Akers, 1998). For example, they teach individuals that they should respond with violence when treated in a disrespectful manner. Anderson's account of street life in a poor, inner-city community illustrates some of the principles of social learning theory.

> These children of the street . . . are said to "come up hard." They often learn to fight at an early age, using short-tempered adults around them as models. The street-oriented home may be fraught with anger, verbal disputes, physical aggression, and even mayhem. The children observe these goings-on, learning that might makes right. . . . Even small children test one another, pushing and shoving, and are ready to hit other children over circumstances not to their liking . . . the child who is the toughest prevails. Thus the violent resolution of disputes, the hitting and cursing, gains social reinforcement. . . . Those street-oriented adults with whom children come in contact . . . [verbalize] the message they are getting through experience: "Watch your back." "Protect yourself." "Don't punk out." "If somebody messes with you, you got to pay them back." "If somebody disses you, you got to straighten them out." (Anderson, 1994:83, 86)

GST and social learning theory, then, tend to focus on different features of the social environment. Also, they offer different accounts of why the social environment leads to crime. While GST argues that strains pressure individuals to engage in crime, social learning theory argues that deviant others teach individuals to *view crime as a desirable or at least justifiable form of behavior in certain circumstances.* But as was the case with social control theory, GST and social learning theory are also related to one another in important ways.

Strains may lead individuals to form or join deviant groups that reinforce crime, model crime, and teach beliefs favorable to crime. For example, individuals who cannot achieve goals like money through legal means may sometimes join gangs in an effort to achieve money through illegal means. I discuss this idea further in Chapter 2. At the same time, membership in deviant groups increases the likelihood that individuals will experience strains. Not surprisingly, individuals who belong to deviant groups are more likely to mistreat one another and elicit negative treatment from others. For example, gang members often get into conflicts with one another and with others such as teachers, police, and rival gang members (Colvin, 2000; Schreck et al., 2004; Shaffer, 2003). Finally, individuals who belong to deviant groups are more likely to respond to strains with crime, partly because they are more disposed to crime. This disposition is easy to understand, since their friends reinforce criminal responses to strains, model criminal responses, and teach beliefs that justify criminal responses.

In sum, GST is distinguished from social control and social learning theories in terms of (a) the features of the social environment that it examines, and (b) its explanation of why the social environment leads to crime. GST is the only theory to focus explicitly on negative relationships with others and to argue that these relationships pressure individuals to engage in crime. At the same time, these theories are related to one another in important ways. Strains may contribute to low social control and association with deviant others who teach crime. Conversely, low control and association with deviant others may contribute to strains. Further, strains are more likely to lead to crime among those who are low in control and associate with deviant others. I'll return to these relationships at several points in this book and, in the concluding chapter, I'll discuss the possibility of constructing a general explanation of crime that draws on all of these theories.

Conclusion

Why do individuals engage in crime, according to GST? They experience strains or stressors, become upset as a result, and may cope with their strains and negative emotions through crime. Criminal coping is especially likely if they lack the ability to cope in a legal manner, their costs of crime are low, and they are disposed to crime. Crime may allow them to reduce or escape from their strains, obtain revenge against those who have wronged them, or alleviate their negative emotions (through illegal drug use). GST presents a rather different explanation of crime than that offered by the other leading crime theories. One way to appreciate this difference is to consider the images of the offender presented by the different theories. Biopsychological theories view offenders as people who are "out of control" and "mean." Social control theories view offenders as people who are "free to engage in crime" because of their weak ties to conventional others and institutions. Social learning theory sees offenders as people who view crime as a desirable or justifiable response in certain circumstances, reflecting the fact that they have been reinforced for crime, exposed to criminal models, and taught beliefs favorable to crime. GST, by contrast, views offenders as people who are *pressured into crime* as a result of the strains they have experienced.

Note

1 . The measurement of both objective and subjective strains also allows researchers to explore the factors that influence the subjective evaluation of objective strains. Such exploration will help us better understand the causes of crime and, as indicated in Chapter 8, may help us better control crime.

Review and Discussion Questions

1. What are the central ideas of general strain theory?

2. What are strains? What are the three major types of strains? Can you give two examples of each of these types? Can you think of any strains or stressors that do *not* fall under one of these types?

3. What are the major strains experienced by college students? Do you think certain of these strains are more likely to result in crime than others? If so, why?

4. What are objective and subjective strains? How might a researcher measure each type of strain? Why do I state that subjective strains are more likely than objective strains to result in crime?

5. What are vicarious and anticipated strains? How might researchers measure these types of strains? What are the characteristics of those vicarious and anticipated strains most likely to lead to crime?

6. Give an example of each of the three major reasons why strains increase the likelihood of crime.

7. Why do I argue that GST can help explain all major types of crime?

8. What sorts of strains might be especially conducive to corporate crime? What sorts might be conducive to terrorism?

9. Why are some individuals more likely than others to cope with strains through crime? Describe the characteristics of someone who is quite likely to cope with strains through crime.

10. How do biopsychological theories, social control theory, and social learning theory explain crime? Draw a diagram depicting the central arguments of each of these theories, similar to the diagram in Figure 1.1.

11. How does GST differ from biopsychological, social control, and social learning theories? How is GST related to these theories?

12. Do you think it is possible to build a general or integrated theory of crime that draws on all of these theories? If so, what might such a theory look like (e.g., can you describe the key arguments of this theory or draw a diagram of the theory)?

13. Use GST to explain a criminal incident described in the mass media. ✦

Chapter 2

Why Do Strains Increase the Likelihood of Crime?

Why do strains increase the likelihood of crime? Why, for example, does harsh parental discipline or the inability to achieve one's monetary goals increase crime? A brief explanation was presented in Chapter 1. Strains lead to a range of negative emotions, like anger, frustration, and depression. These negative emotions create pressure for corrective action, and crime is one possible response. Crime may allow individuals to reduce or escape from their strains (e.g., run away from abusive parents, obtain the money they want), retaliate against those who have wronged them or others, or alleviate their negative emotions (through illicit drug use). This chapter elaborates on this brief explanation.

In the first part of the chapter, I describe why strains may lead individuals to commit a *particular* crime or series of related crimes. The central point is that strains lead to negative *emotional states*, which increase the likelihood of criminal coping. These emotional states not only create pressure for corrective action, but they may also reduce the ability to engage in legal coping, reduce the perceived costs of crime, and increase the disposition for crime. I also argue that strains may temporarily reduce social control, for example, bonds to conventional others—especially if these conventional others are the source of the strains. Further, strains may temporarily foster the social learning of crime, for example, the belief that crime is justified.

In the second part of this chapter, I argue that the chronic or repeated experience of strains may create a general *predisposition* or inclination to engage in crime if one is provoked or tempted. This occurs partly because chronic strains contribute to negative *emotional traits* that are conducive to crime. Emotional traits refer to individuals' general tendency to experience certain emotions, rather than to the actual experience of an emotion (or an emotional state). So people high in trait anger tend to get angry a lot, although they are not necessarily angry at any given time (see Spielberger et al., 1983, 1995). Chronic strains also reduce one's ability to cope in a legal manner, contribute to personality traits conducive to crime, lower one's level of social control, and foster the social learning of crime.

So this chapter describes why strains lead to particular crimes and to a general predisposition to engage in crime.

Why Do Strains Lead to Particular Crimes?

The occurrence of particular crimes is usually explained in terms of rational choice and routine activities theories (see Clarke and Cornish, 1985; Cullen and Agnew, 2003; Felson, 2002). These theories argue that predisposed individuals are most likely to commit crimes when they are in situations where the benefits of crime are seen as high and the costs as low. The benefits of crime are likely to be seen as high when attractive targets for crime are present, like property that is valuable and easily moved (e.g., jewelry, lightweight electronic equipment). The costs are likely to be seen as low when others who might prevent the crime are absent. These others, sometimes called "capable guardians," include police, parents, teachers, and neighbors. Based on these arguments, it is said that particular crimes are most likely when motivated offenders encounter attractive targets in the absence of capable guardians.

The experience of strains, however, may also help account for the occurrence of particular crimes. In fact, much data suggest that provocations by others—a type of strain—are a major source of violent crimes. For example, Lockwood (1997) asked a sample of middle- and high-school students about the violent incidents in which they had been involved. He discovered that almost all of these incidents began with one student provoking another, including pushing, grabbing, hitting, teasing, and insulting (Lockwood, 1997). Wilkinson (2002) interviewed 125 adolescent males who had recently committed violent acts, and she also found that these acts usually began with a provocation of some sort, including bumping, hitting, insulting, "grilling" (staring at someone too long), having one's property stolen, and advances on "one's girl" by another man (also see Tedeschi and Felson, 1994). These sorts of provocations do not, however, appear to be major causes of property crimes and drug use (see Agnew, 1990a). Interviews with offenders suggest that property crimes and drug use are often prompted by other types of strains. In particular, property criminals often state that they engage in acts like burglary and robbery because they experience a temporary, but desperate need for money (see Agnew, 2006a; Tunnell, 1992; Wright and Decker, 1997). And drug use is often prompted by the experience of a range of strains (see Hoffmann, 2000).

Strains may lead to the occurrence of particular crimes for several reasons.

Strains Lead to Negative Emotional States, Which Are Conducive to Crime

Mazerolle and his colleagues (2003) asked a sample of college students to read the following two vignettes, each of which describes a particular strain. The students were then asked how they would feel if they experienced the strain and whether they would react to the strain in the same manner as the central character in each vignette.

It's Friday night. Mike and Lisa, who have been dating for two years, go into the Dutch Goose for a few beers and dinner. While drinking their beers, Mike excuses himself and goes to the bathroom. While he is away, another guy, Joe, who is with his friends, starts talking to Lisa and sits down at her table. Mike returns just as Joe is asking Lisa for her phone number and asks the guy if he has a problem, because he is coming on to his girlfriend. Joe stands up and tells Mike that Lisa does not have a ring and is therefore allowed to talk to whomever she wants. Mike does not like this very much, so he motions to Lisa for her hand so they can leave. Meanwhile, Joe's friends stare Mike down. Then Joe pushes Mike's hand down. Mike grabs a beer bottle off the table and hits Joe in the head with the bottle.

It's Sunday evening. Laura has to go to the mini-market near campus to buy batteries for her alarm clock. Laura needs the batteries because she has to wake up very early the next day to take an exam in her 8:30 a.m. class. Laura will be up studying most of the night, and she knows that if she doesn't have the batteries for her alarm clock, she will probably oversleep. The store is about to close when Laura realizes that she does not have enough money to buy the batteries, but the batteries are small enough to fit in her pocket. Laura has enough money to buy a soda so that no one will be suspicious of her not buying anything. Laura decides to take the batteries.

Many of the students who read the vignettes said that they would feel upset if they experienced the strains described. Further, those students who said they would feel upset were more likely to report that they would engage in the crimes that are described. These vignettes illustrate one of the central ideas of GST: strains increase the likelihood of crime because they make people feel bad. That is, they contribute to a range of negative emotions, and these emotions in turn increase the likelihood of a criminal response. These negative emotions create some pressure for corrective action: you feel bad and want to do something about it. Further, these negative emotions may lower the ability to cope in a legal manner, reduce the perceived costs of crime, and create a disposition for crime.

To fully appreciate these arguments, it is necessary to know something about the negative emotions that may result from strains and their impact on individuals. The following discussion draws heavily on the psychological and sociological research on emotions (e.g., Levinson et al., 1999; Lewis and Haviland-Jones, 2000; Mayne and Bonanno, 2001; Morgan and Heise, 1988; Parrott, 2001; Solomon, 2003). Among other things, this research describes the major emotions, their characteristics, their causes, and their effects. Some of this research suggests that the key negative emotions are anger, depression, and fear. Each of these emotions involves the negative evaluation of an event or condition, but they are distinguished from one another in terms of two dimensions—feelings of power or potency and level of activity.

Anger. Anger usually results when individuals are treated unjustly by others. Anger is associated with feelings of power (potency) and a desire to correct or respond to the perceived injustice (high activity) (see Averill, 1982, 2001; Canary and Semic, 1999; Shaver et al., 2001; Spielberger et al., 1983, 1995). Researchers sometimes determine whether individuals are angry by asking them how much they agree with statements like:

I am mad.

I feel angry.

I am burned up.

I am furious.

A range of emotions are closely related to anger and may even be considered subcategories of anger. These emotions are distinguished from one another in terms of their causes and the feelings associated with them. One such emotion is *frustration*. Frustration results when individuals experience difficulty satisfying their goals or desires, and involves feelings of unfulfilled desire. The woman in the vignette who did not have enough money for the batteries she so desperately needed was a good candidate for frustration. Another related emotion is *malicious envy*, which occurs when individuals feel they have a right to what others have. Such envy often involves feelings of inferiority, longing, and ill will. Yet another related emotion is *jealousy*, which occurs when "we are threatened with the loss of an important relationship to a rival" (Parrott, 2001:283). Jealousy typically involves suspicion, distrust, and fear of loss.

Anger and these related emotions occupy a special place in GST. Such emotions increase the likelihood of crime for several reasons. First, they create much pressure for corrective action. In particular, they are quite unpleasant and they create a strong need to correct a perceived injustice or to satisfy desires. Second, these emotions reduce the ability of individuals to cope in a legal manner. Angry individuals are less able to accurately access their situation and effectively communicate with others; among other things, they tend to attribute malicious intent to the acts of others and they are quick to take offense. Third, angry individuals are less concerned with the costs of crime; in particular, they have a sense of potency or power and they are less likely to consider the long-term consequences of their behavior (they are "consumed with rage"). Finally, angry individuals are more disposed to crime, especially other-directed crime. They have a strong desire for revenge and they are more likely to believe that crime is justified, as it will be done to right a perceived wrong.

Surprisingly, only a few studies have examined whether state anger and related emotions help explain the effect of strains on particular crimes. The limited research in this area, however, is generally supportive of GST. For example, Jang and Johnson (2003) found that individuals who experienced more strains were more likely to report that they felt angry, and that this state anger increased their likelihood of deviance, especially fighting. (Anger had a smaller effect on drug use.) Further, anger explained much of the effect of strains on fighting. Mazerolle and colleagues (2003) obtained similar results, with state anger explaining much of the effect of strains on intentions to assault (respondents were asked whether they would behave as "Mike" did in the vignette at the start of this chapter, where Mike assaulted a man who had "come on" to his girlfriend). Interestingly, Mazerolle and colleagues found that state anger only explained a small portion of the effect of strains on intentions to shoplift (also see Bao et al., 2004; Broidy, 2001; De Coster and Kort-Butler, 2004; Sigfusdottir et al., 2004).

One intriguing possibility suggested by these studies is that different emotional states are relevant to different types of crime. Anger may be especially likely to lead to aggression. The same may be true of jealousy, with the target of one's aggression being the individual's romantic rival or the object of the individual's romantic affection. Frustration and envy may also inspire violence against others, especially when specific others are the clear source of the frustration or envy. Frustration and envy, however, may contribute to property crime when they involve material goals and desires. For example, consider the shoplifting vignette presented at the start of this chapter, in which a women desperately needs batteries for her alarm clock, but discovers she lacks sufficient money to buy them after going to a convenience store. The frustration felt in this situation may well contribute to theft.

Depression. Depression usually results when people have experienced some disliked event or condition, like the death of a loved one. Unlike anger, depressed people feel powerless or unable to alter the disliked state of affairs (low potency), and often become "inactive, lethargic, and listless" (low activity). Some of the emotions related to depression include anguish, despair, hopelessness, and disappointment. So depression, like anger, results from the experience of disliked events and conditions, but these events and conditions are more likely to be seen as beyond the control of individuals.

Like anger, depression should increase the likelihood of crime. Depression creates some pressure for corrective action since it is an unpleasant emotion, although it may not create as much pressure as anger. Depression reduces the ability to cope in a legal manner, in part because depressed people are lethargic and feel powerless to act. Depression reduces the perceived costs of crime, as the misery experienced by depressed people may lead them to feel that they have little to lose by committing crime. It is unclear, however, whether depression creates a disposition for crime—unless it is accompanied by anger. Depression is probably less likely than anger to result in aggression, which requires some sense of potency and activity. Depression, however, may be more likely to result in "passive" crimes like illegal drug use. Jang and Johnson (2003) provide limited support for this argument. They found that depression and related emotional states had a much smaller effect than anger on fighting, but a much larger effect on drug use (also see Bao et al., 2004; Landau, 1997; Peirce et al., 1994; Piquero and Sealock, 2000; Power and Dalgleish, 1997; Sigfusdottir et al., 2004; Simons et al., 2003).

Fear. Fear usually results when people anticipate that they might experience a disliked event or condition and feel relatively powerless to stop it (low potency). As a consequence, there is a strong urge to flee or hide (high activity). Some of the other emotions associated with fear include terror, panic, and anxiety. Like anger and depression, fear should increase the likelihood of crime. However, fear should be less strongly related to other-directed crimes than anger, and more strongly related to criminal efforts to flee or hide, such as running away, truancy, skipping school, and drug use (which allows for the psychological escape from problems) (see Aseltine et al., 2000; Power and Dalgleish, 1997).

Summary. The experience of strains increases the likelihood that individuals will experience a range of negative emotional states, with several major emotions being highlighted: anger, frustration, jealousy, malicious envy, depression, and fear. Still other negative emotions might be listed, such as shame and alienation (e.g., Dutton et al., 1995). These negative emotional states increase the likelihood of crime for several reasons. They create pressure on individuals to engage in corrective action, they reduce the ability to cope in a legal manner, they reduce the perceived costs of crime, and/or they create a disposition for crime. It was argued that particular emotions may be especially conducive to certain types of crime. Anger, for ex-

...ay be most relevant to aggression, while frustration may
... relevant to property crime.

...fortunately, these arguments have not been extensively
tested. Most tests of GST have focused on emotional traits (see
below) rather than emotional states. This neglect of emotional states
is perhaps the largest gap in the research on GST. Hopefully, future
research will remedy this problem by examining the extent to which
negative emotional states explain the effect of strains on particular
crimes. Researchers should also examine whether particular types
of strains foster particular negative emotions—for example,
whether fear is the result of anticipated strains that individuals feel
powerless to prevent. And researchers should examine whether
particular emotions are more conducive to some types of crime than
others—for example, whether depression is more conducive to
drug use than to aggression.

Strains May Temporarily Reduce Levels of Social Control

The primary way strains increase the likelihood of particular
crimes is through their effect on negative emotional states. Strains,
however, may also temporarily lower individuals' levels of social
control (see Chapter 1 for an overview of social control theory).
Most types of social control are thought of as reasonably stable, a
view that some data support (e.g., Loeber et al., 2000). For example,
emotional bonds to conventional others are moderately to highly
stable over time; individuals who like their parents and teachers at
one point in time tend to like them at later points in time. Nevertheless, they may occasionally experience temporary disruptions in ongoing levels of social control. For example, a juvenile who generally
has a strong emotional bond to his parents may briefly dislike them
when they forbid him to go to a party, or an adult who usually has a
strong investment in conventional institutions may have a weak investment for a short while because she has had a dispute with her
boss or has been laid off from work.

The extent to which strains temporarily reduce social control
and the type(s) of control affected depend partly on the nature of the
strains (see Chapter 3 for a fuller discussion). Many strains involve
negative treatment by conventional others, such as parents, teachers, spouses, employers, and police. These strains may temporarily
reduce emotional bonds to these others. They may also reduce investment in conventional institutions like school and work (e.g.,

getting failing grades at school, being demoted or fired from a job). Further, they may reduce direct control if relationships with these others are disrupted (e.g., spending less time with parents, being expelled from school, being laid off from work). Finally, the sense of desperation evoked by many strains may reduce internal control. Individuals may temporarily put aside their moral beliefs and concern for others, and instead focus more exclusively on their own self-interest (Konty, 2005).

So certain types of strains may lead to temporary reductions in social control, and such reductions may help account for the occurrence of particular crimes. Unfortunately, this idea has not been well tested. More generally, there has been little research on the idea that individuals may experience temporary reductions in social control—except for the limited case in which individuals find themselves in situations where "capable guardians" like parents and police are absent (although see Agnew, 2006a; Farrington, 1992; Horney et al., 1995).

Strains May Temporarily Foster the Social Learning of Crime

Finally, strains may lead to particular crimes because they temporarily foster the social learning of crime (see Chapter 1 for an overview of social learning theory). In particular, certain strains involve brief exposure to others who model crime, reinforce crime, or present beliefs favorable to crime (see Chapter 3 for further information). For example, individuals who are criminally victimized are, by definition, briefly exposed to criminal models. Individuals who are abused by peers are frequently exposed to others who model, reinforce, and otherwise encourage crime. Such exposure may lead individuals to (temporarily) conclude that crime may be an appropriate or desirable coping mechanism. Also, strains may temporarily foster the belief that crime is justified. Many strains involve unjust treatment by others. Such treatment may foster the belief that crime is justified in those particular situations, as it is being used to "right" an injustice. For example, individuals who assault others often claim that the assault was justified because they were unjustly provoked by these others. These arguments have not been tested.

Summary

Strains lead to particular crimes primarily because they foster negative emotional states, which create pressure for corrective action, reduce the ability to cope in a legal manner, reduce the perceived costs of crime, and increase the disposition for crime. Strains may also temporarily reduce social control and foster the social learning of crime. These arguments are illustrated in Figure 2.1. Although they have not been well tested, some data suggest that strains contribute to negative emotional states and that these states increase the likelihood of crime. Testing these arguments is critical, for they can dramatically expand situational explana-

Figure 2.1 The Mechanisms by Which Strains Increase the Likelihood of Particular Crimes

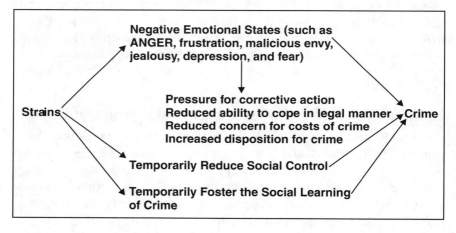

tions of crime—supplementing rational choice and routine activities theories.

Why Do Chronic or Repeated Strains Create a Predisposition to Crime?

GST not only explains why individuals commit particular crimes, but also why some individuals have a greater predisposition to crime than others. Individuals who are predisposed to crime are more likely to engage in crime if tempted or provoked. As a consequence, they tend to have higher overall levels of crime than others. In this section, I argue that chronic or repeated exposure to strains increases the predisposition to crime for several reasons.

Chronic or Repeated Strains Reduce the Ability to Legally Cope With Strains

The chronic or repeated experience of strains reduces individuals' actual and perceived ability to cope in a legal manner. Imagine, for example, a woman who regularly faces financial crises, like difficulty paying her rent. This woman may eventually exhaust the legal means she has for obtaining money, like her savings and borrowing from friends and family. Also, chronic strains may cause individuals to question the utility of their efforts at legal coping. Consider, for example, a student who is bullied by others. This student may try to cope by reasoning with the people who bully him. But if the student continues to be bullied, he will probably come to doubt the effectiveness of reasoning as a coping strategy. As a consequence of these effects, individuals who experience chronic/repeated strains are more likely to view crime as their only or best option for coping. There has been no research in this area.

Chronic or Repeated Strains Lead to Negative Emotional Traits, Which are Conducive to Crime

Chronic or repeated strains contribute to negative emotional *traits,* including anger, frustration, depression, and fear. As indicated, emotional traits are distinct from emotional states, with emotional traits referring to the tendency to experience particular emotions. So someone who possesses the emotional trait of anger tends to get angry a lot (see Mazerolle et al., 2003). They are more easily upset than others and they experience more intense emotional reactions when upset. The trait of anger is sometimes measured by asking individuals how much they agree with statements like the following (see Agnew, 1985; Speilberger et al., 1983):

I am a hotheaded person.

I fly off the handle.

It makes me furious when I am criticized in front of others.

It makes my blood boil when I am pressured.

Individuals who experience chronic or repeated strains develop negative emotional traits like anger partly because their continued experience with strains reduces their ability to cope in a legal manner. As a consequence, new strains are more likely to overwhelm them and elicit strong emotional reactions. You may have experienced this phenomena yourself. When things are going well in your life, it is often easy to cope with the occasional strain. But when things are going poorly (you are experiencing a lot of strains), even a minor strain may overwhelm and upset you.

Thomas Bernard (1990) argued that people who live in poor, inner-city communities regularly experience a range of strains, including "population density and crowding, noise, pollution, technological innovations imposed on nontechnological populations, elaborations of institutional organizations and their regulations, design of housing complexes on the basis of efficiency and space-utilizing criteria, restrictions in recreational space, the anonymity of central and local bureaucracies, the power structure of industrial relations, and the demands of repetitive work performance in situations inducing excessive and unavoidable degrees of fatigue" (79–80). Bernard also lists such additional strains as interpersonal conflict, crime, low social position, and racial and ethnic discrimination. He argues that such strains lower the threshold for "perceived wrong or injury" and increase the intensity of one's anger—thereby contributing to trait anger.

Elijah Anderson found some support for this argument in his study of life in a lower-class urban community. He states that:

> Frustrations mount over bills, food, and, at times, drink, cigarettes, and drugs. Some tend toward self-destructive behavior; many street-oriented women are crack addicted ("on the pipe"), alcoholic, or repeatedly involved in complicated relationships with the men who abuse them. In addition, the seeming intractability of their situation, caused in large part by the lack of well-paying jobs and the persistence of racial discrimination, has engendered deep-seated bitterness and anger in many of the most desperate and poorest blacks, especially young people . . . the frustrations of persistent poverty shorten the fuse in such people, contributing to a lack of patience with anyone, child or adult, who irritates them. (1999:10–11)

So chronic or repeated strains increase the likelihood that individuals will develop negative emotional traits. Such traits, in turn, increase individuals' predisposition for crime. This occurs largely because individuals with negative emotional *traits* are more likely to experience negative emotional *states* in response to particular strains. So, for example, an individual high in trait anger is more likely to experience state anger if insulted by another person. And as indicated above, negative emotional states create pressure for corrective action, reduce the ability to cope in a legal manner, reduce the perceived costs of crime, and create a disposition for crime.

There has been some research on strain and negative emotional traits, most of which focuses on trait anger. Data suggest that individuals who have experienced more strains are higher in trait anger. Further, trait anger typically explains part of the effect of strains on individuals' overall level of crime, especially violent crime (Agnew, 1985; Aseltine et al., 2000; Bao et al., 2004; Baron, 2004; Baron and Hartnagel, 2002; Brezina, 1998; Gibson et al., 2001; Hay, 2003; Hollist, 2004; Mazerolle and Piquero, 1997, 1998; Mazerolle et al., 2003; Piquero and Sealock, 2000; Sharp et al., 2001; Simons et al., 2003). Trait anger, however, seems less relevant to the explanation of property crime. A few researchers have also examined the impact of strains on selected other emotional traits, including depression, resentment, and anxiety. Data suggest that strains do increase such traits, and these traits *sometimes* explain part of the effect of strains on crime (Aseltine et al., 2000; Bao et al., 2004; Brezina, 1998; Gibson et al., 2001; Hollist, 2004; Manasse, 2002; Piquero and Sealock, 2000, 2004; Sharp et al., 2001; Simons et al., 2003; Wallace et al., 2005). More research is needed in this area, however.

Low Constraint and Negative Emotionality. Negative emotional traits overlap somewhat with the personality traits of low constraint and negative emotionality. The trait of anger, in particular, has much in common with negative emotionality (or the tendency to become easily upset, experience intense emotional reactions when upset, and have an aggressive interactional style). It should therefore come as no surprise that chronic or repeated strains may contribute to negative emotionality. Certain types of chronic strains, like harsh and erratic parental discipline, may also contribute to low constraint (the tendency to act without thinking, engage in risky behaviors, reject social norms, and show little concern for others). Parents who employ harsh, erratic disciplinary techniques fail to teach their children to exercise self-restraint. Children only learn to constrain themselves when they are consistently sanctioned for their misbehavior in an appropriate manner. Also, as Colvin (2000:39–40) notes:

Not knowing for sure when behavior will be ignored or harshly punished leaves the person uncertain about how his or her behavior is related to consequences. . . . The person begins to sense that events are beyond his or her control. Thus a strong belief in fate and luck is fostered along with a mindset of "get it now" or "grab it while it's there" rather than deferring gratification.

There is limited support for the argument that chronic or repeated strains contribute to negative emotionality and low constraint, thereby further increasing individuals' predisposition for crime (Agnew, 1995b, 1997; Agnew et al., 2002; Anderson, 1999; Bernard, 1990; Caspi et al., 1994; Colvin, 2000; Konty, 2005).

Chronic or Repeated Strains May Reduce Levels of Social Control

Chronic or repeated strains may also lead to long-term reductions in the major types of social control (see Chapter 1). Versions of this argument have been made by most of the leading strain theorists, including Merton (1938), Cohen (1955), Cloward and Ohlin (1960), Elliott et al. (1985), and Colvin (2000). The following discussion draws heavily on their work (also see Agnew, 1995b; Agnew et al., 2000).

As indicated above, many strains involve negative treatment by conventional others, like parents, spouses, teachers, and employers. Further, these strains are often chronic or occur on a repeated basis. Such strains include child abuse, harsh discipline by parents, demeaning treatment by teachers, the receipt of low grades, conflict with spouses, unemployment, and work in "bad" jobs. These strains may reduce long-term emotional bonds to conventional others. Child abuse, for example, is likely to reduce children's bonds to parents. These strains may also reduce long-term investments in conventional activities. Chronic unemployment, for example, represents a major reduction in investment in conventional activities. Further, these strains may reduce long-term levels of direct control by causing individuals to retreat from conventional others, like parents and teachers. And these effects may reduce the belief that crime is wrong, as individuals' ties to those who teach this belief are weakened. Also, individuals are less likely to adopt societal norms condemning crime when they fail to reap the benefits that society has to offer, like a good education, a good job, and a loving family. Individuals who are very poor, for example, are less likely to condemn criminal methods of obtaining money (Merton, 1938). More generally, strained individuals are more likely to adopt a value orientation that minimizes concern for others and prioritizes their own self-interest (Konty, 2005).

Researchers have found some support for these arguments. Studies suggest that individuals who are experiencing a lot of strains tend to be lower in social control. For example, Paternoster and Mazerolle (1994) found that a measure indexing several strains was strongly correlated with a measure of several types of social control (also see Hoffmann and Miller, 1998; Hoffmann and Su, 1997; Konty, 2005; Lempers et al., 1989; Maxwell, 2001). Further, certain studies that have employed longitudinal or over-time data have found that high levels of strain at one point in time lead to reductions in social control at a later point in time. For example, Elliott et al. (1985) found that a range of family- and school-related strains reduced emotional bonds to parents and teachers, investment in school (e.g., grades), and acceptance of conventional norms.

Chronic or Repeated Strains May Foster the Social Learning of Crime

Finally, chronic or repeated strains may foster the social learning of crime. Most notably, such strains increase the likelihood that individuals will join or form criminal groups, like delinquent peer groups and gangs. The members of such groups, in turn, model crime, reinforce crime, and teach beliefs favorable to crime. Also, chronic or repeated strains directly increase the likelihood that individuals will come to view crime as a desirable, justifiable, or at least excusable form of behavior. These arguments have been made by several prominent strain theorists, most notably Merton (1938), Cohen (1955), Cloward and Ohlin (1960), and Bernard (1990). The arguments below draw heavily on their work (also see Agnew, 1995a, b).

Increased Association With Criminal Others. Chronic or repeated strains increase the likelihood that individuals will join or form criminal groups for several reasons. As indicated above, such strains often reduce levels of social control, including emotional bonds to conventional others, investment in conventional institutions, direct control, and the belief that crime is wrong. This increases the likelihood that individuals will come in contact with criminal groups and it frees them to associate with such groups. Individuals low in social control spend more time in the street, away from conventional others and conventional institutions like school and work. As a result, they are more likely to be exposed to criminal groups. Also, they are freer to associate with such groups because they are lower in direct control, have less to lose, and do not condemn crime. Elliott et al. (1985) found some support for these arguments. Individuals who were higher in school and family strains were more likely to associate with delinquent others, and the primary reason for this was that they were lower in the types of social control listed above.

Chronic and repeated strains, however, do more than free individuals to associate with criminal groups. Such strains also increase the appeal of criminal groups. In particular, the victims of such strains often view criminal groups as a solution to their strains. Individuals experiencing chronic and repeated strains have not, by definition, been able to effectively cope on their own. Criminal groups, however, often seem to allow for the alleviation of their strains. In particular, criminologists have claimed that strained individuals join criminal groups in an effort to address several major types of strains. The more prominent arguments in this area include the following:

- Individuals who cannot achieve status through conventional channels, like educational and occupational success, often join criminal gangs because the gang makes them feel important, respected, and/or feared (see especially Cohen, 1955).

- Individuals who cannot achieve their monetary goals through conventional channels often join criminal groups in an effort to better achieve such goals. Such groups often assist the individual in income-generating activities of a criminal nature, like drug selling, extortion, and theft (Cloward and Ohlin, 1960).

- Individuals who are rejected or mistreated by family members sometimes join criminal groups like gangs in an effort to obtain the support and comfort they cannot get at home. This argument is often made with respect to females (Esbensen et al., 1999; Miller, 2001). It has also been argued that females sometimes join criminal groups in an effort to escape the gender oppression they experience at home and elsewhere (Campbell, 1990; Leblanc, 2000).

- Individuals who are victimized by others sometimes join criminal groups like gangs in an effort to protect themselves (Curry and Decker, 2003; Anderson, 1999).

- Juveniles who desire greater autonomy from adults often join criminal groups in an effort to obtain such autonomy, including the opportunity to participate in "adult activities" like alcohol consumption, sexual intercourse, and partying (Moffitt, 1993).

It is important to note, however, that criminal groups rarely provide a complete solution to individuals' strains. Gang members, for example, frequently report that while gang membership brings status in the eyes of some, it elicits disrespectful treatment from others. They also report that while the gang is like a supportive family in some ways, they often suffer abuse and mistreatment at the hands of their fellow gang members. Further, membership in criminal groups may lead to additional problems or strains over the long term, like family and employment problems. Nevertheless, criminal groups often function as a partial, short-term solution to strains.

Blazak (2001) illustrates these points in his discussion of racist skinhead gangs. He argues that many working-class, white, male youth feel that their status is threatened. In particular, their economic status is threatened by the decline of manufacturing jobs that pay a decent wage, and they feel that the privileged status they enjoy as white, heterosexual males is threatened by changes in race, gender, and sexual relations. The skinheads make a deliberate effort to recruit such youth and provide them with a sense of importance, leading them to believe that they are warriors defending the white race. In the words of one skinhead document, "Nazi skinheads will give them a sense of accomplishment, attainment, success, and belonging" (Blazak, 2001:988).

Miller (2001:49–50) also illustrates these points in her description of a female gang member:

Brittany described a terrible violent family life. . . . Her aunt's boyfriend had sexually assaulted her at the age of five, but family members didn't believe her. Although she

didn't know her father, who was in jail, she had early memo-
ries of him physically abusing her mother. Moreover, she felt
very disconnected and unloved by her family and also
described being isolated at school. . . . Brittany saw the gang
as a means of finding love. She explained: "I felt that my
family didn't care for me . . . that when I was on the streets I
felt that I got more love than when I was in the house. So I
felt that's where my love was, on the streets [with her gang],
so that's where I stayed.

Having made these arguments, I should note that whether
strained individuals actually join criminal groups depends on a
number of factors. One key factor is whether criminal groups are
available in their community. Data suggest that criminal groups are
more common in certain communities, especially very poor communities. If criminal groups are not available, strained individuals
may form such groups. The likelihood of this happening, however,
depends on the extent to which strained individuals regularly interact with one another (in the street, at school, etc.). This is one reason
why criminal groups are more common in poor, urban communities; there are more strained individuals in regular interaction with
one another. The formation of criminal groups is also influenced by
other factors. A precipitating event, like an assault by juveniles from
another neighborhood, often prompts juveniles to organize into a
gang. And media images of gang life have been said to motivate
strained youth to organize into gangs (see Agnew, 2005a for a fuller
discussion).

There is some support for the argument that strains increase association with criminal groups like gangs. Gang members typically
report that they joined gangs in an effort to cope with the strains
they were experiencing, including a lack of money, family problems, victimization by others, and a lack of autonomy. Field studies
of gangs confirm these interview data. And surveys find that juveniles experiencing more strains are more likely to join criminal
groups, like delinquent peer groups and gangs. For example, Paternoster and Mazerolle (1994) found that strains increased the likelihood that juveniles would associate with delinquent others, even
after they took account of the juveniles' level of social control (also
see Agnew, 2005a; Eitle et al., 2004; Hill et al., 1999; Maxwell, 2001;
Vowell and May, 2000).

The Belief That Crime Is a Desirable, Justifiable, or Excusable Response to Strains. In addition to increasing the likelihood of association with criminal groups, chronic or repeated strains may directly foster the belief that crime is a desirable or justifiable or excusable response to strains. To understand why this is so, imagine an individual experiencing chronic or repeated strains; for example, a juvenile who is regularly abused by her father, or a high-school student who is regularly bullied by others, or a single parent who has been unemployed for over a year. As suggested above, such individuals may believe they have few legal options for dealing with their strains. They may also believe that they are being unjustly victimized by others. And their ties to conventional others and institutions may be weak. Such individuals may well conclude that certain types of crime are excusable, justifiable, or even desirable given their circumstances. Some data support this argument. Agnew and Peters (1985), for example, found that individuals who reported that they were mistreated by teachers and others were more likely to hold beliefs justifying crime (also see Anderson, 1999; Elliott et al., 1985).

But Is Crime an Effective Solution to One's Strains?

At several points in this chapter I have stated that strained individuals often turn to crime because they believe it is an effective way to cope with their strains. But is this belief accurate? As indicated in Chapter 1, data tend to suggest that over the long term crime may create more problems than it solves, and interviews with criminals reveal that their efforts at criminal coping are often far from an effective solution to their strains. Females who run away from abusive parents, for example, usually confront a new set of problems on the street—like difficulty obtaining food and shelter and abuse by other males. But some data suggest that crime may help certain individuals cope with their strains over the *short term.* Crime, for example, often allows individuals to obtain the money, status, and autonomy they desire—at least for a brief period. It often allows individuals to escape from or reduce the negative treatment they experience. Brezina (1999), for example, found that parents who abused their teenage children often provoked a violent response from those children, and this violent response reduced parental abuse. Crime often allows individuals to satisfy their desire for revenge (see Neergaard, 2004). And drug use frequently makes individuals feel better—at least for a brief period.

Brezina (1996) conducted a fascinating study in which he examined the effect of several strains on anger, resentment, depression, and anxiety. He found that these strains increased each of these negative emotions. But he further found that the effect of strains on these emotions was much smaller when the respondents engaged in delinquency—suggesting that delinquency may make strained individuals feel better (also see Morris and Reilly, 1987; Simons et al., 2003). Brezina (2000) elaborated on this work in a subsequent paper, where he drew on a wide range of evidence to argue that crime often functions as a short-term solution to one's problems or strains. Brezina notes, however, that crime is more likely to have this effect for some individuals than others. For example, crime is more likely to benefit individuals who are low in social control, as such individuals are less likely to be caught and sanctioned for their crime.

So while I do not want to suggest that crime is an effective solution to the individual's strains, *crime may provide a partially effective, short-term solution to the strains experienced by some individuals*. Again, however, the long-term consequences of crime are generally negative. Also, as discussed in Chapter 8, there are a number of steps we can take to help individuals cope with their strains in a noncriminal manner—steps which will better serve these individuals over both the short and long term.

Summary

The above arguments are illustrated in Figure 2.2, which shows the mechanisms by which chronic or repeated strains may create a predisposition for crime.

Figure 2.2 The Mechanisms by Which Chronic or Repeated Strains Increase the Predisposition for Crime

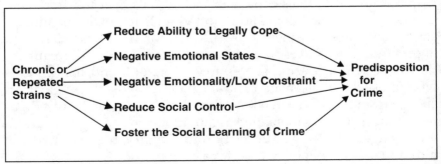

Summary

Strains increase the likelihood of particular crimes for several reasons. Most notably, strains lead to negative emotional states, including anger, frustration, malicious envy, jealousy, depression, and fear. These states create pressure for corrective action, reduce the ability to engage in legal coping, reduce the perceived costs of crime, and increase individuals' disposition for crime. Certain types of strains may be more conducive to some emotional states than others, and certain emotional states may be more conducive to some types of crime than others. Strains may also lead to particular crimes by temporarily reducing social control and fostering the social learning of crime.

The chronic or repeated experience of strains creates a general predisposition for crime. This occurs because chronic or repeated strains reduce the ability to engage in legal coping, lead to negative emotional traits, contribute to negative emotionality and low constraint, reduce social control, and foster the social learning of crime.

Review and Discussion Questions

1. What are the major reasons why strains increase the likelihood of committing particular crimes?

2. How do emotional states differ from emotional traits? What are the major negative emotions, and how do they differ from one another? Why do these emotions increase the likelihood of crime?

3. I argue that certain strains may be more conducive to some emotions than others, and that certain emotions may be more conducive to some types of crime than others. Give an example of each of these arguments.

4. Why do strains sometimes lead to temporary reductions in social control and temporary increases in the social learning of crime?

5. What are the major reasons why chronic or repeated strains create a predisposition for crime?

6. How do chronic or repeated strains reduce the ability to legally cope, contribute to negative emotional traits, contribute to the personality traits of low constraint and negative emotionality, reduce social control, and foster the social learning of crime?

7. What factors influence whether strained individuals join or form criminal groups?

8. How would you respond to someone who claimed that crime is an effective solution to strains?

9. Suppose you wanted to explore the reasons why strains increase the likelihood that individuals will engage in particular crimes. List all the factors or variables you would have to measure. Develop a short list of questions you would ask to measure any two of these factors if you were doing a survey.

10. Describe the major research findings on the reasons why strains increase the likelihood of crime (distinguish between that research dealing with the reasons why strains lead to particular crimes and that dealing with why chronic or repeated strains create a predisposition for crime). Note gaps in this research (i.e., areas where further research is needed). ✦

Chapter 3

What Types of Strains Are Most Likely to Cause Crime?

General strain theory (GST) focuses on numerous strains, some having to do with the loss of valued possessions, some with the experience of negative or aversive treatment, and some with the inability to achieve goals. Many specific strains fall into these broad categories. As an illustration, Table 3.1 lists some of the specific strains examined by Agnew and White (1992) in their test of GST. This list, however, is far from complete; some inventories of stressful events and conditions contain hundreds of specific strains (see Cohen et al., 1995; Herbert and Cohen, 1996). This focus on numerous strains is a major advantage of GST. GST considers many strains that were neglected by previous strain theories, and data suggest that a good number of these strains are related to crime.[1]

Table 3.1   The Types of Strains Examined in Agnew and White's (1992) Test of General Strain Theory

> **A. Negative Life Events.** A 15-item scale with high scorers stating that they experienced a number of negative life events that upset them, including assault, theft, the death of a close friend, serious illness or injury, the divorce of their parents, or a parent losing a job.

Table 3.1 The Types of Strains Examined in Agnew and White's (1992) Test of General Strain Theory—*continued*

B. **Life Hassles.** A nine-item scale with high scorers stating that they are "very much bothered" by such concerns and difficulties as "not having enough time to do all the things I really want to do," adults and friends "don't respect my opinions," "my classmates do not like me," "I don't get along with" parents and siblings, and "I am not the right size for my age."

C. **Negative Relations With Adults.** High scorers on this scale state that teachers talk down to them and embarrass them for not knowing the right answers, and that their parents often complain about them, "blow their tops," get cross and angry over little things, act very strict, try to control whatever they do, act as though they are in the way, etc.

D. **Parental Fighting.** Higher scorers state that they are bothered by the fact that their parents often fight or argue with one another a lot.

E. **Neighborhood Problems.** High scorers state that their neighborhoods are unsafe and that they are afraid to walk in them during the day or night.

F. **Unpopular with Opposite Sex.** High scorers state that they are very bothered by the fact that they are not "good looking" and are not popular with the opposite sex.

G. **Occupational Strain.** High scorers state that they are "very unsure" they will get the job they want.

H. **Clothing Strain.** High scorers state that their parents can never afford to buy them the kinds of clothes they want.

At the same time, this focus on numerous strains creates certain problems. Researchers and policymakers are left wondering which of the hundreds of specific strains they should consider in their work. In particular, they are left wondering whether some strains are more relevant than others to the explanation and control of crime. Also, the broad focus of GST makes it difficult for researchers to test the theory. As Jensen (1995:152) points out, "if strain can be defined in so many different ways, then strain theory is virtually unfalsifiable. There is always a new measure that might salvage the theory." It is therefore critical that GST more precisely specify those types of strain most likely to cause crime. And that is what I try to do in this chapter.

I begin by briefly reviewing the research on strain theory to see what it tells us about those types of strains most likely to lead to crime. I then draw on this review and other work to describe the general characteristics of those types of strains most likely to cause crime. Briefly, such strains (a) are seen as unjust, (b) are seen as high in magnitude, (c) are associated with low social control, and (d) create some incentive or pressure to engage in crime. I next list the specific strains that possess these characteristics and are most likely to cause crime. I also list numerous strains that do not possess these characteristics and are less likely to cause crime. Finally, I discuss how my predictions about those types of strain most and least likely to cause crime might be tested.

Research on the Types of Strains Most Likely to Cause Crime

The research on GST provides us with some information about the types of strains most likely to cause crime, although much of this research suffers from two problems that limit its utility. First, the research on GST only examines some of the strains described by the theory. This is because most research makes use of survey data that were not collected for the purpose of testing GST. As a consequence, many key strains are not examined, so we do not know whether they are related to crime. For example, researchers rarely examine that type of strain involving peer abuse. Second, most tests of GST combine their individual strain measures into a more general measure of strain. For example, researchers commonly measure strains by counting the number of stressful life events experienced by the individual, with such events including things like "death, illness, or accidents among family or friends; changes in school or residence; parental divorce or separation; and family financial problems" (e.g., Hoffmann and Su, 1997; Aseltine et al., 2000). Researchers then determine whether individuals who experience more events are more likely to engage in crime. This strategy is based on the idea that crime is more likely among individuals who experience several strains. This is a very plausible idea, and most studies find that individuals who experience more strains are moderately more likely to engage in crime. However, this strategy prevents us from determining whether some strains have a greater effect on crime than others.

Some studies, however, have examined the effect of different strains on crime. Many of these studies were designed to test GST or other versions of strain theory. Others were not explicitly designed to test strain theory, but they examined strains that fall under GST. Many studies, for example, have examined the effect of child abuse on crime. If we draw on these studies, we can begin to point to those strains that increase crime and those that do not. In particular, certain strains have been found to affect crime in at least several studies, including studies that take account of other factors that may affect crime and that examine the effect of strains on *subsequent* crime. Likewise, several studies suggest that certain strains do not increase the likelihood of crime. Criminologists place greatest confidence in those findings that are confirmed in at least several studies.

Types of Strains That Increase Crime

Certain of the strains that increase crime affect *juveniles* (for overviews, see Agnew, 2001, 2005a). Some of these strains involve relations with *family members.* They include parental rejection of the child; parental punishments that are erratic, excessive, and/or harsh; child abuse and neglect; family conflict; and parental separation and divorce. Certain of these family strains, like parental rejection and poor disciplinary techniques, are among the strongest predictors of crime. Other strains involve relations with *school officials.* They include poor grades; poor relations with teachers, including demeaning treatment and unfair punishment by teachers; and the experience of school as boring and a waste of time. And still other strains involve relations with peers. A small number of studies suggest that peer abuse, including physical and verbal abuse, may contribute to crime (see Agnew and Brezina, 1997; Colvin, 2000; Wallace et al., 2005).

Other strains that increase crime affect *adults* (for overviews, see Agnew, 2001, 2005b; Colvin, 2000). Certain of these strains involve *marital problems.* Crime is more likely among those who do not get along with their spouses, particularly those who get into frequent conflicts with their spouses and are verbally and physically abused by them. Certain of these strains involve *work experiences,* including chronic unemployment and work in the secondary labor market. The secondary labor market consists of jobs characterized by low pay, few benefits, unpleasant tasks (e.g., simple, repetitive, or physically demanding work), little autonomy, and coercive control. These marital and work strains are among the strongest predictors of adult crime.

Still other strains that increase crime are relevant to *both juveniles and adults.* A rapidly growing body of research suggests that *criminal victimization* increases the likelihood of subsequent crime. In fact, it may be among the most important causes of crime (e.g., Agnew, 2002; Eitle and Turner, 2002; Wallace et al., 2005). A few recent studies suggest that *experiences with prejudice and discrimination* increase crime (Eitle, 2002; Katz, 2000; Nyborg and Curry, 2003; Simons et al., 2003). And data suggest that *homelessness* has a relatively large effect on crime, although most studies in this area have focused on youth homelessness (Baron, 2004; Baron and Hartnagel, 2002; Hagan and McCarthy, 1997). Homelessness appears to increase crime through the many problems it creates, including a desperate need for money and victimization by others.

So there is good evidence that a number of strains increase crime, with certain of these strains having a relatively strong effect on crime. I should note, however, that it is sometimes unclear *why* these strains increase crime. GST assumes that they affect crime *primarily* through their effect on negative emotions, such as anger. That is, these strains upset people and they cope through crime. As indicated in Chapter 2, there is some evidence for this position. But as further indicated in Chapter 2, many of these strains may also affect crime because they contribute to low constraint and negative emotionality, reduce social control, and foster the social learning of crime. For example, harsh parental discipline may increase crime because it contributes to low constraint and negative emotionality. Low grades may increase crime because they reduce investment in conventional institutions, a social control argument. And peer abuse may increase crime because it implicitly teaches children that violence is an appropriate way to respond to certain problems, a social learning argument. Researchers can determine the extent to which these different arguments are correct by examining the "intervening mechanisms" between strains and crime. That is, they can examine the extent to which strains increase negative emotions, contribute to low constraint and negative emotionality, reduce social control, and foster the social learning of crime. They can then examine the effect of these later factors on crime (e.g., the effect of negative emotions on crime). The best evidence, at present, is that strains increase crime for all of the above reasons (see Chapter 2; Agnew, 1985, 1993, 1995a, 2005b; Brezina, 1998; also see Thaxton and Agnew, 2004). I discuss this issue further in Chapter 9, when I discuss the possibility of constructing an integrated theory of crime.

Types of Strains That Do Not Increase Crime

There is good reason to believe that several major strains do not increase crime. In fact, the experience of certain strains may reduce the likelihood of crime. This is the case with parental punishments that are consistently applied, *not* excessive, and *not* harsh (e.g., not verbally or physically abusive). While most juveniles do not like being punished by their parents, much data indicate that the consistent and reasonable use of punishments is associated with less rather than more crime (Agnew, 2005a). This fact is easily explained in terms of social control and social learning theories. Both of these theories argue that the *proper application of punishments* reduces the likelihood of crime.

A second type of strain that does not increase crime involves the inability of individuals to achieve their educational and occupational goals. Several studies have asked individuals about their educational and occupational "aspirations," or the amount of education and the type of job they would *ideally* like to achieve, and about their educational and occupational "expectations," or the amount of education and the type of job they *realistically* expect to achieve. Drawing on the classic strain theories of Merton (1938), Cohen (1955), and Cloward and Ohlin (1960), these studies argue that crime should be higher among individuals who do not expect to achieve their educational and occupational aspirations. Much data, however, suggest that this is not the case. The *expectation that one will not achieve one's educational or occupational aspirations* does not appear to increase the likelihood of crime (see Agnew, 1995d, 2001; Jensen, 1995).

Finally, a few studies have examined whether unpopularity with peers is related to crime. Such studies focus on adolescent samples and argue that popularity with peers is a major goal for most adolescents. The inability to achieve this goal, therefore, should be an important type of strain. The data, however, suggest that *unpopularity with peers* is not related to crime or is associated with lower levels of crime (see Agnew, 2001; Agnew and Brezina, 1997; Agnew and White, 1992). This includes unpopularity with peers in general and with members of the opposite sex. It is important to note, however, that unpopularity with peers is distinct from peer abuse.

Conclusion

It is clearly the case that certain strains are more likely than others to lead to crime. This fact raises a major question for GST: what are the characteristics of those types of strains most likely to cause crime? Answering this question is important because it will help us predict which strains are most likely to lead to crime. While we know that some strains are related to crime and others are not, there are many more strains whose relationship to crime is uncertain. Answering this question may also help us control crime. The most obvious way to control crime is to reduce the strains that people experience, but that is not always possible. But if we better understand why some strains increase crime while others do not, we may be able to alter strains in ways that reduce the likelihood of crime. For example, we may be able to teach parents to punish in ways that reduce rather than increase the likelihood of further misbehavior. (This issue is discussed further in Chapter 8). The next section draws on the above review and other material in an effort to describe the characteristics of those types of strains most likely to cause crime.

What Are the Characteristics of Those Types of Strains Most Likely to Cause Crime?

Chapter 2 described *why* strains increase the likelihood of crime. Briefly, strains may elicit strong negative emotions, which create pressure for corrective action, reduce the ability to engage in legal coping, reduce the perceived costs of crime, and create a disposition

for crime. Strains may also contribute to personality traits conducive to crime, reduce social control, and foster the social learning of
crime. In this section, I argue that some strains are more likely to
have these effects than others. In particular, strains are more likely
to have these effects when they (a) are seen as high in magnitude, (b)
are seen as unjust, (c) are associated with low social control, and (d)
create some pressure or incentive to engage in criminal coping.
Strains with these characteristics, then, are most likely to cause
crime.

The Strains Are Seen as High in Magnitude

Imagine that you are chatting with a group of acquaintances and
someone reacts to a remark you make by stating "you don't know
what you're talking about." Now imagine the same situation, but
this time someone reacts to your remark by stating "you're an
asshole" and shoving you. Both reactions are likely to upset you,
but I think most people would agree that the second reaction is
more likely to lead to crime. Part of the reason for that is that the second reaction is more severe than the first. And, generally speaking,
strains that are seen as more severe or higher in magnitude are more
likely to result in crime. The magnitude of the strain refers to the extent to which a strain is negatively evaluated; that is, the extent to
which it is disliked and viewed as having a negative impact on one's
life. A severe strain increases the likelihood of criminal coping for
several reasons:

- A severe strain is more likely to generate strong negative emotions, including anger, depression, and fear.

- A severe strain directly reduces the ability of individuals to
  cope in a legal manner. For example, it is more difficult to legally cope with a large rather than a small financial problem.
  A large financial problem is more likely to exhaust individuals' savings and ability to borrow from others, making criminal coping more likely. Severe strains, then, are more likely to
  tax legal coping abilities.

- A severe strain, particularly one that is high in degree and of
  long duration, is more likely to contribute to the traits of negative emotionality and low constraint. For example, strains of

long duration are more likely to make one irritable—a key component of negative emotionality.

- A severe strain is more likely to contribute to low social control. For example, an individual's emotional bond to parents is unlikely to be affected by a minor argument, but might be jeopardized by a severe argument.

- A severe strain is more likely to foster the social learning of crime. For example, the desperation created by a severe strain is more likely to lead individuals to join criminal groups or come to believe that crime is justified.

How Can Researchers Determine if Strains Are Seen as High in Magnitude (or Likely to Be Seen as High in Magnitude)? Researchers can employ several techniques. First, researchers can ask individuals to rate the severity of the strains they are experiencing. Second, researchers can ask a sample of group members or a panel of judges familiar with the group being examined whether they think particular strains are likely to be seen as severe. It should be kept in mind, however, that the ratings obtained from these two techniques will reflect both the characteristics of the strains and of the raters. People high in negative emotionality, for example, will be more likely to rate a given strain as severe (see Agnew, 2001, for a discussion of how to overcome this problem). Finally, researchers can take account of the factors listed below to estimate the likelihood that particular strains will be seen as severe.[2]

What Characteristics of Strains Influence Perceptions of Magnitude? There is reason to believe that several features of the strain influence perceptions of magnitude (see Agnew, 2001, for a fuller discussion). These features include:

A. The *degree or size of the strain*. It is sometimes possible to measure the size of a strain in terms of a standard metric, like the amount of money lost. This is often not possible, however. Further, the metrics used to measure the size of strain vary from one type of strain to another, making it difficult to make comparisons across types of strains. Drawing on the stress research, we might deal with this problem by having judges or group members rate the size of the strain using a common metric. For example, a variety of strains might be described, some involving the loss of valued possessions, some the experience of negative treatment, and some the inability to achieve one's goals. Judges might then be asked to rate the value of lost possessions, the adversity of negative treatment, or the extent of goal blockage on a scale from 1 (low) to 10 (high).

B. The *duration, frequency, recency, and expected duration of the strain* are also likely to influence the perceived magnitude of the strain. Consider, for example, the following two strains. In one case, an individual was insulted once in the distant past by a neighbor. In another case, an individual has been frequently insulted by a neighbor over a long period of time, the insults continue, and the individual believes they will continue into the future. Clearly, the second strain is likely to be seen as higher in magnitude. Generally speaking, we would expect strains that are more frequent, more recent, of longer duration, and expected to continue in the future to be seen as higher in magnitude. The stress literature provides some support for these arguments, with data suggesting that such strains have a larger negative impact on people. For example, they make people more depressed (see Agnew, 2001).

C. The *centrality of the strain.* Centrality refers to whether the strain threatens the *core* goals, needs, values, activities, and/or identities of the individual (see Agnew, 2001). For example, does the strain interfere with the achievement of one of an individual's core goals, perhaps monetary success, or does it interfere with the achievement of a secondary goal, perhaps proficiency as a tennis player? Does the strain threaten a core identity, perhaps masculine identity, or a secondary identity, perhaps identity as a good chess player? Certain strains are such that they threaten a broad range of goals, values, needs, identities, and activities, so they are likely to be high in centrality for most people who experience them. This is the case, for example, with "extreme stressors" (Dohrenwend 1998, 2000) and "traumatic events" (Wheaton et al., 1997). Examples include physical abuse by parents, sexual assault or abuse, chronic unemployment, and combat in a war zone. Other events and conditions may be seen as central in some groups or among some individuals, but not among others. This reflects the fact that there are group and individual differences in such things as goals, values, and identities. For example, most men in the United States attach strong importance to their masculine identity and dislike it very much when that identity is threatened (e.g., they are accused of being "sissies"). Most females, however, attach much less importance to masculine identity.

In sum, strains are more likely to lead to crime when they are seen as high in magnitude, with magnitude affecting negative emotions, the ability to cope in a legal manner, the personality traits of low constraint and negative emotionality, social control, and the social learning of crime. The perceived magnitude of strains is a function of several characteristics, including the size of the strain; the duration, frequency, recency, and expected duration of the strain; and the centrality of the strain. However, we do not yet know how these factors combine to influences perceptions of magnitude.

The Strains Are Seen as Unjust

Imagine you are walking down the street. Someone accidentally trips on a crack in the sidewalk, bumps into you, and knocks you to the ground. Now imagine that you are walking down the street and someone deliberately shoves you aside, knocking you to the ground. Both incidents qualify as strains; being knocked to the ground is disliked by most people. But which incident do you think is more likely to result in a criminal response?

I think most people would agree that the second incident, involving the deliberate shove, is more likely to result in crime. Even though both incidents involve the same amount of physical harm, the behavior in the second incident is more likely to be seen as unjust. And there are several reasons why unjust strains are more likely to lead to crime:

- Unjust strains are more likely to lead to anger and related emotions (see Agnew, 1992, 2001). And as indicated in Chapter 2, such emotions occupy a special place in GST. In particular, they are especially likely to lead to other-directed crime. This occurs because they create much pressure for corrective action, reduce the ability to engage in legal coping, reduce the perceived costs of crime, and, especially, increase the disposition for crime.

- Unjust strains are more likely to contribute to the traits of negative emotionality and low constraint. Unjust treatment, for example, is more likely to make people irritable and to reduce their concern for others (a key component of low constraint).

- Unjust strains are more likely to reduce social control, especially when the unjust strains are associated with those who exercise social control. In particular, efforts to exercise direct control will be less effective when such efforts are seen as unjust. And unjust treatment by conventional others and institutions is likely to jeopardize the individual's ties to such others and institutions. For example, juveniles may come to dislike their teachers if they feel that their teachers unfairly punish them.

- Unjust strains are more likely to foster the social learning of crime. For example, unjust treatment is more likely to foster the belief that crime and deviance are justified. In this area, Agnew and Peters (1986) found that students were more likely to believe that cheating was justified when they were treated unfairly by their teachers (e.g., their teachers showed favoritism when giving out grades, or gave overly difficult and tricky exams).

How Can Researchers Determine if Strains Are Seen as Unjust (or Likely to Be Seen as Unjust)? Again, researchers can employ several techniques. As before, the most direct technique is to ask individuals to rate the injustice of the strains they have experienced. Researchers might also ask a sample of group members or a panel of judges familiar with the group being examined whether they think particular strains are likely to be seen as unjust. The ratings obtained from these two techniques, however, will reflect both the characteristics of the strains and the characteristics of the individuals making the ratings. Just as some individuals are more likely than others to dislike a given event, some are more likely to rate a given event as unjust. This is especially true of those who are low in constraint and high in negative emotionality (Piquero et al., 2004). Finally, researchers might use their knowledge of the justice literature to determine whether particular strains are likely to be seen as unjust. In particular, there has been a good deal of research on those factors that determine whether individuals view events and conditions as unjust.

What Characteristics of Strains Influence Perceptions of Injustice? The justice research suggests that a strain is most likely to be seen as unjust when it involves *the voluntary and intentional violation of a relevant justice norm or rule.* Most strains involve perpetrators who do something to victims. We are more likely to view the perpetrators' behavior as unjust if they freely chose to treat their victims in a way that they knew would probably be disliked (the "voluntary and intentional" part). We are less likely to view the behavior as unjust if it is the result of such things as reasonable accident or chance. That is why we are less upset by an accidental bump than by a deliberate shove, even though both may cause the same physical harm. We are also less likely to view strains as unjust if they are the result of our own behavior (e.g., we injure ourselves while behaving in a reckless manner) or natural forces (e.g., our home suffers damage during a storm).

Unjust behavior, however, involves more than a voluntary and intentional effort to harm someone. For example, parents voluntarily and intentionally punish their children on a regular basis, but we usually do not view their behavior as unjust. Likewise, teachers voluntarily and intentionally assign low grades to students on a regular basis, but we usually do not view their behavior as unjust. In order for voluntary and intentional behaviors to be seen as unjust, they must also violate a relevant justice rule. In particular, researchers have discovered that most people employ certain rules to determine whether a particular behavior is just or unjust (see Agnew, 2001 for a fuller discussion). The voluntary and intentional infliction of strain is most likely to be seen as unjust when:

A. Victims believe the strain they experienced is *undeserved.* In the United States, victims often believe that their strain is deserved if it is the result of negatively valued behavior on their part (e.g., a child is punished for misbehaving) or if it is the result of the possession of certain negatively evaluated characteristics deemed relevant in the particular situation (e.g., a job applicant is turned down because he or she does not have relevant work experience). Furthermore, the strain must not be excessive given the negatively evaluated behavior or the characteristics of the victims (e.g., parents should not impose a *harsh* punishment when their children engage in *mild* misbehavior). Violations of these conditions foster the impression that the strain is undeserved.

B. Victims believe that their strain is *not in the service of some greater good.* The infliction of strain is often justified by appeals to higher purposes or authorities; for example, nations may ask individuals to serve in combat to protect their country or gangs may ask members to risk injury for the protection of "turf." Related to this, perpetrators may justify the strains they inflict by claiming that their victims will achieve some greater good. Parents, for example, may claim that they need to limit the autonomy of their children in order to protect them from greater harm. Doctors may claim that patients need to undergo painful medical procedures to protect their health.

C. Victims believe that the *process used to decide whether to inflict their strain is unjust.* Among other things, victims are more likely to view the process as unjust if (a) they have no voice in the decision to inflict the strain, (b) they do not respect and trust those inflicting the strain, (c) they believe that those inflicting the strain lack certain important information, and/or (d) no rationale is provided for the decision to inflict the strain. For example, juveniles are more likely to feel that the punishments they receive from teachers are unjust if the teachers did not give them a chance to tell "their side of the story," if they believe their teachers "have it in for them," or if the teachers fail to explain the reason for their punishments.

D. The strain *violates strongly held social norms or values,* especially those embodied in the criminal law. Related to this, the strain involves *treatment that is generally perceived as disrespectful, inconsiderate, or aggressive.* For example, people are more likely to feel that their treatment by the police is unjust if the police are verbally abusive to them.

E. The strain that victims experience is *very different from their past treatment in similar circumstances and/or from the treatment of similar others.* For example, suppose a juvenile who teases his sister is usually punished by receiving a stern lecture from his parents, but on one occasion the teasing results in his being grounded for a week. The juvenile is likely to feel that this punishment is unjust, as it is much more severe than the usual sanction. Or suppose a teacher punishes most students who talk in class by giving them detention for one day, but one student is punished by being given detention for a week. This student is also likely to feel that the punishment is unjust.

Individuals are likely to perceive their strain as unjust if criteria A *and* B are satisfied, *or* if one of the other criteria are satisfied. I know this sounds rather complicated, but the characteristics of the strain often allow us to roughly judge the likelihood that individuals will view it as unjust. For example, a criminal victimization is quite likely to be viewed as unjust; criminal victimizations are typically seen as undeserved, not in the service of some greater good, violating strongly held social norms, and so on. By contrast, consider a situation where a poorly educated person is politely turned down for a highly paid job. This event is much less likely to be seen as unjust as the strain is deserved, it does not violate strongly held social norms, it does not involve disrespectful treatment, and so on.

In sum, strains are more likely to lead to crime when they are seen as unjust. Strains are likely to be seen as unjust when they involve the voluntary and intentional violation of a justice rule. This violation contributes to anger and related emotions, which are especially conducive to other-directed crimes. Unjust strains are also more likely to contribute to the traits of negative emotionality and low constraint, reduce social control, and foster the social learning of crime.

The Strains Are Associated With Low Social Control

Consider the following two strains. First, someone is unemployed for a long period of time. Second, a well-paid lawyer has to work long hours on a regular basis, often performing difficult and complex tasks. I think most people would agree that the first strain is more likely to result in crime. This example highlights a third factor affecting the likelihood that strains will lead to crime. Strains are more likely to lead to crime when they are associated with low social control.

As you may recall from Chapter 1, there are several types of social control, with each referring to a factor or set of factors that restrains individuals from crime. There is *direct control,* which refers to the extent to which others set rules that prohibit crime, monitor behavior, and consistently sanction individuals for rule violations. It is easier for individuals to engage in crime when others exercise little direct control over them—for example, when their parents fail to monitor them and sanction them for rule violations. There is the *emotional bond or attachment to conventional others,* such as family members and teachers. It is easier to engage in crime when such bonds are weak, because individuals do not have to worry about hurting close others or jeopardizing relationships with them. There is *investment in conventional institutions,* such as school and work. It is easier to engage in crime if one is doing poorly at school, is unemployed or employed in a "bad" job, and has little hope for the future. Individuals in such circumstances have little to lose through crime. And there are individuals' *beliefs regarding crime.* It is easier to engage in crime when one does not believe that it is wrong to do so.

Certain strains are associated with low levels of social control. For example, this is the case with parental rejection. Children who are rejected by their parents probably have little emotional bond to them and are probably subject to little direct control by them. To give another example, those strains involving unemployment and work in the secondary labor market ("bad jobs") are associated with a low investment in conventional institutions. Strains associated with low social control are more likely to result in crime for several reasons:

- Such strains reduce the costs of crime. Juveniles who are rejected by parents, for example, can engage in crime with little worry about whether their crime will hurt their parents and whether their parents will catch and punish them. Individuals who are unemployed can engage in crime without worrying that crime will jeopardize their jobs.

- Strains associated with low social control reduce the ability to engage in legal coping. Individuals who are low in control often lack the social supports and resources that facilitate legal coping. Juveniles who are rejected by their parents, for example, probably do not receive much help from their parents in coping with strains. Individuals who are unemployed or employed in bad jobs do not have the financial resources that often allow for legal coping (e.g., moving to a better neighborhood or going to a marriage counselor).

- Strains associated with low social control may also contribute to the traits of negative emotionality and low constraint. Individuals who are poorly controlled by others, for example, are less likely to learn how to control themselves (or develop high constraint).

While some strains are associated with low social control, others are associated with high control. For example, a major juvenile strain involves parental supervision. Parents often impose rules that juveniles do not like and sanction juveniles for violating these rules. Parental supervision, however, is associated with high social control, particularly direct control. To give another example, a major occupational strain involves the long hours and difficult tasks associated with many professional and managerial jobs. This strain is associated with a strong investment in conventional activities. Individuals experiencing these types of strain are less likely to engage in crime, primarily because the costs of crime are higher for them. Also, their close ties to others and large investment in conventional institutions increase their ability to engage in legal coping. Further, they are more likely to possess personality traits that are opposed to crime.

These arguments help explain why the inability to achieve educational and occupational goals is unrelated to crime. The pursuit of such goals implies some level of social control. As Kornhauser (1978:47) states:

> If the child is sufficiently socialized to have a strong desire for conventional goals [like educational and occupational success], he should be well enough socialized also to have internalized values governing the conventional means of achieving them. . . . He should also be strongly enough attached to conventional persons and institutions to resist the temptation to use nonnormative means.

The pursuit of educational and occupational success therefore implies at least some attachment to conventional others and the acceptance of conventional values.

How Can Researchers Determine if Strains Are Associated With Low Social Control? Researchers should estimate the extent to which the strain being examined is associated with the major types of control: direct control, attachment to conventional others, investment in conventional institutions, and the belief that crime is wrong. This is easily done in certain cases. For example, suppose that the strain being examined stems from employment in a prestigious, high-paying job; that clearly suggests a strong investment in conventional institutions. In other cases, researchers can employ observational or survey research to determine whether the strain is associated with low or high social control. For example, survey data can be used to determine whether individuals who desire educational and occupational success are, in fact, high in such types of control as attachment to conventional others and the belief that crime is wrong.

In sum, strains are more likely to lead to crime when they are associated with low social control because the low control reduces the costs of criminal coping, reduces the ability to cope in a legal manner, and contributes to the traits of low constraint and negative emotionality.

The Strains Create Some Pressure or Incentive for Criminal Coping

A final factor affecting the likelihood that a strain will lead to crime is the extent to which the strain creates some incentive or pressure to engage in criminal coping. *Certain strains are more easily resolved through crime and/or less easily resolved through legal channels than others* (see Brezina, 2000). As a consequence, individuals have more incentive to cope with these strains through crime. For example, the type of strain involving a desperate need for money is more easily resolved through crime than is the type involving the inability to achieve educational success. It is much easier to get money through crime than it is to get educational success. Also, *certain strains are associated with exposure to others who model crime, reinforce crime, teach beliefs favorable to crime, or otherwise try to pressure or entice the individual into crime.* For example, individuals who experience child abuse are exposed to criminal models who may foster the belief that crime is an appropriate way to deal with one's problems. To give another example, many interpersonal disputes occur before an audience, with the audience members often urging or pressuring the disputants to engage in violence.

Strains that create some pressure or incentive to engage in criminal coping are more likely to result in crime primarily because they foster the social learning of crime. That is, they increase the likelihood that individuals will view crime as a desirable, justifiable, or excusable method for coping with their strains. Such strains may also reduce the ability to engage in legal coping, given that some of these strains are, by definition, more difficult to cope with through legal channels than others.

How Can Researchers Determine if Strains Create Some Pressure or Incentive for Criminal Coping? Researchers should consider the following factors when determining whether a particular strain creates some pressure or incentive for criminal coping:

A. What noncriminal and criminal options are available for coping with the strain? How easily implemented are these options? And how effective are they in reducing the strain? It should be kept in mind that the ease of implementation and the effectiveness of criminal and noncriminal options depends on both the characteristics of the strain and the characteristics of the people experiencing the strain (a topic I discuss further in Chapter 4). For example, work is a more easily implemented and effective option for coping with monetary strain among well-educated people than among poorly educated people.

B. Does the strain stem from or is it associated with exposure to others who model crime, reinforce crime, present beliefs favorable to crime, or otherwise try to pressure or entice the individual into crime?

Anderson's (1999) discussion of life in a poor, inner-city community provides a nice illustration of these points. Anderson focuses on a particular type of strain in this community: disrespectful treatment, ranging from being stared at too long to physical assault. Perhaps his central point is that young males who experience this type of strain are under much pressure to cope in a violent manner. Violence, in particular, is often the only effective response to this type of strain. Efforts to ignore disrespectful treatment or reason with the perpetrators often result in further abuse—by both the perpetrators and others in the community. The police rarely provide meaningful assistance to individuals in the community (also see Black, 1983). And efforts to ignore or minimize this type of strain are also ineffective. Perpetrators typically escalate their level of abuse and others regularly remind victims of the terrible treatment they have suffered. Further, Anderson stresses that others in the community model violent responses to disrespectful treatment, reinforce violent responses, claim that violence is an appropriate way to respond to such treatment, and sometimes pressure individuals to engage in violence.

Summary

In sum, strains are most likely to lead to crime when they (a) are seen as unjust, (b) are seen as high in magnitude, (c) are associated with low social control, and (d) create some pressure or incentive for criminal coping. At present, I would argue that all four of these characteristics are roughly equal in importance and that the absence of any one characteristic substantially reduces the likelihood that strains will result in crime—although strains with only some of these characteristics may still increase the likelihood of crime.

What Specific Strains Are Most and Least Likely to Cause Crime?

This section uses the above characteristics to predict which specific strains are most and least likely to cause crime. Drawing on existing research where possible, I roughly estimate the extent to which a range of strains are seen as unjust, are seen as high in magnitude, are associated with low social control, and create some pressure or incentive for criminal coping. (It would of course be desirable to verify my judgments using the research strategies described above.) I focus on several key types of strain, including family, peer, school, and work-related strains. They include most of the strains examined in tests of GST and other strain theories, as well as several strains that have been largely neglected by criminologists. I first list those specific strains that are most likely to cause crime. I then list certain strains which should be much less likely to cause crime.

Strains Most Likely to Cause Crime

I believe that the following strains are likely to be seen as high in magnitude and unjust, to be associated with low social control, and to create some pressure or incentive for criminal coping. In particular, these strains are likely to threaten individuals' core goals, needs, values, and/or activities. These strains typically involve the voluntary and intentional violation of justice rules. For example, they frequently involve disrespectful or aggressive treatment and are likely to be seen as undeserved. Most of these strains are associated with low social control, including low direct control, low attachment to conventional others, low investment in conventional institutions, and/or the weak condemnation of crime. Criminal coping is often an effective, short-term solution to these strains. Many of these strains involve exposure to others who model crime (e.g., abuse by parents, peers, and spouses). And many increase the likelihood of association with others who model crime, reinforce crime, and present beliefs favorable to crime (e.g., homelessness, unemployment, work in the secondary labor market) (see Agnew, 2001, for a fuller discussion of these issues).

The first set of strains affect mainly juveniles.

A. *Parental rejection.* Parents who reject their children do not express love or affection for them, show little interest in them, provide little support to them, and often display hostility toward them. Data indicate that parental rejection is strongly related to delinquency (Agnew, 2001, 2005a; Maxwell, 2001; Sampson and Laub, 1993).

B. *Supervision/discipline that is erratic, excessive, and/or harsh* (use of humiliation/insults, threats, screaming, and/or physical punishments). Data indicate that the parental use of erratic, excessive, and harsh discipline is strongly related to crime. Limited data also suggest that school and criminal justice officials who employ this type of discipline/supervision increase the likelihood of crime—although more research is needed in this area (e.g., Agnew, 1989, 2001, 2005a; Colvin, 2000; Lanza-Kaduce and Radosevich, 1987; Maxwell, 2001; Mazerolle et al., 2000; Patterson et al., 1992; Sampson and Laub, 1993; Sherman, 1993, 2000; Tyler, 1990).

C. *Child abuse and neglect.* Child abuse and neglect include physical abuse; sexual abuse; emotional abuse; and the failure to provide adequate food, shelter, medical care, and affection/attention (neglect). Data suggest that abuse and neglect are related to crime, especially abuse and neglect that have been recently experienced (e.g., Baron, 2004; Colvin, 2000; Ireland et al., 2002; Piquero and Sealock, 2000; Smith and Thornberry, 1995; Thornberry et al., 2001).

D. *Negative secondary school experiences.* Negative school experiences include low grades, negative relations with teachers (e.g., teachers treat the juvenile unfairly, or belittle or humiliate the juvenile), and the experience of school as boring and a waste of time. Data indicate that negative school experiences are related to delinquency (Agnew, 1989, 2005a; Colvin, 2000; Morash and Moon, 2005a; Sampson and Laub, 1993).

E. *Abusive peer relations, especially among youth.* Peer abuse includes insults, ridicule, gossip, threats, attempts to coerce, and physical assaults. A recent newspaper article focused on how juveniles are now using the Internet to abuse one another. For example, "online lists rating a school's girls as 'hottest,' 'ugliest,' or 'most boring' are common. One that surfaced at [a New York] school listed names, phone numbers and what were said to be the sexual exploits of dozens of girls" (Harmon, 2004). Peer abuse has been neglected as a type of strain, although data suggest that it is widespread and that it often has a devastating effect on victims (e.g., Ambert, 1994; Lockwood, 1997). Limited data suggest that such abuse may increase the likelihood of crime (see Agnew, 1990a, 2001; Agnew et al., 2002; Agnew and Brezina, 1997; Colvin, 2000; Wallace et al., 2005).

The second set of strains affect mainly adults:

F. *Work in the secondary labor market.* Such work commonly involves unpleasant tasks (e.g., simple, repetitive, or physically demanding work, or work that requires a subservient stance), little autonomy, coercive control (e.g., threats of being fired), low pay, few benefits, little prestige, and very limited opportunities for advancement. Further, such work is often intermittent in nature. Data suggest that work in the secondary labor market is associated with crime (Agnew, 2005b; Colvin, 2000; Crutchfield and Pitchford, 1997).

G. *Unemployment, especially when it is persistent and blamed on others* (e.g., Baron and Hartnagel, 1997; Box, 1987; Colvin, 2000; Hagan and McCarthy, 1997; Uggen, 2000).

H. *Marital problems.* Such problems include frequent conflicts and verbal and physical abuse. There has not been much research on the impact of marital problems on crime, although data indicate that individuals who do not get along with their spouses are more likely to engage in crime (e.g., Agnew, 2005b; Sampson and Laub, 1993).

The final set of strains affect both juveniles and adults:

I. *The failure to achieve selected goals, including thrills/excitement, high levels of autonomy, masculine status, and the desire for much money in a short period of time* (see Agnew, 1997, 2001, 2006a; Agnew et al., 1996; Anderson, 1999; Baron, 2004; Cernkovich et al., 2000; Colvin, 2000; Katz, 1988; Matza and Sykes, 1961; Messerschmidt, 1993; Moffitt, 1993; Tittle, 1995). Unlike the goals of educational and occupational success, the pursuit of these goals is *not* associated with high levels of social control. In particular, the pursuit of these goals does not imply a strong attachment to conventional others or the acceptance of conventional values (see Cernkovich et al., 2000, on money goals). Rather, the pursuit of these goals frequently stems from the possession of certain personality traits, like sensation seeking (White et al., 1985); exposure to deviant groups, like delinquent peer groups (see Matza and Sykes, 1961); and structural conditions, like poverty in the midst of plenty (see Kornhauser, 1978). Also, these goals are easily achieved through crime. Several studies, in particular, report that crime is frequently used to get money, obtain thrills/excitement, demonstrate or obtain autonomy, and "accomplish" masculinity (e.g., Agnew, 1984; Agnew et al., 1996; Anderson, 1999; Baron, 2004; Cernkovich et al., 2000; Colvin, 2000; Jakupcak, 2003; Katz, 1988; Messerschmidt, 1993; Mullins et al., 2004).

J. *Criminal victimization.* Being criminally victimized is one of the most severe types of strain, and a rapidly growing body of research suggests that such victimization is strongly related to criminal offending (see Agnew, 2002; Baron, 2004;

Eitle and Turner, 2002; Lauritsen et al., 1991, 1992; Sampson and Lauritsen, 1993; Shaffer, 2003; Wallace et al., 2005). Also, the criminal victimization of one's family members and friends may increase the likelihood of crime. Further, the anticipation of being criminally victimized may increase crime (see Agnew, 2002; Eitle and Turner, 2002).

K. *Residence in economically deprived communities.* Such residence is associated with a wide range of strains, including economic strains, high rates of criminal victimization, family problems, school problems, and peer abuse. Much data indicate that crime rates are higher in such communities and that the residents of such communities are more likely to engage in crime (see Chapter 7).

L. *Homelessness.* Homelessness is associated with a range of strains, including a desperate need for money, a need for food and shelter, frequent conflicts with others, and criminal victimization. Data suggest that homelessness and its attendant problems are associated with crime (Baron, 2004; Baron and Hartnagel, 1997; Hagan and McCarthy, 1997).

M. *Discrimination based on characteristics such as race/ethnicity and gender.* Discrimination based on race and sex is quite common in the United States (Ambert, 1994). Further, experiences with discrimination contribute to psychological distress (Brown et al., 1999; Harrell, 2000). Criminologists, however, have not devoted much attention to the effects of discrimination on individual offending, although a few recent studies have linked discrimination based on race and gender to crime (e.g., Anderson, 1999; Eitle, 2002; Eitle and Turner, 2003; Katz, 2000). For example, Simons et al. (2003) found that discrimination increased crime among a sample of African American youth. They measured discrimination with a set of 13 questions, including:

- How often has someone yelled a racial slur or racial insult at you just because you are African American?

- How often have the police hassled you just because you were African American?

- How often has someone threatened you physically just because you were African American?

In sum, a range of strains are predicted to increase the likelihood of crime. Existing data suggest that many of these strains do in fact increase the likelihood of crime, with several of these strains being among the most important predictors of crime. Other of these strains, like peer abuse and discrimination, have not been well researched by criminologists.

Strains Least Likely to Cause Crime

It is also important to list those types of strains that should be least likely to cause crime. At a general level, I would predict that those strains which are *low in magnitude* will be weakly related to crime. Researchers, then, should estimate the magnitude of the strains they are examining using one of the methods listed above. This is something that is rarely done in the criminology research. If we look at those factors said to influence the perceived magnitude of strains, we would predict that the following types of strains will have a relatively weak effect on crime: strains that are small in degree; strains that were briefly experienced in the distant past, with no hope of recurrence; and strains that threaten secondary goals, needs, values, identities, or activities.

Also, I would predict that those strains that are *seen as just* (or not seen as unjust) will be less likely to cause crime. This includes those types of strains that are clearly the result of reasonable accident or chance, the victims' own behavior, or "natural causes" like bad weather and disease. Many of the strains commonly included in the stressful life-events scales used to test GST likely fall into this category, like accident, serious illness or injury, serious illness or injury of brother or sister, brother or sister leaving home for college or a job, and a family member dying.

At a more specific level, the following strains should be less likely to cause crime for the reasons indicated below.

The Failure to Achieve Goals Such as Educational Success, Occupational Success, and Middle-Class Status. As argued above, the pursuit of these conventional success goals implies some level of social control. Also, the inability to achieve these goals is not likely to create strong pressure for criminal coping. In particular, these goals are not easily achieved through criminal means, like theft and violence. In fact, criminal behavior may undermine the achievement of these goals. As indicated, data suggest that the expected failure to achieve one's educational and occupational aspirations is not related to crime.

Supervision/Discipline by Parents, Teachers, Criminal Justice Officials, and Other Conventional Authority Figures That Is (a) Consistent, (b) Not Excessive, and (c) Not Verbally or Physically Abusive. Such supervision/discipline may be strongly disliked (e.g., juveniles being grounded, offenders being arrested). But this supervision/discipline is not likely to be seen as unjust since it is administered in a fair *way* by legitimate authority figures, is not excessive, is not aggressive or disrespectful, and does not violate widely shared social values. Further, such supervision/discipline creates a high level of direct control and reduces the likelihood of association with delinquent others. Much data demonstrate that parental supervision/discipline of this type is associated with lower levels of crime (Agnew, 2005a; Sampson and Laub, 1993). And some data suggest that this may also be the case when such supervision/discipline is administrated by school and criminal justice officials (Lanza-Kaduce and Radosevich, 1987; Sherman, 1993, 2000; Tyler, 1990).

The Burdens Associated With the Care of Conventional Others, Such as Children or Sick/Disabled Spouses. While such burdens may be disliked, they are not likely to be viewed as unjust. There is a strong cultural expectation that one is supposed to care for children and sick/disabled spouses. In fact, one is usually labeled a "bad" parent or spouse if such care is not provided. This type of strain implies at least a moderate level of social control: caregivers likely have strong emotional bonds to the persons in their care. This type of strain also does not create much pressure or incentive for most forms of criminal coping. Caregivers have little opportunity to engage in crime, except for family violence, neglect, certain types of illicit drug use, and possibly shoplifting. Crime is generally not an effective solution to this type of strain. And the burdens associated with caregiving limit association with criminal others. The impact of this type of strain on crime has not been well examined. Data from the stress literature, however, indicate that females are more likely than males to experience this type of strain (see Broidy and Agnew, 1997). This may partly explain why females are less involved in crime than males. It may also help explain why gender differences in crime are smallest for the crimes of family violence, larceny (especially shoplifting), and certain types of illicit drug use, like the misuse of prescription drugs (e.g., Kimmel, 2002; Saunders, 2002; Simoni-Wastila et al., 2004; Wallace et al., 2003).

The Excessive Demands Associated With Conventional Pursuits That Provide Rewards Like High Pay, Prestige, and/or Intrinsic Satisfaction (or That Have a Strong Likelihood of Providing Such Rewards in the Future). The prime examples of such pursuits are attending college and work in prestigious and/or high-paying jobs. Excessive demands include long working hours and work on difficult tasks. This strain may be seen as high in magnitude, but it is not likely to be seen as unjust. The voluntary or quasi-voluntary nature of these conventional pursuits contributes to self-blame, and the victims of this strain may feel that the excessive demands made on them are justified or offset by the rewards they receive (or will receive). This strain is associated with high social control, particularly a strong investment in conventional institutions (e.g., jobs or educational pursuits). And this strain does not create much pressure or incentive for criminal coping. The excessive demands limit the opportunity for association with criminal others. Further, crime is typically not an effective solution to such demands (with the exception of cheating and certain types of white-collar crime). This type of strain has not been well-examined, although we do know that time spent studying is negatively related to crime (Agnew, 2005a; Hirschi, 1969).

Unpopularity With Peers, Especially Criminal Peers, and Isolation From Unsupervised Peer Activities. This type of strain may be seen as high in magnitude, particularly among adolescents, who tend to attach much importance to peers and peer activities. This type of strain may also be seen as unjust. Adolescents may blame their unpopularity and isolation on peers who unfairly reject them or on parents who unfairly limit their social lives. This strain, however, may contribute to an increase in social control by increasing the time that adolescents spend with their parents or other conventional figures. Also, this strain does not create much pressure or incentive for crime. Little time is spent with peers who may reinforce crime, model crime, foster beliefs conducive to crime, or provide opportunities for crime. Data support this prediction: crime is less common among adolescents who report that they are unpopular with peers, have few close friends, have few delinquent friends, never or seldom date, or seldom engage in unsupervised social activities with peers (Agnew,

2001; Agnew and Brezina, 1997; Agnew and Petersen, 1989; Osgood et al., 1996).

A Note Regarding Extreme Instances of the Above Types of Strains. Certain of the above types of strains may lead to crime *in extreme cases.* For example, extraordinary demands at work or school and extraordinary demands for the care of conventional others may be viewed as unjust because they are far outside the range of past experience or the experience of similar others; they may severely tax efforts at conventional coping; and they may eventually undermine conventional attachments and commitments. As such, these extraordinary demands may lead to crime.

Summary

The above lists identify those types of strains that are most and least likely to cause crime. These lists incorporate and extend the work of classic and contemporary strain theorists. Building on the classic strain theorists, they indicate that the inability to achieve certain success goals, like the rapid acquisition of much money, is related to crime, while the inability to achieve other success goals—particularly educational and occupational goals—is not. The lists also include many of the strains that contemporary researchers have identified, like the denial of autonomy goals (Greenberg, 1977; Moffitt, 1993; Tittle, 1995); threats to masculine status (Anderson, 1999; Messerschmidt, 1993); disrespectful, unfair, or abusive police practices (Sherman, 1993, 2000); the types of coercion discussed in Colvin's (2000) theory of differential coercion; and the types of oppression discussed in Hewitt and Regoli's (2002) theory of differential oppression. Further, the lists contain types of strains that have not been extensively discussed in the strain literature—noting which are related to crime and which are not.

How Do We Test the Above Predictions?

The most obvious way to test these predictions is to examine the effects of the different strains on crime. As indicated, this has already been done in several cases. The predictions that certain of the above strains increase crime have been verified in numerous studies. In fact, some of these strains are among the strongest predictors of crime. And the predictions that other strains are much less likely to increase crime has been verified in many studies. Some of these strains, in fact, reduce the likelihood of crime. But the effect of many other strains on crime is less clear. In particular, we need more research on the relationship between crime and abusive peer relations; erratic, excessive, and harsh discipline administered by school and police officials; marital problems; experiences with prejudice and discrimination; the burdens associated with the care of conventional others; the excessive demands associated with conventional pursuits; and the inability to achieve monetary goals, thrills/excitement, autonomy, and masculine status.[3]

Certain Strains May Be More Conducive to Some Types of Crime Than Others

While the problems and negative emotions generated by strains are conducive to a range of crimes, researchers should investigate the possibility that certain strains are more conducive to some types of crime than others. There are several reasons why this might be the case. Certain strains are more readily resolved through some types of crime than others. For example, the inability to achieve monetary goals is best resolved through income-generating crimes, while the inability of adolescents to achieve autonomy goals is best resolved through offenses such as truancy, running away, and curfew violation. Also, strains that occur in one domain—like the family, school, peer, or work domain—may be conducive to crimes in that domain (De Coster and Kort-Butler, 2004). Strains experienced in the family, for example, may be especially conducive to family violence or efforts to escape from the family, such as running away. Further, the conditions associated with certain types of strains may create opportunities for some types of crime and close off opportunities for other types. For example, unemployment reduces opportunities for work-related crimes. Homelessness, however, creates numerous opportunities for a range of "street" crimes.

The Proper Measurement of Strains

When testing the above predictions, it is important to properly measure each type of strain. Many researchers employ rather simplistic measures. In fact, it is quite common to measure the experience of a strain with a single question, even though the responses to this question often provide little information about the magnitude, injustice, or other dimensions of the strain. For example, economic strain is sometimes measured by asking people their family income.

Perhaps as a consequence, researchers often find that this strain is unrelated or weakly related to crime (see Agnew, 2005a). Other researchers, however, have employed more detailed measures of economic strain that provide a much better indication of the magnitude of such strain. For example, some researchers have examined such things as the extent to which a family has enough money for clothing, food, medical care, and bills, and whether family members have had to make any changes to cope with economic hardship, like moving, taking an additional job, canceling medical insurance, or obtaining government assistance (e.g., Conger et al., 1994; Fox and Chancey, 1998; Voydanoff and Donnelly, 1998 ; also see Agnew et al., 1996; Cernkovich et al., 2000). It is typically the case that such measures have substantial impacts on behavior.[4]

The Cumulative Effect of Strains on Crime

While a particular strain may increase the likelihood of crime, it has been argued that crime is especially likely when individuals experience two or more strains close together in time. Experiencing several strains at once is especially likely to generate negative emotions and tax the ability to cope in a legal manner. Unfortunately, it is not uncommon for strains to occur together. One strain, such as a job loss, frequently leads to other strains, such as family conflict (see De Coster and Kort-Butler, 2004; Pearlin, 1989; Wethington, 2000). As a consequence, most researchers who test GST employ cumulative measures, which count the number of different strains experienced. However, these measures often include many strains predicted to have relatively weak effects on crime and exclude many strains predicted to have relatively strong effects on crime. This may explain why such measures usually have only a moderate effect on crime.

As an alternative strategy, I suggest that we first determine which strains are most strongly related to crime. We can then explore the cumulative impact of strains on crime by combining these strains into a single scale. For example, researchers might find that 10 strains have relatively strong effects on crime. Each of these strains might be scored from "1" (the individual does not experience this type of strain) to "5" (the individual experiences this type of strain to an extreme degree). We might then sum the individual's score on each of the ten strains to produce a cumulative measure of strain (e.g., someone who experiences all ten strains to an extreme degree gets a score of "50").[5] If the experience of several strains is especially likely to result in crime, this cumulative measure should have a *nonlinear effect* on crime of the type illustrated in Figure 3.1.

Figure 3.1 The Nonlinear Effect of a Cumulative Strain Measure on Crime

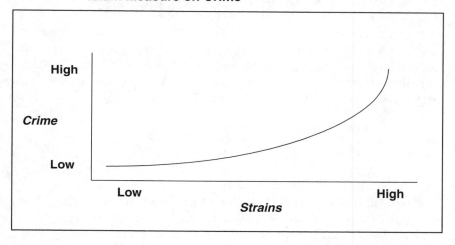

As can be seen, as the cumulative measure increases it has an increasingly large effect on crime. For example, it might be the case that individuals who experience two strains are twice as likely to engage in crime as individuals who experience one strain. However, individuals who experience three strains may be four times as likely to engage in crime as individuals who experience two strains (these numbers are hypothetical). This prediction of a nonlinear effect has not been directly tested to my knowledge. However, certain data provide some support for it. For example, Mazerolle and Piquero (1997) asked a sample of college students how they would respond to certain strains. For example, how would they respond if someone flirted with their romantic partner? A good number of students said they would likely respond to these strains with crime. Further, students who were experiencing more strains in their lives were more likely to state they would respond with crime. This suggests that a given strain is more likely to lead to crime when other strains are being experienced.

Summary

This chapter listed those types of strains most and least likely to cause crime. Those types of strains most likely to cause crime (a) are seen as high in magnitude, (b) are seen as unjust, (c) are associated with low social control, and (d) create some pressure or incentive to engage in crime. Such strains increase the likelihood of crime because they are more likely to elicit negative emotions, reduce the ability to engage in legal coping, contribute to negative emotionality and low constraint, reduce social control, and foster the social learning of crime. Those specific strains most likely to increase crime were listed, as were several of the strains least likely to cause crime.

Notes

1. Those studies testing general strain theory or theories closely related to GST include Agnew 1985, 1989, 1990a, 1999, 2002, 2004; Agnew and Brezina, 1997; Agnew et al., 1996; Agnew et al., 2002; Agnew et al., 2000; Agnew and White, 1992; Aseltine et al., 2000; Bao et al., 2004; Baron, 2004; Baron and Hartnagel, 2002; Bernard, 1990; Brezina, 1998, 1999; Brezina et al., 2001; Broidy, 2001; Colvin, 2000; De Coster and Kort-Butler, 2004; Eitle, 2002; Eitle and Turner, 2002, 2003; Eitle et al., 2004; Gibson et al., 2001; Hay, 2003; Hoffmann and Cerbone, 1999; Hoffmann and Miller, 1998; Hoffmann and Su, 1997; Jang and Johnson, 2003; Katz, 2000; Landau, 1998; Maxwell, 2001; Mazerolle, 1998; Mazerolle and Maahs, 2000; Mazerolle and Piquero, 1997, 1998; Mazerolle et al., 2000, 2003; Morash and Moon, 2005a, b; Paternoster and Mazerolle, 1994; Piquero and Sealock, 2000, 2004; Pratt and Godsey, 2003; Robbers, 2004; Sigfusdottir et al., 2004; Simons et al., 2003; Wallace et al., 2005; Warner and Fowler, 2003.

2. Just as a distinction was made between objective and subjective strains, a distinction can be made between objective magnitude (a strain is seen as high in magnitude by most people) and subjective magnitude (a strain is seen as high in magnitude by the person experiencing it). The first technique measures subjective magnitude, while the second and third techniques measure objective magnitude. There should be much overlap between ratings of subjective and objective magnitude, but not complete overlap. See Agnew (2001) for a fuller discussion.

3. Researchers should also examine the extent to which these strains are seen as high in magnitude and unjust, are associated with low social control, and create some pressure or incentive for criminal coping. Further, researchers should determine the extent to which these dimensions help account for the impact of strains on crime (e.g., are strains seen as unjust more likely to result in crime?). Baron and Hartnagel (2002) and Paternoster and Mazerolle (1994) provide examples of research in these areas.

4. A similar situation characterizes the stress literature, although stress researchers are starting to collect more detailed information on stressors so as to better estimate things like their magnitude. For example, some stress researchers have abandoned simple checklist measures and are employing intensive interviews with semistructured probes (see Herbert and Cohen, 1996; Wethington et al., 1995; Wheaton, 1996). Such techniques were developed because respondents often report trivial stressors when checklist measures are used—even when such checklists attempt to focus on serious stressors (Dohrenwend, 2000; Herbert and Cohen, 1996; Wethington et al., 1995). Also, many stress researchers now recognize that the circumstances associated with a stressor have an important effect on its impact. It is difficult to employ intensive interviews in the large-scale surveys often conducted by criminologists, but criminologists can do a much better job of measuring strains in such surveys.

5. When creating this cumulative measure, researchers might weight the individual strain measures by their effect size. A similar strategy has been successfully employed in the stress literature (Herbert and Cohen, 1996; Turner et al., 1995; Wheaton et al., 1997; also see Agnew and White, 1992). Also, an alternative strategy for investigating the cumulative impact of strains is to determine whether strains interact with one another in their impact on crime through the creation of interaction terms (see Wheaton et al., 1997; note the argument that moderate levels of prior stress sometimes *reduce* the negative effects of current stressors).

Review and Discussion Questions

1. Why is it important to specify those types of strains most and least likely to contribute to crime?

2. What does the research say about those types of strains most and least likely to cause crime?

3. What are the major characteristics of those types of strains most likely to cause crime? Why do these characteristics increase the likelihood of crime?

4. How can researchers determine if a strain is high in magnitude? Related to this, what characteristics of strains influence perceptions of magnitude? Why are strains high in magnitude more likely to cause crime?

5. Why are strains seen as unjust more likely to cause crime? How can researchers determine if strains are seen as unjust or are likely to be seen as unjust? What characteristics of strains influence perceptions of injustice?

6. What do I mean when I state that some strains are associated with low social control (be sure to list the major types of social control)? Why are strains associated with low social control more likely to cause crime? How can we determine if strains are associated with low social control?

7. How can we determine if strains create some pressure or incentive for criminal coping?

8. List any three of the strains said to be most likely to cause crime and any three of those said to be least likely to cause crime. Drawing on the discussion in this chapter, explain why these strains are said to be most or least likely to cause crime.

9. Can you think of any strains not listed in this chapter that are relatively likely to cause crime? Can you think of any strains that are unlikely to cause crime?

10. How should researchers go about trying to test the arguments in this chapter?

11. List any two strains that you believe may increase the likelihood of crime. Do you think these strains are more conducive to some types of crime than others?

12. List any one strain and describe how you might measure it if you were conducting a survey.

13. Why are individuals who experience several strains close together in time said to be especially likely to engage in crime? ✦

Chapter 4

Why Are Some Individuals More Likely Than Others to Respond to Strains With Crime?

Think back to a strain or stressor you recently experienced. How did you respond to this strain? Chances are quite good that you did *not* respond by engaging in crime. While strains increase the likelihood of crime, most individuals do not respond to strains with crime. Rather, they respond in other, noncriminal ways. A number of researchers have asked individuals how they respond to strains and the negative emotions associated with strains, like anger. Such researchers inevitably find that noncriminal responses are more common than criminal responses.

Broidy (2001) examined how college students cope when they are "unable to reach a certain goal" and "bad things happen" to them. The coping strategies listed by Broidy include:

- I try to figure out where I went wrong so I can change the outcome.

- I realize that it wasn't very important after all.

- I ignore it and think about the goals I did accomplish.

- I try to get physical exercise to make myself feel better.

- I try talking to friends or family members to make myself feel better.

- I try talking to a therapist to make myself feel better.

Morris and Reilly (1987) reviewed the prior literature in an effort to describe the coping methods individuals employ when they are in a "bad mood." Such methods include:

- engaging in pleasant activities like eating and shopping (one scale lists 320 commonly enjoyed events or activities)

- trying to distract oneself by watching TV, keeping busy, or engaging in an engrossing activity

- comparing oneself to those who are worse off

- seeking out friends

- avoiding other people

- engaging in problem-directed action of a legal nature (e.g., studying harder in an effort to raise grades)

- consuming alcohol

- retaliating against those deemed responsible for the bad mood

In an article titled "I'm So Mad I Could Scream," Guerrero (1994) examined the ways in which individuals "dealt with feelings of anger in their close relationships over the past month." Based on interviews with 50 undergraduates and an examination of the literature on anger expression, Guerrero produced a list of 21 ways in which individuals cope when they are angry with their partners, including:

- discussing problems with their partners

- sharing feelings with their partners

- trying to "patch things up" with their partners

- hiding feelings from their partners

- denying feeling angry

- giving their partners the silent treatment

- giving their partners cold/dirty looks

- leaving the scene

- yelling and screaming at their partners

- slamming doors or throwing objects

- threatening their partners

So while some individuals cope with their strains and negative emotions in a criminal manner, most cope in a noncriminal manner. These data raise a major question for GST: why are some individuals more likely than others to cope with their strains in a criminal manner? I partly addressed this question in Chapter 3, when I stated that individuals experiencing *certain types of strains* are more likely to engage in criminal coping. I then listed the strains most likely to result in crime. But it is still the case that only some of the individuals who experience these strains cope with crime. *Whether individuals respond to strains with crime depends not only on the types of strains they experience, but also on the characteristics of the individuals and their environments.*

This chapter describes those individual and environmental characteristics that increase the likelihood of criminal coping. As you will see, these characteristics increase the likelihood of criminal coping because they affect the ability to cope in a legal manner, the costs of criminal coping, and the disposition for criminal coping. But before I discuss these characteristics, I provide a brief overview of the major ways of coping with strains.

What Are the Major Ways of Coping With Strains?

Clearly, there are many ways to cope with strains and the negative emotions associated with strains. Researchers often group these coping strategies into a number of smaller categories. Harnish et al. (2000), for example, group coping strategies into six categories: avoidance (not thinking about the strain), positive reappraisal (reinterpreting the strain in a more positive light), religion (relying on religious beliefs or faith to cope), active cognitive coping (trying to think of ways to deal with the strain), active behavioral coping (doing things to reduce the strain), and social support (seeking comfort from others). (Other grouping schemes overlap a good deal with this one; for examples, see Compas et al., 2001; Tolan et al., 2002). I employ a somewhat different grouping scheme, one that reflects my interest in explaining crime. In particular, I group coping strategies into three broad categories, each of which has several subcategories (Agnew, 1992; also see Pearlin, 1989).

First, individuals may employ *behavioral coping strategies of a criminal or noncriminal nature.* Behavioral coping strategies focus on reducing the level of strain and they parallel the major types of strain listed in Chapter 1. So individuals may engage in behaviors designed to protect or retrieve those things they value, terminate or escape from aversive treatment, or achieve their goals. Their actions in these areas may involve criminal or noncriminal behavior. Juveniles seeking to escape from an aversive school environment, for example, may illegally skip school or they may try transferring to another school. Many of the coping strategies described at the start of this chapter involve behavioral coping, like discussing problems with one's partner and engaging in problem-directed action of a legal nature.

Second, individuals may employ *cognitive coping strategies* in an effort to reinterpret objective strains in ways that minimize their subjective adversity. In particular, individuals may try to ignore or minimize the importance of their strains. Take, for example, someone who is unable to achieve her monetary goals. This person might try to ignore or deny her monetary problems, perhaps by engaging in distracting activities. This person might try to convince herself that money is not that important, and that other things—like family and religion—are more important. This person might try to convince herself that she does not need that much money to "get by." And this person might take solace in the fact that she has more money than others (see Agnew, 1992, for a fuller discussion). Many of these cognitive coping strategies were also illustrated in the first part of this chapter, like trying to distract oneself by watching TV and realizing that "it" wasn't very important after all.

Third, individuals may employ *emotional coping strategies* that act directly on the negative emotions created by strains. These strategies try to alleviate negative emotions rather than cognitively reinterpret or behaviorally alter the strains that produced these emotions. Emotional coping strategies may be of a criminal or noncriminal nature. They include the use of illegal and legal drugs, physical exercise, listening to music, meditation, and seeking comfort from friends. Emotional coping may also involve efforts to seek revenge against others. Strains often create a desire for revenge that is distinct from the desire to reduce or escape from the strains. Vengeful behavior may be of a criminal (e.g., assault, vandalism) or noncriminal nature (e.g., malicious gossip), and recent data suggest that such behavior frequently makes one feel better (Mullins et al., 2004; Neergaard, 2004). The first part of this chapter lists several emotional coping strategies, including engaging in pleasant activities, exercising, seeking comfort from friends and family, consuming alcohol, and throwing objects at one's partner.

I should note that individuals often employ more than one coping strategy. An individual experiencing strains at school, for example, may cope by trying to avoid school, convincing himself that school is not that important, and seeking comfort from friends. Individuals are sometimes classified according to their overall "coping style," which refers to the different types of coping they tend to employ and how often they employ them (see Tolan et al., 2002). Some individuals, for example, make frequent use of a broad range of coping strategies. Others focus on one or a few types of coping, like emotional coping. And still others report that they make little or no effort to cope with their strains.

There has been some research on the effectiveness of coping efforts. Most such research examines whether particular strategies or coping styles reduce negative emotions, although a few studies have examined whether coping strategies reduce individuals' levels of crime (e.g., Compas et al., 2001; Harnish et al., 2000; Umberson et al., 2002). The results of such research are somewhat mixed. Also, it is sometimes the case that the effectiveness of a coping strategy varies by the type of strain examined. One study, for example, found that religion was an effective way to cope with the death of a loved one, but not with interpersonal problems like family conflicts (Mattlin et al., 1990). Nevertheless, the data tend to suggest that behavioral coping of a legal nature may reduce negative emotions and crime—probably because such coping reduces the strains that one is experiencing. Certain of the cognitive and emotional coping strategies described above may not be as effective in reducing negative emotions and crime; in fact, some may be associated with increased levels of distress and crime. More research, however, is needed on the effectiveness of different coping strategies and styles, particularly their effectiveness in reducing the likelihood of crime.

Given the current research, the discussion below focuses on those individual and environmental characteristics which directly increase the likelihood of criminal coping, reduce the likelihood of behavioral coping of a legal nature, and—to a lesser extent—undermine the effectiveness of emotional and cognitive coping. For the sake of simplicity, I simply refer to these characteristics as those which increase the likelihood of criminal coping.

What Individual and Environmental Characteristics Increase the Likelihood of Criminal Coping?

This section lists those individual and environmental characteristics believed to increase the likelihood of criminal coping. This list draws on the research on GST, the larger criminology literature, and the stress literature, which describes those factors that influence the reaction to stressors or strains. Five sets of characteristics are presented: (a) poor coping skills and resources, (b) low levels of conventional social support, (c) low social control, (d) association with criminal others and beliefs favorable to crime, and (e) exposure to situations where the costs of criminal coping are low and the benefits are high. Again, these factors increase the likelihood of criminal coping by reducing the ability to cope in a legal manner, reducing the costs of crime, and/or increasing the disposition for crime. Certain of these factors also increase the likelihood of criminal coping by influencing individuals' perception of and sensitivity to strains. That is, these factors influence the subjective perception of objective strains; especially the perceived magnitude and injustice of objective strains. As indicated in Chapter 3, strains that are viewed as unjust and high in magnitude are more likely to prompt criminal coping.[1]

When reading this section, you will notice that the research on those factors predicted to increase the likelihood of criminal coping has produced mixed results. For example, certain studies have found that individuals who associate with other criminals are more likely to cope with strains in a criminal manner, while other studies have not found such an effect. I believe that a major reason for these mixed results is that it is difficult to detect what are known as "conditioning" or "interaction" effects in survey research. (When a factor like association with other criminals influences the effect of strains on crime, we say that this factor "conditions" the effect of strains on crime or "interacts" with strains in its effect on crime.) Survey research usually involves selecting a sample of respondents (e.g., 1,000 high-school students in a particular city), and then interviewing them or having them fill out questionnaires. Survey research is far and away the most common method for determining whether some characteristic conditions the effect of strains on crime. But as McClelland and Judd (1993) demonstrate, survey research frequently fails to detect conditioning effects (also see Mazerolle and Maahs, 2000). Additional reasons for the mixed results are described below.

The mixed findings that I describe, then, should be interpreted with much caution. In fact, it is encouraging that several studies based on survey research have found conditioning effects, given the difficulty of detecting such effects. More research, however, is clearly needed in this area. Ideally, such research should use data from experiments, vignette studies, or field studies, where possible (see Agnew, 2006b; Mazerolle and Maahs, 2000, for further information).

Poor Coping Skills and Resources

Some individuals lack the skills and resources that allow them to cope with strains in a legal manner. Further, they may possess certain coping skills and resources that facilitate criminal coping. A large number of coping skills and resources can be listed. The following list is not exhaustive, but rather focuses on what I believe are the most critical.

Poor Problem-Solving and Social Skills. Strains essentially create a problem for individuals; they have lost something they value, they are being treated in a negative manner by others, or they cannot achieve an important goal. Some individuals possess the skills to solve this problem in a legal manner, while others do not. Data, in particular, suggest that delinquents are more likely than non-delinquents to have poor problem-solving and social skills. Dodge (1986) lists the following five steps in effective problem-solving: (a) search for cues in the environment, (b) interpret these cues, (c) generate possible responses to the situation, (d) consider the possible consequences of the responses, and (e) enact the chosen response. Data suggest that delinquents have problems at each of these steps. They attend to fewer environmental cues; they tend to focus on aggressive cues; they often attribute hostile intent where there is none; they generate fewer alternative responses; they generate more aggressive responses; and they fail to recognize the negative consequences of delinquent behavior. Further, delinquents often lack the social skills to enact prosocial responses. Certain of these social skills are quite basic, like maintaining eye contact when talking with someone; while others are more complex, like recognizing the feelings of others and negotiating with others in an assertive, but nonaggressive manner (also see Agnew, 2005a:447–448).

So individuals who lack good problem-solving and social skills have less ability to cope in a legal manner. They may also be less aware of the costs of criminal coping. For these reasons, poor problem-solving and social skills should increase the likelihood of criminal coping. I am not aware of any tests of this proposition.

Low Constraint and Negative Emotionality. In addition to individuals' skills, the ability to cope is a function of the resources possessed by individuals. Among the key resources are personality traits, including the core personality traits of low constraint and negative emotionality. I briefly described these traits in Chapter 1. Individuals who are low in constraint are impulsive (tend to act without thinking), like to take risks, reject social norms or rules, and have little concern for the feelings or rights of others. Individuals who are high in negative emotionality are easily upset and quick to anger, tend to attribute their problems to others, and have an aggressive or antagonistic interactional style. In popular terms, we might describe people low in constraint and high in negative emotionality as "out of control" and "mean."

Individuals with these traits are less able to cope with strains in a legal manner. Among other things, they tend to act without thinking and they lack the social skills that are often necessary for legal coping (these traits affect criminal coping partly through their effect on problem-solving and social skills). Individuals with these traits are also less aware of and concerned with the costs of crime; in particular, they give little thought to the consequences of their behavior and care little about social norms or the reactions of others. Further, such individuals are more disposed to crime, given their attraction to risky activities and aggressive interactional style. Finally, such individuals are more likely to perceive objective strains in a way that is conducive to crime. In particular, they are more likely to rate objective strains as high in magnitude, given their greater sensitivity to strains. And they are more likely to view such strains as unjust, given their tendency to blame their problems on others (see Piquero et al., 2004).

Agnew and his associates (2002) examined whether the traits of low constraint and negative emotionality condition the effect of strains on crime (or influence whether strains lead to crime). In particular, they used data from a survey that involved interviews with a nationally representative sample of children aged 12 to 16 and their parents and teachers. They measured the strains these children were experiencing, including family-, school-, peer-, and neighborhood-related strains (for example, the children were asked whether their family life was "tense and stressful," whether their parents often yelled at them, whether they hated going to school, whether other kids "picked on" them, and whether their neighborhood was a poor place for kids to grow up). They also estimated the extent to which the children were low in constraint and high in negative emotionality. In particular, a parent and teacher of each child was asked such things as whether the child was "impulsive, acted without thinking," and had "a very strong temper and loses it easily." And the children themselves were asked about the extent of their delinquency in the last year. As predicted, Agnew and his associates found that the children who were high in negative emotionality and low in constraint were much more likely to respond to strains with delinquency. However, other studies that have examined low constraint and negative emotionality (or similar traits) have produced mixed results; some finding that these traits increase the likelihood of criminal coping and some not (Mazerolle and Maahs, 2000; Mazerolle et al., 2000, 2003; Paternoster and Mazerolle, 1994).

Low Socioeconomic Status (SES). Individuals with resources like money, education, and "good jobs" are better able to cope in a legal manner than others. Imagine, for example, two individuals who experience the same strain: unemployment. The first individual is well-educated and has substantial savings, while the second is a high-school drop-out with no savings. Clearly, the first individual is in a much better position to cope with unemployment in a legal manner. She has savings to tide her over while she looks for another job, and her educational credentials, knowledge of the job market, and connections make it easier for her to find work. To give another example, imagine that these same two individuals experience a dispute with a neighbor. Once more, the first individual is in a better position to cope. She is better able to negotiate with her neighbor given the skills, knowledge, and habits associated with a good education; she is better able to secure the cooperation of the police if necessary, partly because of her elevated social position; and she is better able to purchase the services of others who will help her respond to her strain. In fact, the Yellow Pages and newspapers are filled with the ads of individuals and organizations eager to alleviate strains in a legal manner—*if* one has the money to purchase their services. Such individuals and organizations include attorneys, tutors, marriage counselors, physicians, psychologists, real estate agents, and security consultants. So for a variety of reasons, individuals who are low in socioeconomic status are less able to cope with their strains in a legal manner. I should also note that SES influences the costs of criminal coping, with higher SES individuals having more to lose through criminal coping.

Surprisingly, there has not been much research on the extent to which SES influences the effect of strains on crime. Hoffmann and Cerbone (1999) found that family income did not affect the impact of strains on crime. The stress research, however, suggests that lower SES individuals may be more vulnerable to stressors; that is, they may be more likely than higher SES individuals to experience depression and certain other negative reactions in response to stressors (see Thoits, 1995; Turner and Avison, 2003). Also, the criminology literature suggests that lower SES individuals have higher rates of serious offending (Agnew, 2005a). Future research, then, should certainly devote more attention to the effect of SES on criminal coping.

While I have focused on SES, other sociodemographic characteristics like age, gender, and race/ethnicity may also affect the ability to cope with strains in a legal manner. I say more about such effects in Chapter 6 (also see Thoits, 1995),

Low Self-Efficacy. Not only is the individuals' ability to cope in a legal manner important, also important is the individuals' *belief* that they have the ability to cope in a legal manner. Some individuals, high in self-efficacy, believe that they can successfully deal with the problems they encounter in a legal manner. Such individuals are therefore more likely to make an effort at behavioral coping of a legal nature. Other individuals, low in self-efficacy, believe that there is little they can do to legally respond to their strains. They are therefore more likely to engage in criminal coping. The few studies that have examined this prediction have produced mixed results, with most finding that low self-efficacy does not increase the likelihood of criminal coping (Agnew and White, 1992; Baron, 2004; Baron and Hartnagel, 2002; Eitle and Turner, 2003; Hoffmann and Cerbone, 1999; Hoffmann and Miller, 1998; Jang and Johnson, 2003; Paternoster and Mazerolle, 1994).

As indicated, these mixed results may stem from the difficulty of detecting interactions in survey research. They may also stem from the fact that researchers sometimes employ questionable measures of self-efficacy. Agnew and White (1992), for example, measured self-efficacy by asking respondents whether they felt in control of their lives, whether success was a matter of their own doing rather than luck or chance, and whether they believed that others were running their lives. As Jang and Johnson (2003) point out, researchers might benefit from looking at more specific measures of self-efficacy (also see Bandura, 1997; Hoffmann and Miller, 1998). For example, researchers might ask respondents whether they feel they can respond to the *specific problems or strains* they are experiencing in a legal manner.

A Note on Criminal Skills and Resources. The discussion up to this point has examined those skills and resources that influence the ability to cope in a legal manner. But as certain strain theorists have argued, the *inability* to cope in a legal manner does not guarantee that criminal coping will occur (Cloward and Ohlin, 1960; Cullen, 1984). Individuals also need to possess those skills and resources necessary for criminal coping. This idea has not attracted a great deal of support, in part because most criminal activities do not require much in the ways of skills or resources—although there are exceptions, like certain types of white-collar crime. Even so, certain skills and resources may make it easier for individuals to engage in crime and so increase the likelihood of criminal coping. Some of these skills and resources facilitate the commission of violent crimes, and they include physical size, physical strength, fighting ability, and the possession of an "aggressive demeanor" (see Agnew, 1990b, on coercive power). Researchers have not examined the extent to which these resources increase the likelihood of criminal coping. Data, however, suggest that individuals with mesomorphic or muscular body builds are somewhat more likely to engage in crime (Shoemaker, 2000:22–26). And Felson's (1996) analysis of violent incidents found that bigger people are more likely to assault smaller people, suggesting that physical size influences the likelihood of violence.

A more general resource that may promote criminal coping is the level of "criminal self-efficacy;" that is, the extent to which individuals feel that they can successfully respond to their strains through crime. Certain accounts suggest that criminals may be quite high in criminal self-efficacy (e.g., Cromwell, 2003). They often view themselves as tough, street-smart people who are quite adept at criminal coping if the need arises. One armed robber, for example, stated "There is only three types of people in this world: those who wonder what happen; those that know what happen; and then people like me that make shit happen. I make happen whatever I want to happen" (Wright and Decker, 1997:56). But at the same time, criminals may feel that they are unable to *legally* cope with many of their strains, so they are low in "legal self-efficacy." The measures of self-efficacy now used by researchers often fail to distinguish between these two types of self-efficacy, but such a distinction is critical, as one type may promote criminal coping while the other type may promote legal coping.

Low Levels of Conventional Social Support

Individuals often receive assistance or support from conventional others when coping with their strains. Such support may come from family members, friends, teachers, neighborhood residents, religious figures, government agencies, and others. And this support may assume a number of forms. Others may give information or advice on how to cope with strains. For example, parents may advise their child on how to cope with a bully at school. Others may directly assist in coping efforts, or even cope for someone. For example, friends may lend an unemployed person money or even conduct a job search on his or her behalf. And others may provide individuals with emotional support, comforting them and assuring them that things will eventually be all right. Individuals, however, differ in the amount of social support they receive from conventional others. Those who receive less support should be less able to cope with their strains in a legal manner.

Elijah Anderson (1990) provides an example of the importance of social support in his discussion of life in an inner-city community. He states that at one time the young people in this community received much social support from "old heads," or older, respected residents of the community. These old heads would often function as surrogate fathers to many of these young people, providing guidance, encouragement, financial aid, and help in finding jobs. In some cases, they would teach young people the skills and attitudes they needed to earn a living. But in recent years, many of the working- and middle-class old heads have moved to more affluent communities. And the old heads who have remained have less influence, partly because decent-paying jobs in the inner city have become scarcer, making it more difficult for the old heads to assist youth and undermining their lessons about the rewards of hard work and a conventional lifestyle. Anderson suggests that crime rates in the community have increased partly as a consequence.

The few studies that have examined the effect of social support on criminal coping have produced mixed results (Eitle and Turner, 2003; Jang and Johnson, 2005; Paternoster and Mazerolle, 1994; Robbers, 2004). Nevertheless, there is some reason to believe that social support may be an important conditioning variable. The stress literature indicates that social support often reduces the negative consequences of stressors, like the effect of stressors on depression (Thoits, 1995). Studies on "resilient youth" also point to the importance of social support. Resilient youth are young people who have grown up in aversive environments, such as troubled families and very poor neighborhoods, but have nevertheless avoided serious involvement in crime. Data suggest that such youth are distinguished from their more criminal peers partly by the fact that they were able to form close relationships with conventional others, perhaps teachers or coaches, who provided them with social support (Rutter et al., 1998). Related to this, data suggest that mentoring programs, which focus on the provision of social support, may reduce crime if properly implemented (see Agnew, 2005b). Finally, Cullen and his associates present much data suggesting that individuals high in social support are less likely to engage in crime. Among other things, government assistance to the poor reduces violence, parental social support reduces delinquency, and the support provided by spouses and employers reduces crime (Cullen, 1994; Wright and Cullen, 2001). The provision of social support may reduce crime for several reasons, but as Cullen (1994) points out, one of the primary reasons is probably the fact that support allows individuals to better cope with strains.

So there is some reason to believe that social support may reduce criminal coping, although more research is clearly needed in this area. Such research might benefit from employing more specific measures of social support, asking respondents about the extent to which conventional others can help them legally cope with the strains they are experiencing (see Thoits, 1995, for further information on the measurement of social support). Also, researchers should take into account the extent to which individuals receive social support from criminal others, with such support being designed to aid criminal coping (see Cullen, 1994). Criminal others, for example, may advise individuals to cope with strains in a criminal manner, help them carry out criminal acts, or help them deal with the negative emotions—like guilt and fear—that sometimes accompany criminal acts.

Low Social Control

A third set of factors increasing the likelihood of criminal coping has to do with low social control. As you may recall, social control has several components: direct control, the emotional bond to conventional others, the investment in conventional activities, and the belief that crime is wrong. Individuals who are low in social control are more likely to cope with strains through crime because the costs of criminal coping are lower for them. They can commit crimes with little risk of detection and sanction, they have little to lose if they are caught, and they do not believe that crime is wrong—so crime is unlikely to make them feel guilty or bad. Individuals low in social control are also less able to cope with strains in a legal manner. Their weak bonds to conventional others reduce the likelihood that these others will teach them coping skills or provide them with social support. And their weak investment in conventional institutions like school and work means that they lack certain of the resources that facilitate legal coping, like money, education, and good jobs.

A few studies have examined whether social control influences the effect of strains on crime, focusing on emotional bonds to parents, investment in conventional institutions like school, the belief that crime is wrong, and residence in "disorganized" communities where people are less likely to exercise control over one another. These studies have produced mixed results (Agnew et al., 2000, 2002; Aseltine et al., 2000; Baron and Hartnagel, 2002; Hoffmann, 2003; Mazerolle et al., 2000; Mazerolle and Piquero, 1997; Morash and Moon, 2005a). Again, however, these mixed results may stem from the difficulty of detecting interactions in survey research.

Association With Criminal Others/Beliefs Favorable to Crime

A fourth set of factors increasing the likelihood of criminal coping is association with criminal others and beliefs favorable to crime. Individuals who associate with criminal others, like delinquent peers and gang members, are more likely to develop a disposition for crime. Social learning theory, described in Chapter 1, explains why this is so. Criminal others model crime for individuals, which individuals then imitate. Criminal others reinforce individuals' crime in certain circumstances, which leads them to anticipate that crime will be similarly reinforced in the future. And criminal others teach individuals beliefs favorable to crime. In particular, they may teach that crime is a justifiable or excusable response to certain strains—like provocations by others and a desperate need for money.

Criminal others not only increase individuals' disposition for crime, they also lower the perceived costs of crime. Individuals who associate with other criminals may feel that it is easier to "get away" with crime, partly because of the strength found in numbers and partly because they frequently see their peers get away with crime. Further, criminal others may reduce individuals' ability to engage in legal coping. They may provide little support for legal coping. In fact, they may actively discourage and even punish efforts at legal coping. For example, they may ridicule individuals who try to respond to provocations by leaving the scene. Or they may regularly remind individuals of the strains they have suffered, making efforts to cognitively minimize these strains less effective. Finally, individuals who associate with criminal others may be more likely to rate objective strains as high in magnitude and unjust, reflecting the fact that criminal others are often more sensitive to strains and quicker to make hostile attributions (see Bernard, 1990).

Association with criminal others, then, should increase the likelihood of criminal coping for several reasons. Several studies have tested this idea, but—not surprisingly—they have produced mixed results (Agnew et al., 2002; Agnew and White, 1992; Aseltine et al., 2000; Baron, 2004; Baron and Hartnagel, 2002; Eitle and Turner, 2002, 2003; Hoffmann and Miller, 1998; Mazerolle and Maahs, 2000; Mazerolle et al., 2000; Mazerolle and Piquero, 1997; Morash and Moon, 2005a; Paternoster and Mazerolle, 1994).

Individuals should also be more likely to engage in criminal coping if they have beliefs favorable to crime, particularly beliefs that define crime as a desirable, justifiable, or excusable response to strains. Individuals who associate with criminal others are more likely to hold such beliefs, but criminal others are not the only source of such beliefs. Individuals who experience chronic or repeated strains may turn to crime out of desperation, and in doing so they may come to adopt beliefs that justify or excuse their crime. Elijah Anderson (1999), for example, argues that many poor, inner-city residents, especially young males, are frequently treated in a disrespectful manner by others. They are often unable to effectively respond to such treatment in a legal manner. As a consequence, many come to believe that violent responses to disrespectful treatment are sometimes justified.

A few studies have examined whether beliefs favorable to crime increase the likelihood of criminal or deviant coping. Agnew and Peters (1986), for example, asked a sample of college undergraduates whether they experienced certain academic strains—like feeling that their grades are not good enough to achieve their career goals, having other students refuse to help them with their work, having professors show favoritism when giving out grades, and having professors deliberately give them overly difficult or tricky exams. They also asked these students whether they believed that cheating was justified when these sorts of strains occurred (e.g., is cheating justified when professors deliberately give overly difficult or tricky exams?). They found that academic strains were much more likely to lead to cheating among those who believed that such strains justified cheating. Other studies, however, have produced mixed results regarding the effect of beliefs favorable to crime on criminal coping (Baron, 2004; Baron and Hartnagel, 2002; Eitle and Turner, 2003; Mazerolle and Maahs, 2000; Morash and Moon, 2005a; Paternoster and Mazerolle, 1994).

Exposure to Situations Where the Costs of Crime Are Low and the Benefits Are High

Finally, criminal coping is more likely when strained individuals are in situations where the costs of crime are low and the benefits are high. For example, imagine two juveniles who are identical in terms of the above-listed factors; that is, they have identical levels of coping skills and resources, conventional social support, social control, association with criminal others, and beliefs favorable to crime. Now imagine that each of these juveniles experiences the same strain: they see something they badly want at a shopping mall, but they do not have the money to pay for it. But the first juvenile is shopping with his parents, while the second is shopping with his criminal friends. The second juvenile is more likely to shoplift the item, because the costs of doing so are lower and the benefits are higher. There are no parents around who might sanction the shoplifting, and the juvenile's criminal friends might react to the shoplifting with approval.

So the likelihood of criminal coping is also influenced by the situations that people encounter. Criminal coping is more likely in situations where conventional adults are absent, since the costs of crime are lower in such situations. Criminal coping is also more likely where attractive targets for crime are available, like valuable property that is easily moved. And criminal coping is more likely in situations when criminal others are present, as these others more often model, reinforce, and otherwise encourage crime. The presence of attractive targets and criminal others influence individuals' disposition for crime. So other things being equal, individuals who are in situations conducive to crime are more likely to engage in criminal coping. I am not aware of any studies that have tested this idea.

Conclusion

A range of factors, then, are predicted to increase the likelihood that individuals will cope with their strains in a criminal manner. Criminal coping should be more likely when individuals (a) have poor coping skills and resources; (b) have low levels of conventional social support, (c) have low levels of social control, (d) associate with criminal others and hold beliefs favorable to crime, and (e) are in situations where the costs of crime are low and the benefits are high. Researchers have only examined whether some of these factors increase the likelihood of criminal coping, and the results from their studies are mixed. As indicated above, these mixed results may be partly due to the fact that it is difficult to detect conditioning effects in survey research. They may also be due to the overly general way in which some of the above factors have been measured. For example, researchers typically employ very general measures of self-efficacy; they do not examine whether individuals believe they can cope with the specific strains they are experiencing and they do not distinguish "legal self-efficacy" from "criminal self-efficacy." A final reason for the mixed results may be that most researchers examine these factors in isolation from one another.

Whether a given factor increases the likelihood of criminal coping likely depends on the level of the other factors. For example, whether individuals with poor coping skills respond to strains with crime probably depends on such things as their level of conventional social support, social control, and association with delinquent peers. To illustrate, children generally have poor coping skills, but most do not respond to strains in a criminal manner. That is because they usually receive much social support from parents (who often cope on their behalf), they are closely supervised by parents, and they rarely associate with delinquent peers. Given this argument, it may be best for researchers to consider individuals' overall standing on all of those factors that increase the likelihood of criminal coping. Individuals, in particular, might be divided into several groups: those who possess all or most of the factors that increase the likelihood of criminal coping, those who possess some of the factors, and those who possess few or none. Criminal coping should be most likely among those who possess all or most of the factors conducive to criminal coping.

Mazerolle and Maahs (2000) employed this strategy, although they only considered three factors that increase the likelihood of criminal coping: low constraint or self-control, association with delinquent peers, and beliefs favorable to crime. Using data from a nationally representative sample of adolescents, Mazerolle and Maahs computed each individual's "total risk" for criminal coping based on the extent to which they possessed these three factors. Individuals with a high-risk for criminal coping, then, were relatively low in constraint and relatively high in association with delinquent peers and beliefs favorable to crime. Mazerolle and Maahs found that such individuals were much more likely to cope with strains in a criminal manner than those with a medium or low risk for criminal coping. For example, when they focused on a subgroup of adolescents who scored high on several measures of strains, they found that 92 percent of the adolescents at high risk for criminal coping actually engaged in crime, versus only 26 percent of the adolescents at low risk for criminal coping.

So while the research on those factors predicted to influence the effect of strains on crime has produced mixed results, there is reason to believe that further research which addresses the problems indicated above will produce more supportive findings.

Note

1. The factors discussed in this chapter not only influence the effect of strains on crime, but also the effect of strains on negative emotions and the effect of negative emotions on crime. For the sake of simplicity, I focus on the effect of strains on crime, which encompasses the other effects.

Review and Discussion Questions

1. List at least five different ways you might cope with a strain (such as receiving low grades).

2. What is a "conditioning" or "interaction" effect?

3. How do I classify the major types of coping? Can you think of other ways to classify coping strategies?

4. What is meant by "coping style"?

5. What does the research say about the effectiveness of different coping strategies in preventing distress and crime?

6. Briefly, what major individual and environmental characteristics increase the likelihood that individuals will cope with strains through crime? Why do such characteristics increase the likelihood of criminal coping?

7. What major coping skills and resources increase the likelihood of criminal coping?

8. What is meant by "social support"?

9. Why are individuals low in social control more likely to cope with strains through crime?

10. Why are individuals who associate with other criminals more likely to engage in criminal coping?

11. Describe the characteristics of those situations where criminal coping is most likely (i.e., those situational characteristics that influence the costs and benefits of criminal coping).

12. Describe the characteristics of an adolescent who is likely to engage in criminal coping. Be as concrete as possible (e.g., do not simply say the adolescent has a low investment in

conventional activities—indicate that the adolescent has low grades and no plans for further education). Describe the characteristics of an adult who is likely to engage in criminal coping.

13. The research on those factors said to influence the likelihood of criminal coping has produced mixed results. Why might this be the case? ✦

Chapter 5

How Does General Strain Theory Explain Patterns of Offending Over the Life Course?

Most crime theories focus on explaining why some individuals are more likely than others to engage in crime. This is true of general strain theory (GST), which argues that some individuals are more likely to engage in crime because they are more likely to (a) experience those strains conducive to crime, and (b) cope with these strains in a criminal manner. In recent years, however, criminologists have started to devote more attention to the explanation of patterns of offending over the course of a given individual's life.

Several studies have followed individuals over long periods of time, tracking their levels of criminal offending. And these studies have found that different people exhibit different patterns of offending (see Agnew, 1997, 2003; Moffitt, 1993). Most commonly, individuals start committing offenses as they become adolescents and then dramatically reduce their offending as they become adults. This is known as the "adolescence-limited" pattern of offending, since offending is largely limited to the adolescent years. Another group of individuals commit offenses at relatively high rates over most of their lives. This is known as the "life-course–persistent" pattern of offending. While life-course–persistent offenders make up only 5 to 10 perecent of the population, they are an important group because they account for a large share of all crime, including a majority of all serious crime. Yet another group of individuals, roughly 10 percent of the population, largely abstains from offending during their lives (the "abstaining" pattern). Still other patterns of offending have been found, including individuals who offend at low rates over much of their lives, but the adolescence-limited and life-course–persistent patterns are the major ones.

The first part of this chapter focuses on the explanation of the adolescence-limited pattern of offending. Why is it that most individuals increase their offending when they become adolescents, and then reduce it when they become adults? I begin by briefly describing how biopsychological, social control, and social learning theories explain adolescence-limited offending. Then I describe how GST explains such offending. You should keep in mind that I am *not* trying to explain why some individuals have higher rates of offending than others ("between individual" differences in offending); rather, I am trying to explain why many individuals increase their offending during the adolescent years ("within-individual" differences in offending). Even so, the explanation I offer is very similar to that used to explain between-individual differences in offending. Basically, I argue that offending peaks during adolescence because adolescents are more likely to (a) experience those strains conducive to crime, and (b) cope with these strains in a criminal manner. I describe why this is so below.

The second part of this chapter focuses on the explanation of the life-course–persistent pattern of offending. I begin by briefly describing how biopsychological, social control, and social learning theories explain life-course–persistent offending, followed by the GST explanation. Not surprisingly, GST argues that some individuals offend at high rates over much of their lives because they are more likely to (a) experience those strains conducive to crime over much of their lives, and (b) cope with these strains through crime. I describe why this is so below.

Why Do Most Individuals Increase Their Levels of Offending During Adolescence?

Again, adolescence-limited offending is the most common pattern of offending. Most individuals substantially increase their levels of offending as they enter the adolescent years—typically in the early teens. They then dramatically decrease their levels of offending as they enter the adult years, typically in the late teens to early 20s. Levels of offending tend to peak in the mid- to late teenage years. Why is this so? What is it about adolescence that is so conducive to criminal offending? Part of the answer has been provided by biopsychological, social control, and social learning theorists. But GST also has much to say in this area. (This section draws heavily on Agnew, 1997, 2003).

Biopsychological, Social Control, and Social Learning Explanations for the Adolescent Peak in Offending

Biopsychological Theory. Certain biopsychological theorists explain the adolescent peak in offending by arguing that adolescents are more likely to possess those individual traits conducive to crime, particularly the traits of low constraint and negative emotionality. As you may recall from earlier chapters, individuals with these traits are impulsive, like to take risks, tend to reject social norms, have little concern for the feelings or rights of others, are more sensitive to stressors, tend to blame their problems on others, and have an antagonistic interactional style. In brief, they are "out of control" and "mean." Adolescents may be more likely to possess these traits partly for biological reasons, like hormonal surges during puberty and differences in brain functioning during adolescence (see the excellent discussion in Walsh, 2000). And they may be more likely to possess these traits for social reasons. Reduced levels of supervision during adolescence (see below), for example, may contribute to impulsive behavior. And increased association with delinquent peers (see below) may contribute to risky behavior and beliefs favorable to crime. So adolescents may be higher in low constraint and negative emotionality. I will shortly argue that this fact also helps explain why adolescents are more likely to experience strains and react to such strains with crime.

Social Control Theory. Social control theorists argue that adolescents are more likely to engage in crime because they are less subject to the major types of social control. Adolescents are *less subject to direct control.* Parents relax the rules they impose on adolescents, allowing them more freedom to do such things as choose their friends and stay out late at night. Related to this, adolescents spend more time away from their parents, making it more difficult for parents to monitor their behavior. According to one study, time spent with parents declines by almost half as juveniles move from childhood to adolescence, with the decline being most evident on weekend nights and on weekday afternoons and evenings (Larson et al.,

1996). Further, adolescents may also be less subject to direct control at school, because they usually attend larger schools and frequently change classes throughout the day. So adolescents are less subject to direct control than children. Adolescents may also be less subject to direct control than adults. While adults are legally permitted to engage in a wider range of behaviors than adolescents, adults are often under the watchful eye of family members and employers, much of their time is structured by family and work responsibilities, and they are subject to the more severe sanctions of the adult justice system.

Although the data are less clear-cut, there is reason to believe that adolescents also have *weaker bonds to conventional others and institutions* than children and adults. Relations with parents often deteriorate during adolescence, as adolescents develop strong bonds to peers and more often challenge parental authority. Also, adolescents' ties to school become weaker, with both school performance and satisfaction declining. This occurs because school becomes more demanding—with teachers grading in a more rigorous manner and creating a more competitive environment. However, when adolescents become adults they usually develop strong bonds to conventional others and institutions, forming their own families and becoming involved in their jobs.

Finally, it has been argued that adolescents are less likely than adults to believe that crime is wrong. This may stem, in part, from the fact that adolescents are more likely to associate with delinquent peers who challenge parental beliefs. So there is reason to believe that adolescents may be lower in social control than both children and adults. I will shortly argue that this fact also helps explain why adolescents are more likely to experience strains and react to strains with crime.

Social Learning Theory. Social learning theorists argue that adolescents are more likely to engage in crime primarily because of their increased involvement with delinquent peers—who model crime, reinforce crime, and teach beliefs favorable to crime. Adolescents have more freedom to select their friends and spend more time with them than do children. Further, adolescents are exposed to a more diverse group of peers than are children, partly because adolescents usually attend larger schools that draw students from wider areas. Many of these peers are involved in delinquency. And such peers are often attractive to adolescents, partly because they engage in forbidden, but attractive "adult" activities, like drinking and sexual behavior. Adolescents, then, are much more likely than children to associate with delinquent peers. One study, for example, found that approximately one out of ten 11-year-olds reported that at least some of their friends had used alcohol during the past year, but by age 18 this figure had risen to approximately nine out of ten (Warr, 1993). As adolescents become adults, they marry and get involved in jobs—which dramatically decreases their association with delinquent peers (Warr, 2002).

So adolescents are more likely to associate with delinquent peers than children and adults, which plays a substantial role in explaining the adolescent peak in offending. I will shortly return to this fact because it too helps explain why adolescents are more likely to experience strains and react to them with crime.

The General Strain Theory Explanation for the Adolescent Peak in Offending

GST argues that adolescents are more likely to offend than children and adults because they are more likely to (a) experience those strains conducive to crime, and (b) cope with such strains through crime. GST, however, does not dispute the arguments that adolescents are more likely to possess those personality traits conducive to crime, be lower in social control, and associate with delinquent peers. As indicated, GST draws on these arguments to help explain why adolescents are more likely to experience strains and cope with them through crime.[1] GST, then, is quite compatible with bio-psychological, social control, and social learning theories.

Adolescents Experience More Strains Conducive to Crime

There are several major reasons why adolescents experience more strains than children and adults, certain of which have already been mentioned.

Adolescents Are More Likely to Possess the Traits of Negative Emotionality and Low Constraint. As indicated in Chapter 1, individuals with these traits experience more objective and subjective strains. Such individuals are not pleasant people. They often antagonize and provoke negative reactions from others like parents, teachers, and peers. Imagine, for example, parents who have a child with these traits. The child is quarrelsome, regularly misbehaves, and is difficult to discipline. The parents may eventually become so frustrated with the child that they end up rejecting him or her, or employing harsh disciplinary techniques. Further, individuals with these traits often select themselves into aversive environments where the likelihood of negative treatment is high, such as delinquent peer groups, bad marriages, and bad jobs. For example, such individuals are often rejected by conventional peers and attracted to the risky activities of delinquent peers. In addition, individuals with these traits are more likely to perceive the objective strains they experience as high in magnitude and unfair. That is because they are more sensitive to strains and more likely to blame the strains they experience on others (see Agnew et al., 2002; Piquero et al., 2004).

Adolescents Are Lower in Social Control. The lower social control of adolescents also increases the likelihood that they will experience strains. Individuals who are low in social control are, by definition, weakly tied to others like parents and teachers. This increases the likelihood that these others will treat them in a negative manner. For example, parents are more likely to mistreat their children when they are not strongly bonded to them. Low social control also reduces the likelihood that these others will protect the individual from harm (or strains). To illustrate, parents who poorly supervise their children are less likely to prevent them from getting into situations where they might suffer harm. As a consequence, such children are more likely to engage in activities like "hanging out" on the street with their peers, where the potential for experiencing strains is high (see Agnew, 1997; Agnew et al., 2000).[2]

Adolescents Are More Likely to Associate With Delinquent Peers. Association with delinquent peers not only fosters the social learning of crime, it also increases the likelihood that adolescents will experience strains. Data suggest that delinquent peers are more likely to treat one another in a negative manner; for example, they more often get into conflicts with one another and abuse one another. This is not surprising when one considers that delinquent peers are, by definition, disposed to crime. The members of delinquent peer groups may also be more likely to get into conflicts with others outside the group, like rival groups of peers, parents, teachers, and police (see Colvin, 2000; Giordano et al., 1986; Schrek et al., 2004; Shaffer, 2003).

Adolescents Live in a Larger, More Demanding Social World Than Children and Adults. There are additional reasons why adolescents are more likely to experience strains, beyond those related to biopsychological, social control, and social learning theories. Such reasons have to do with certain of the other biological and social changes associated with adolescence. One of the most important of these is the fact that adolescents come to live in a larger, more demanding social world than children and adults—a world where the likelihood of experiencing strains is higher. Perhaps the best way to appreciate this social world is to think about the changes that occur as juveniles move from childhood to adolescence.

Such juveniles leave elementary schools and enter secondary schools, which are more demanding. In particular, adolescents in secondary schools are subject to more rules, given more work, graded in a more difficult manner, and placed under more competitive pressure. Secondary schools are also larger in size, draw students from a wider area, and have students change classes several times a day. As a consequence, adolescents come to interact with many more students, including students from backgrounds different than their own. Related to this, adolescents get involved in larger, more diverse peer groups. Further, interactions among such peers is governed by a more subtle set of social cues. In childhood, for example, peer rejection is a function of highly visible negative behaviors. In adolescence, it is a function of more subtle behaviors. Finally, romantic relationships develop, which also increase the difficulties of social interaction (see Agnew, 1997, 2003, for further discussion).

Adolescents, in short, experience a dramatic increase in the size and demands of their social world. These changes are likely to be stressful in and of themselves, particularly in view of the fact that they often occur in tandem with major biological changes. More important for our purposes, however, is that these changes increase the likelihood that adolescents will be treated in a negative manner by others. There are more people to negatively treat adolescents. These people are freer to treat adolescents in a negative manner, because their ties to the adolescents may be less strong and adolescents are less well-supervised. Also, interaction with these people is more demanding in the ways indicated above, so there is a greater likelihood that interactions will break down in ways that result in negative treatment. Adolescents, for example, may have difficulty meeting the increased academic demands of their teachers or the newly experienced demands of romantic partners, with the result being poor grades or severed relationships.

As adolescents become adults, however, their social world begins to narrow and they have more control over the nature of this world. Their circle of friends become smaller, they usually settle with a single romantic partner, and the number of people they interact with at their jobs is likely to be smaller than the number at school. They also experience less turnover in friends, romantic partners, and coworkers. Further, adults have more choice over their associates than adolescents. Adults, for example, typically have some choice over where they live and work. All of these factors reduce the likelihood of negative treatment by others. There are fewer people to treat adults in a negative manner and these people are less likely to engage in negative treatment. The reduction in crime among adults, then, is partly due to the fact that adults live in a smaller social world and have more control over the nature of this world.

Adolescents Come to Desire Many of the Privileges of Adulthood, but Are Often Prevented From Achieving Such Privileges Through Legitimate Channels. There are several reasons adolescents come to desire such adult privileges as autonomy and status. Adolescents physically resemble adults and assume some adult responsibilities, which fosters the belief that they deserve certain adult privileges. The peer-oriented social world of adolescents creates a desire for freedom from adult supervision and status, including masculine status among boys. Finally, adolescents are regularly exposed to peers at school and in the media who have more adult privileges than they possess, which further increases their desire for such privileges.

Adolescents, however, are frequently denied the privileges they desire. While they desire autonomy or the freedom to do what they want, their behavior is still subject to much control, with a broad range of behaviors prohibited or restricted (see Agnew, 1984, 2003; Greenberg, 1977; Moffitt, 1993). The regulations encountered in the school system may be especially difficult to deal with, as many of these regulations become *more* strict during adolescence (see Greenberg, 1977). Parents, however, may also continue to restrict the freedom of adolescents. Data support these arguments, suggesting that adolescents often demand greater autonomy from parents and teachers, and that they frequently clash with these individuals over issues involving autonomy (Agnew, 1997, 2003). It should be noted that these clashes usually do not involve "raucous, open conflict" over major issues. Rather, they usually involve clashes over more mundane issues, like doing chores, clothing, appearance, schoolwork, activities, interpersonal relations, and rules regarding such things as bedtime and curfew. In short, they involve clashes over the everyday details of life. Such conflicts generate much emotional tension, however, and they are common. Limited data also suggest that these clashes tend to peak in early to mid-adolescence. Further, limited data suggest that frustration over the inability to obtain the desired autonomy does contribute to delinquency (Agnew, 1984: Piquero and Brezina, 2001). Delinquency may be a means of asserting autonomy (e.g., sexual intercourse, alcohol consumption, disorderly behavior), achieving autonomy (e.g., stealing money to gain financial independence from parents), or venting frustration against those who deny autonomy.

Data also suggest that adolescents are very concerned about their social standing or status among peers (Agnew, 2003). Adolescents who have trouble achieving status through legal channels, like social class, academic performance, and athletic prowess, may try to achieve status through crime. For example, they may coerce others into treating them with respect or join gangs in an effort to achieve status (see Anderson, 1999; Cohen, 1955; Greenberg, 1977, 1985; Messerschmidt, 1993).

When adolescents become adults, they achieve the autonomy that is often denied them as adolescents and they become less concerned about their peer status as peer relations become less important. The peak in crime during adolescence, then, may be partly due to the fact that adolescents come to pursue goals that are often difficult for them to achieve through legal channels.

Evidence on Increased Strain Among Adolescents. So there is good reason to believe that adolescents are more likely to experience strains than both children and adults, particularly strains conducive to crime like negative school experiences, abusive peer relations, and the inability to achieve goals like autonomy and status. But what do the data indicate? Are adolescents more likely to experience such strains? This is a difficult question to answer at present, because of the lack of representative surveys that employ comprehensive measures of strains. Certain data, however, suggest that such strains may be more common among adolescents. Grades become worse during adolescence, victimization and association with delinquent peers increase, and certain studies suggest that stressful life events may peak during early and middle adolescence—although these studies typically focus on limited age ranges (Agnew, 1997, 2003).

In addition, data suggest that adolescents not only experience more *objective strains* conducive to crime, but that they are more upset by these strains as well—that is, they experience more *subjective strains*. In particular, several studies suggest that adolescents are more annoyed by and experience higher levels of emotional distress in response to strains than do children and adults (see Agnew, 1997, 2003). One of the best of these studies was carried out by Larson and Lampman-Petraitis (1989; also see Larson and Ham, 1993). They equipped preadolescents and early adolescents with electronic pagers, which were signaled at random times during the day. Respondents were then asked to record their feelings. The early adolescents reported more occurrences of anger, hurt, and worry than did the preadolescents. This higher instance of negative affect was due to (a) a higher instance of perceived negative events, and (b) the fact that these negative events had a much larger effect on the emotional state of young adolescents than preadolescents.

The few empirical studies that have tried to account for the relationship between age and crime have tended to neglect variables related to GST. Even so, limited data provide some support for GST. In perhaps the best study in this area, Hoffmann and Cerbone (1999) found that increases in the number of stressful life events help explain the increases in delinquency that most juveniles experience during early to mid-adolescence. Further, data from Rutter (1985) and Sampson and Laub (1993) suggest that crime is most likely to decline among those adolescents who enter satisfying relationships as adults. These data are typically interpreted in terms of social control theory: such relationships are said to increase the costs of crime. But these data may also reflect declining levels of strain. Finally, as noted above, the increased association with delinquent peers that occurs during adolescence explains a large part of the relationship between age and crime. This increased association may lead to an increase in crime not only for reasons related to social learning theory, but also because it leads to an increase in interpersonal conflicts.

But Not All Adolescents Experience Increased Levels of Strains (and Not All Adults Experience Decreased Levels). It is important to note that I am *not* arguing that *all* adolescents experience increased levels of strains. Some adolescents may not experience an increase in strains because they are in protected environments. For example, they may attend small high schools, attend all-female schools, or possess personality characteristics that limit their interaction with peers (see Caspi et al., 1993; Moffitt, 1993). This helps explain why a small percentage of adolescents are able to abstain from crime. Likewise, it is obviously the case that not all adults experience decreased levels of strains. Many adults fail to get involved in good marriages or get decent jobs, which helps explain why a small percentage of individuals continue to offend well into the adult years.

Adolescents Are More Likely to Cope With Strains in a Criminal Manner

Not only do adolescents experience more strains than children and adults, but they are more likely to cope with the strains they do experience in a criminal manner. There are several reasons for this, certain of which have already been mentioned (see Agnew, 1997, 2003, for extended discussions).

Adolescents Have Poorer Problem-Solving and Social Skills. Their relatively poor skills stem primarily from the fact that they lack experience at coping. This is not, of course, to claim that children have more experience; children, however, are under the protection of parents who cope on their behalf. But parents are much less likely to cope on behalf of their adolescent children. Parents are less aware of the problems experienced by their adolescent children and they expect such children to handle many of their own problems, given their greater maturity. As a consequence, adolescents not only experience more strains, but they also assume greater responsibility for coping with these strains. Unfortunately, they have little experience at coping, which increases the likelihood of ineffective coping, including criminal coping.

Adolescents Are More Likely to Be Low in Constraint and High in Negative Emotionality. As indicated in Chapter 4, these traits increase the likelihood of criminal coping for several reasons.

Adolescents Lack Key Coping Resources, Like Power and Money. Legal coping often requires power or the ability to influence others. Individuals with power are better able to escape negative treatment or get others to end their negative treatment. One of the distinguishing features of adolescents is that they often lack power and are compelled to remain in environments they find aversive. In particular, adolescents are compelled to live with their families in certain neighborhoods, to go to certain schools, and, within limits, to interact with the same groups of peers and neighbors (see Agnew, 1985). If any of these environments is aversive, there is often little that adolescents can do to legally cope. Except under unusual circumstances, adolescents cannot quit school or change teachers, move to new neighborhoods, leave their families, or exercise substantial control over parents, teachers, and others. Likewise, adolescents lack money, which facilitates legal coping for all of the reasons indicated in Chapter 4. As a consequence of these deficits, adolescents often end up coping using one of the few resources available to them—physical strength (see Agnew, 1990b).

Adults, however, are much more likely to possess coping resources like money and power. Adults experiencing strains are therefore better able to do such things as move to new neighborhoods, quit their jobs, or get divorced. Their greater resources also increase their bargaining power when dealing with others who treat them in a negative manner. Children lack money and power, but parents typically employ their power on behalf of their children (see Marwell's, 1966, discussion of the "power of agency"). Once again, then, we find that adolescents have less access to legal means of coping.

Adolescents Are Lower in Conventional Social Support. Adolescents are lower in conventional social support partly because their ties to people like parents and teachers are often weaker. Also, individuals like parents and teachers are less likely to provide social support because of the cultural expectation that adolescents more frequently cope on their own. So parents who might quickly come to the aid of their troubled children may well tell their troubled adolescents to "handle it yourself." Further, adolescents are less likely to share their problems with others like parents and ask for social support. This is partly because adolescents realize that they are expected to more often cope on their own. Adolescents do come to rely more heavily on friends for support, but data suggest that such support is not as effective in dealing with stressors as is parental support (Agnew, 1997, 2003).

Adolescents Are Lower in Social Control. As indicated above, adolescents are lower in several types of social control. This increases the likelihood of criminal coping for the reasons indicated in Chapter 4. Most notably, low social control increases criminal coping because it lowers the costs of crime.

Adolescents Are More Likely to Associate With Delinquent Peers. As indicated in Chapter 4, delinquent peers increase the likelihood of delinquent coping for several reasons. In particular, they increase adolescents' disposition for crime.

Adolescents Live in a Very 'Public World,' Where Their Strains Often Become Known to Others. Adolescents live in a very public world. Much of the negative treatment they receive occurs before an audience, such as classmates or peers. Other negative treatment, although occurring in private, may be shared with peers and so become part of the public sphere. The public nature of adolescent life makes efforts to minimize the significance of strains more difficult, since such efforts are more likely to be challenged by others. Peers, in fact, often regularly remind adolescents of the negative treatment they have suffered. Further, these others often pressure adolescents to respond to certain strains in a criminal manner. And in order to "save face," many adolescents comply. In particular, data indicate that conflicts between adolescents often occur in front of others and these others frequently encourage a violent response (Tedeschi and Felson, 1994). Children and adults live in more private worlds, and so may have an easier time coping in a legal manner.

Evidence on Poor Coping Among Adolescents. Data from the larger stress literature suggest that adolescents are more likely to cope with strains in "immature" or maladaptive ways, including delinquency (see Agnew, 1997, 2003; Agnew et al., 2002). Certain studies, in fact, suggest that adolescent coping efforts often exacerbate rather than alleviate their levels of stress. It should be noted, however, that not all adolescents experience an increased likelihood of criminal coping. Some adolescents, for example, possess the skills that allow for legal coping, receive much social support from adults, remain high in social control, and avoid association with delinquent peers.

Summary

GST explains the peak in offending during adolescence in two ways. First, adolescents are more likely to experience strains conducive to crime than children and adults. This occurs because adolescents are higher in negative emotionality and lower in constraint; lower in social control; more likely to associate with delinquent peers; more likely to live in a larger, more demanding social world where the likelihood of negative treatment is higher; and more likely to have trouble achieving certain of their goals through legal channels. Further, adolescents are more likely to cope with their strains in a criminal manner for the reasons just indicated.

Why Do Some Individuals Offend at High Rates Over Much of Their Lives?

As indicated, data indicate that a small group of offenders engage in high rates of crime over much of their lives. The stable offending of these life-course–persistent offenders is most often explained in terms of biopsychological, social control, and social learning theories (see Agnew, 1997; Cullen and Agnew, 2003; Farrington, 2005; Moffitt, 1993; Thornberry, 1997).

Most theorists explain life-course–persistent offending by arguing that some individuals develop the traits of low constraint and negative emotionality early in life. These traits are usually said to be a function of both biological factors and children's early family environments (e.g., Farrington, 2005; Gottfredson and Hirschi, 1990; Moffitt, 1993; Wilson and Herrnstein, 1985). And these traits are said to be reasonably stable over time, such that individuals who possess these traits as children tend to possess them as adults. Such traits contribute to high rates of offending over the life course in two major ways.

First, these traits have a direct effect on offending, such that individuals who possess these traits are more likely to engage in crime in a given situation. Some theorists explain this direct effect in terms of control theory. Individuals with these traits give less thought to and care less about the costs of crime. Among other things, they tend to act without thinking about the consequences of their behavior, they care less about their ties to others, and they have little concern for social norms. Other theorists explain this effect in terms of social learning theory. People with these traits are said to find crime more rewarding, since it allows them to satisfy their desire for risky activities and act out their aggressive impulses.

Second, these traits contribute to high rates of offending over the life course through their effect on the social environment. In particular, individuals with these traits affect their environment in ways that reduce levels of social control and foster the social learning of crime. Keep in mind that such individuals are "out of control" and "mean." These individuals are less likely to form close attachments to others over the course of their lives, with these others including parents, teachers, and spouses. They are also less likely to do well in conventional pursuits like school and work. And because of their weak ties to conventional others and institutions, they are poorly supervised and fail to learn to condemn crime. Individuals with these traits, however, are more likely to associate with criminal others. Such others reinforce their crime, model crime, and teach them beliefs favorable to crime (see Agnew, 1997, 2003; Caspi et al., 1989; Moffitt, 1993; Sampson and Laub, 1993; Walsh, 2000; Wright et al., 1999).

So life-course–persistent offending is most often explained in terms of the traits of low constraint and negative emotionality. Thornberry (1987), however, has argued that life-course–persistent offending sometimes develops in the absence of these traits. He states some individuals experience very low levels of social control in childhood. That is, they are poorly supervised, weakly bonded to their parents, do poorly in school, and are not taught to condemn crime. This low social control increases their likelihood of association with delinquent peers. Delinquent peer association, in turn, contributes to further reductions in social control. Adolescents who associate with delinquent peers, for example, often get into conflicts with their parents and do poorly in school. The result is what Thornberry calls an "amplifying loop," where the causes of delinquency mutually reinforce one another. Low social control leads to association with delinquent peers, which in turn contributes to further reductions in social control. This amplifying loop results in high levels of offending. Such offending, in turn, contributes to further reductions in social control and increases in association with delinquent peers. For most adolescents, this amplifying loop is interrupted by the transition to adulthood, when individuals typically marry and become committed to work. Thornberry, however, argues that this does not happen in all cases. If initial levels of social control are very weak, adolescents may not develop adult commitments capable of interrupting the loop. According to Thornberry, this is most likely to happen in the case of lower-class adolescents, who more often experience very low levels of social control early in life. As a result, they are more likely to become involved in delinquency at an early age, setting the amplifying loop described above in motion and leading to extremely high levels of delinquency. Their ties to conventional society are so weak by late adolescence that they are unable to break out of the loop (also see Patterson et al., 1989; Thornberry and Krohn, 2001).

The General Strain Theory Explanation of Life-Course–Persistent Offending

GST explains life-course–persistent offending in ways that parallel the above explanations. GST also argues that many individuals offend at high rates over the course of their lives because they develop the traits of low constraint and negative emotionality as children. While these traits reduce levels of control and foster the social learning of crime, they also increase the likelihood of crime for reasons related to strain theory. In particular, these traits increase the likelihood that individuals will (a) experience objective strains conducive to crime, (b) interpret these strains as high in magnitude and unjust, and (c) cope with them in a criminal manner (Agnew, 1997).

High Levels of Objective Strains. Individuals with these traits are more likely to experience strains over the course of their lives. Again, keep in mind that these individuals are "out of control" and "mean." As a consequence, they are more likely to provoke negative reactions from others. In particular, they are more likely to antagonize their parents and elicit harsh, rejecting reactions from them. They are more likely to be rejected by peers and experience problems at school. And they are more likely to have difficulties with their employers and spouses as well.

In addition to provoking negative reactions from others, individuals with these traits are more likely to select themselves into aversive environments where they are negatively treated by others. Among other things, such individuals are more likely to be attracted to delinquent peers who treat one another harshly. They are more likely to be sorted into lower tracks at school, where relations with teachers and fellow students are more aversive. And they are more likely to obtain less desirable jobs and marry less desirable partners. Individuals who are low in constraint and high in negative emotionality, then, are more likely to experience objective strains over the course of their lives because they provoke negative reactions from others and select themselves into aversive environments.[3]

High Levels of Subjective Strains and Criminal Coping. Individuals with the traits of negative emotionality and low constraint are not only more likely to experience objective strains, they are also more likely to dislike such strains and view them as unjust. As discussed in prior chapters, individuals with such traits are more sensitive to strains and quicker to blame their problems on others. Further, as discussed in Chapter 4, individuals with these traits are more likely to cope with their strains in a criminal manner. Among other things, they are less able to cope in a legal manner, are less aware of and concerned about the costs of crime, and are more disposed to crime.

The Urban Underclass and Life-Course–Persistent Offending. Following the lead of Thornberry (1987), GST also argues that some individuals may engage in high rates of offending over the life course even though they do not possess the traits of low constraint and negative emotionality. Such offending is most likely among very poor individuals, especially those who reside in poor communities. As described in Chapters 6 and 7, such individuals are not only lower in social control and more likely to associate with delinquent peers, they are also more likely to experience a range of strains, including economic, family, school, and peer-related strains. They are more sensitive to such strains. And they are more likely to cope with their strains though crime. Such individuals become involved in an amplifying loop of the type described by Thornberry. The strains they experience lead to reductions in social control, increased association with delinquent peers, and high levels of crime (see especially Chapters 1, 2, and 3). These effects, in turn, contribute to further strains. The criminal acts of individuals, for example, often provoke negative treatment from others, including parents, teachers, employers, peers, police, and the victims of their crimes. This amplifying loop, then, contributes to high rates of offending over the life course.

Summary

GST argues that individuals with the traits of low constraint and negative emotionality are more likely to engage in high rates of offending over the life course for several reasons. They are more likely to provoke negative reactions from others and to select themselves into aversive environments, where they are treated in a negative manner by others. Further, they are more likely to dislike the objective strains they experience, view them as unfair, and cope with them through crime. Some individuals without these traits, however, may also offend at high rates over the life course. Very poor individuals living in poor communities are most likely to fall into this category, since they are most likely to be subject to high levels of strains and other criminogenic factors at an early age. Such individuals become involved in an amplifying loop. Their strains lead to a reduction in social control, an increase in association with delinquent peers, and crime. These effects, in turn, lead to further strains—setting the amplifying loop in motion.

Summary

GST is not only able to explain why some individuals are more likely than others to engage in crime, but can also help explain patterns of offending over the life course. This chapter focused on the two major patterns: adolescence-limited offending and life-course–persistent offending. It was argued that adolescence-limited offending is partly explained by the fact that the biological and social changes associated with adolescence lead to an increase in strains conducive to crime and an increased tendency to engage in criminal coping. And it was argued that life-course–persistent offending is partly explained by the fact that individuals low in constraint and high in negative emotionality are more likely to experience strains conducive to crime over the course of their lives and to cope with these strains through crime. In addition, very poor individuals in poor communities (members of the "urban underclass") are also more likely to be life-course–persistent offenders. They experience numerous strains early in life, which help set an amplifying loop in motion. Strains contribute to a reduction in social control, an increase in delinquent peer association, and crime. These factors, in turn, contribute to further strains. This amplifying loop helps maintain high rates of offending over the course of the individuals' lives.

Notes

1. Further, individuals who are low in social control are less likely to restrain themselves from getting into situations where they might be harmed. Just as such individuals have less to lose by engaging in crime, they have less to lose by engaging in risky activities. So individuals who are low in social control are more likely to engage in activities like staying out late at night and frequenting locations where the likelihood of victimization is high—such as clubs.

2. Conversely, the strains associated with adolescence contribute to low constraint and negative emotionality, a reduction in social control, and an increase in association with delinquent peers.

3. These effects not only increase the likelihood of criminal behavior, they also serve to maintain the traits of low constraint and negative emotionality, as discussed in Chapters 1, 2, and 3 (also see Agnew, 1997).

Review and Discussion Questions

1. Describe the adolescence-limited and life-course–persistent patterns of offending.

2. How do biopsychological, social control, and social learning theories explain the adolescence-limited pattern of offending?

3. How does general strain theory explain adolescence-limited offending?

4. Why do I argue that adolescents experience more strains than children and adults? Related to this, why do I argue that adolescents live in a larger, more demanding social world? And why do adolescents have trouble achieving many goals?

5. Why is it that *some* adolescents do *not* experience an increase in strains?

6. Why do I state that adolescents are more likely to cope with strains in a criminal manner? Related to this, why do I contend that adolescents have relatively poor coping skills and resources and that they are lower in conventional social support?

7. Does the evidence or research support the propositions that adolescents experience more strains and are more likely to cope with such strains in a criminal manner (than children and adults)?

8. How do biopsychological, social control, and social learning theorists explain life-course–persistent offending? Related to this, what is meant by an "amplifying loop"?

9. How does GST explain life-course–persistent offending? Related to this, why are individuals low in constraint and high in negative emotionality more likely to experience objective

and subjective strains, and to cope with such strains through crime? Why does membership in the "urban underclass" increase the likelihood of life-course–persistent offending? ✦

Chapter 6

How Does General Strain Theory Explain Gender, Class, and Race/Ethnic Differences in Offending?

As indicated in earlier chapters, general strain theory (GST) can help explain why some individuals are more likely than others to engage in crime. And as indicated in Chapter 5, GST can also help explain patterns of offending over the course of an individual's life. In this chapter, we shift our focus from individuals to groups and ask why some groups have higher *rates of offending* than other groups. In this area, criminologists have devoted most attention to gender, age, class, and race/ethnic groups. We know that males have much higher rates of offending than females, especially in the areas of serious property and violent crime. And adolescents have much higher rates of offending than children and adults. In fact, age and gender are among the strongest correlates of crime, with adolescent males having rates of offending that far exceed those of other gender and age groups. To illustrate, males aged 17–21 accounted for about 18 percent of all arrests in 2003, while females aged 60–64 accounted for about one tenth of 1 percent of all arrests (2003 FBI Uniform Crime Reports). Social class and race/ethnicity are also related to crime, although not as strongly as many people assume. Lower-class individuals and the members of certain racial and ethnic groups, like African Americans and Latinos, are somewhat more likely to engage in serious crime. However, social class and race/ethnicity have little or no relationship to minor crime (see Agnew, 2005a, for an overview).

I begin this chapter by using GST to help explain why males are more likely than females to engage in crime. I also draw on GST to explain why some females engage in crime. Even though females are less likely than males to engage in crime, it is clearly the case that many females do engage in crime. The causes of female crime were neglected for many years. Most criminologists simply assumed that the factors that caused females to engage in crime were the same as those that caused males to engage in crime (with females simply being less likely to possess these factors). But as argued below, there is some advantage in devoting special attention to the causes of female crime.

I next use GST to explain class and race/ethnic differences in serious crime. I do not discuss age differences in crime in this chapter. Chapter 5 used GST to explain why most individuals dramatically increase their levels of offending during adolescence. The arguments made in that chapter can also be used to explain why adolescents are more likely to engage in crime than children and adults. Namely, adolescents are more likely to experience those types of strains conducive to crime and to cope with these strains through crime. You will notice that I explain other groups' differences in crime in a similar manner: some groups have higher crime rates than other groups because they are more likely to experience those strains conducive to crime and to cope with them in a criminal manner.

How Does General Strain Theory Explain Why Males Have Higher Rates of Crime?

There is little doubt that males are more likely to engage in crime than females. This is especially true for serious violent and property crimes. For example, males accounted for 96 percent of all murder arrests, 90 percent of all robbery arrests, and 79 percent of all aggravated or serious assault arrests in 2003. Gender differences in offending are much smaller for less serious crimes. For example, males accounted for 63 percent of all larceny (theft without force or illegal entry) arrests. Running away from home (a juvenile offense) and prostitution are the only crimes for which females were more likely to be arrested than males (2003 FBI Uniform Crime Reports). Self-report and victimization data also indicate that males have higher crime rates than females (Agnew, 2005a). Some evidence, however, suggests that the gender gap in crime may be becoming smaller over time (Heimer, 2000). In 1960, females accounted for 10 percent of all arrests for index crimes. In 2003, females accounted for 27 percent of all index crime arrests. Females arrests, as a percentage of all arrests, have increased for most major crimes, except murder.

Why are males more likely to engage in crime, especially serious crime, than females? *Biopsychological theorists* explain the gender gap primarily by arguing that males tend to be lower in constraint and higher in negative emotionality. And data tend to suggest that this is the case, with differences in constraint and negative emotionality explaining a substantial part of the gender gap in crime (Burton et al., 1998; LaGrange and Silverman, 1999; Moffitt et al., 2001). Gender differences in these traits may be partly a function of biological differences between the sexes, like differences in levels of testosterone, and partly a function of differences in the ways in which males and females are raised. Among other things, females are socialized to exercise greater self-restraint, avoid risky activities, show concern for others, and control their anger (see Agnew and Brezina, 1997; Broidy and Agnew, 1997). Biopsychological theorists have also argued that females are less likely to engage in crime because they tend to be smaller in size and weaker than males, which makes participation in other-directed crimes more risky and limits opportunities for participation in criminal groups, where a premium is often placed on the ability to use force (see Steffensmeier, 1983).

Social control theorists explain the gender gap by arguing that males are less subject to certain types of control than females. Among other things, males are less closely supervised than females, are less strongly tied to the household (i.e., have less responsibility for household tasks and childcare), are less likely to be punished for aggressive behavior, are less strongly bonded to school, and are less likely to believe that crime is wrong (see Agnew, 2005a; Broidy and Agnew, 1997). These differences in social control partly reflect differences in the way males and females are viewed in our society. Females, for example, are viewed as more vulnerable and weaker than males, and so in greater need of protection or supervision.

Social learning theorists argue that gender differences in crime are due to the fact that males are more likely to associate with criminal others, like delinquent peers and gang members (Heimer and De Coster, 1999; Mazerolle, 1998). These criminal others reinforce crime, model crime, teach beliefs favorable to crime, and provide opportunities for crime. Males may be more likely to associate with criminal others because they are lower in constraint and higher in negative emotionality, which increases the appeal of criminal others (and leads to rejection by conventional others). Also, males are freer to associate with criminal others because they are lower in social control. Further, the strains experienced by males may foster association with criminal others (see below). (See Steffensmeier, 1983, for additional reasons why males are more involved in criminal groups.)

Further, modified versions of social learning theory explain gender differences in other-directed crime in terms of gender-related beliefs and identities (e.g., Heimer and De Coster, 1999; Jensen, 2003; Murnen et al., 2002). In our society, females tend to be seen as weak, submissive, dependent, and nurturing. Males are seen as strong, aggressive, independent, and competitive. Individuals act on these beliefs, treating males and females differently. For example, aggression is more often encouraged in males. And males and females come to internalize these beliefs, viewing themselves differently. For example, most men feel that they must be tough, even aggressive, in order to be "real men." These gender-related beliefs and identities are conducive to other-directed crime in males, but discourage such crime in females.

General strain theory does not dispute the above explanations. In fact, it draws on them when explaining why males are more likely than females to cope with strains in a criminal manner. GST, however, also builds on the above explanations by pointing to additional reasons for the gender gap in offending. I first argue that males are more likely than females to experience most of those strains conducive to crime. I then argue that males are also more likely to cope with these strains in a criminal manner (this discussion draws heavily on Broidy and Agnew, 1997).

Males Are More Likely to Experience Strains Conducive to Crime

It might seem like the easiest way to explain gender differences in crime is by arguing that males experience more strains than females, but much data suggest that this is *not* the case. Numerous studies, for example, have asked males and females whether they have experienced a wide range of stressful life events and conditions. These studies often overlook many stressors that are of special

relevance to females, like sexual abuse, abortion, gender-based discrimination, child-care problems, and the burdens associated with
nurturing others. Nevertheless, females typically indicate that they
have experienced as many or more stressors than males (Aseltine et
al., 2000; Broidy, 2001; Broidy and Agnew, 1997; Hoffmann and Su,
1997; Jang and Johnson, 2003; Mazerolle, 1998; Turner and Avison,
2003; Turner et al., 1995; Van Gundy, 2002). So we cannot simply
argue that males are more likely to engage in crime because they experience more strains.

Males, however, may be more likely to experience those types of
strains conducive to crime (see Chapter 3). That is, males may be
more likely to experience strains that (a) are seen as unjust, (b) are
seen as high in magnitude, (c) are associated with low social control,
and (d) create some incentive or pressure to engage in crime. Although studies in this area do not always agree with one another,
data suggest that males are more likely than females to experience
the following strains conducive to crime (see Agnew 2005a, 2005b;
Broidy and Agnew, 1997, for overviews):

- Harsh discipline. Males are more likely to be punished in a
  harsh manner (Hay, 2003; Mazerolle, 1998).

- Negative secondary school experiences. Males tend to have
  lower grades than females, dislike school more, and more
  often have negative relations with teachers (Mazerolle, 1998).

- Abusive peer relations. Males are more likely to report that
  their relations with peers are characterized by conflict, com-
  petition, jealousy, and imbalance (Agnew and Brezina, 1997;
  Aseltine et al., 2000; Broidy and Agnew, 1997; McCarthy et al.,
  2004; Morash and Moon, 2005b). This may partly reflect the
  fact that males are more likely to associate with delinquent
  peers, who more often abuse and get into conflicts with one
  another.

- Males are more likely to pursue and have trouble achieving
  several goals conducive to crime, including the goals of autonomy, thrills/excitement, masculine status, and monetary
  success. Males are more often encouraged to pursue these
  goals than females. And males frequently have trouble
  achieving these goals through legal channels, especially during the adolescent years. Certain data support these

arguments. Males more often report monetary problems and are more upset by such problems (Broidy and Agnew, 1997; Leiber et al., 1994; Vowell and May, 2000). And males are more likely to report problems "accomplishing masculinity" through legal channels. That is, in particular situations, males sometimes find that they cannot not live up to such masculine ideas as toughness and independence. For example, teachers at school often expect them to act in a docile, obedient manner. Many males tolerate this, especially those who are doing well in school and expect to continue their educations. Other males, however, assert their masculinity in a delinquent manner. Messerschmidt describes the ways in which males in certain class and race/ethnic groups may try to accomplish masculinity through criminal channels (also see Jakupcak, 2003; Mullins et al., 2004). For example, in describing lower-class, minority males in the school system, he states:

> These youth search out ways to escape what appears to them an "emasculating" monotony and formal discipline better suited to "wimps." Moreover, given that they do not have the resources of white, middle-class and working-class boys, marginalized, racial-minority boys are more likely to employ other means of accomplishing gender. In particular . . . these young men are more likely to turn to . . . physical violence. (1993:104)

- Criminal victimization. Males are more likely to be criminally victimized than females. For example, the 2003 National Crime Victimization Survey reports that 26.3 out of every 1,000 males were the victims of violent crimes in 2003, versus 19 out of every 1,000 females (females, however, had higher rates of rape/sexual assault) (Catalano, 2004).

- Homelessness. Males are more likely to be homeless. Hagan and McCarthy (1997:68), for example, found that males were 90 percent more likely than females to be living on the street.

So there is reason to believe that males are more likely than females to experience several types of strains conducive to crime. Males may be more likely to experience these strains because they are lower in constraint and higher in negative emotionality. As indicated earlier, this increases the likelihood that they will provoke negative reactions from others and select themselves into environments where the likelihood of negative treatment is high. Males may also be more likely to experience these strains because they are subject to less control and spend more time in the public sphere, where the likelihood of negative treatment is generally higher (although see the discussion of sexual abuse below). And males may be more likely to experience these strains because they more frequently associate with criminal others, who often abuse and victimize one another. In any event, these gender differences in strains may partly explain the higher rate of male offending.

At the same time, it is important to emphasize that females are more likely to experience certain strains than males. Most of these strains, however, are not conducive to other-directed crime (see Chapter 3). In fact, certain of these strains may reduce the likelihood of such crime. Such strains include:

- Close supervision by parents and others. The lives of females are more closely regulated than the lives of males, with females being more closely supervised than males and more often confined to the "private sphere" or home. While such supervision may be disliked by many females, it generally has the effect of reducing crime (although some females may rebel against this supervision by leaving home or rejecting traditional gender roles—see below).

- The burdens associated with the care of conventional others, like children, spouses, and elderly parents (Mirowsky and Ross, 1989). Females, in particular, assume a greater share of all household and childcare responsibilities, even if they are working full time outside the home. While such burdens may be disliked, they also have the effect of reducing crime since they restrict females to the home and raise the costs of crime (crime may jeopardize their ties to these others). These burdens, however, may be conducive to one type of crime: family violence. Females may sometimes be tempted to strike out at those family members who make excessive demands on them or otherwise treat them in a negative manner. This may help explain the fact that females and males have similar rates of family violence (Kimmel, 2002; Melton and Belknap, 2003; Saunders, 2002).

- Certain network-related strains. Females report more strains involving family members and friends, such as the death or illness of family members and friends. These strains, however, are also unlikely to lead to crime. Among other things, they reflect close ties to conventional others and crime is not an effective strategy for reducing these types of strains.

Females, however, are more likely than or as likely as males to experience certain strains which are conducive to crime. These strains include:

- Sexual abuse. Females are more likely to be the victims of sexual assault and abuse. Unlike the above strains, this type of strain is conducive to crime (see Acoca, 1998; Chesney-Lind and Sheldon, 2004; Eitle and Turner, 2002; Gaarder and Belknap, 2002).

- Partner abuse. Some data suggest that females are more likely to be the victims of emotional and physical abuse by romantic partners, although there is some controversy in this area (Kimmel, 2002; Melton and Belknap, 2003; Miller and White, 2003; Mullins et al., 2004; Saunders, 2002). Such abuse, as discussed below, is also conducive to crime.

- Gender discrimination. Females are more likely to experience gender-based discrimination, including sexual harassment and lower pay for comparable work. This strain is also conducive to crime (Acoca, 1998; Eitle, 2002; Katz, 2000; Hoffmann and Su, 1997).

So while females are more likely than males to experience many strains, a good number of these strains are not conducive to crime. Overall, I argue that *males are more likely to experience strains conducive to crime and this is one reason for the higher rate of male crime.* This argument has not yet received a good test, reflecting the fact that there are no publicly available surveys that contain measures of all or most of the strains conducive to crime. A few studies, however, provide limited support for this argument. Eitle and Turner (2002), for example, found that sex differences in crime were partly explained by the higher rates of violent victimization—both experienced and witnessed—among males (also see Wallace et al., 2005).

I should emphasize that while females may be less likely to experience strains conducive to other-directed crime, that is *not* to minimize the importance of the strains they do experience. Females, again, experience as many or more strains than males. Many of these strains are associated with high levels of social control and are not easily solved through other-directed crime. Nevertheless, these strains may lead to mental health problems like depression, to deviant forms of coping like eating disorders and suicide attempts, and to certain types of self-directed crime such as illegal drug use (see Dornfeld and Kruttschnitt, 1992). This may explain why females have higher levels of depression than males, more often experience eating disorders, and are higher in certain types of drug abuse—like the nonmedical use of prescription drugs (Mirowsky and Ross, 1989; Sharp et al., 2001; Simoni-Wastila et al., 2004; Wallace et al., 2003).

Males Are More Likely to Cope With Strains Through Other-Directed Crime

Males may not only experience more strains conducive to crime, they may also be more likely to cope with strains through other-directed crime. Several studies have examined the reaction of males and females to strains, to determine if it is in fact the case that males more often cope with strains through crime. Such studies have produced mixed results (for overviews, see Broidy and Agnew, 1997; Robbers, 2004). Most studies find some evidence that men are more likely to cope with strains through crime (e.g., Agnew and Brezina, 1997; Broidy, 2001; Hay, 2003; Kring, 2000; Mazerolle, 1998; Morash and Moon, 2005b; Sigfusdottir et al., 2004; Van Gundy, 2002). For example, Piquero and Sealock (2004) found that males were much more likely than females to cope with physical and emotional abuse in their household with crime. But not all studies find this, and in certain cases women appear more likely to cope with crime. For example, Dornfeld and Kruttschnitt (1992) found that girls were more likely to respond to marital discord and divorce with delinquency (also see Hoffmann and Cerbone, 1999; Hoffmann and Su, 1997). These mixed results may be partly due to the fact that researchers usually only examine a few strains, with different researchers often examining different strains. Some strains may be more consequential for males and some for females. For example, females appear to be more sensitive to strains involving the formation and maintenance of close ties to others (Hoffmann and Su, 1997). Also, researchers often employ measures of crime that are biased toward minor offenses such as truancy, running away, and minor drug use, where gender differences are small. I believe that studies examining a broad array of strains and focusing on more serious forms of delinquency will generally reveal that males are more likely to cope with strains through serious crime.

There are several reasons for this.

Males Are More Likely to Experience Moral Outrage in Response to Strains. It is often argued that males have a different emotional reaction to strains than females. In particular, it is claimed that "men get angry and women get depressed." As a consequence, men are said to be more likely to respond to strains with crime, especially other-directed crime of a serious nature. As indicated in Chapter 2, anger is especially conducive to other-directed crime. Among other things, it energizes the individual for action, fosters a sense of power, and creates a strong desire for revenge. Recent research, however, reveals that things are not quite so simple. Data suggest that females are just as likely or somewhat more likely than males to get angry when they experience strains. However, there is reason to believe that the anger of females differs from that of males in an important way (see Agnew and Brezina, 1997; Averill, 2001; Broidy, 2001; Broidy and Agnew, 1997; Hay, 2003; Hoffmann and Su, 1997; Kring, 2000; Manasse, 2002; Mirowsky and Ross, 1989; Morash and Moon, 2005b; Piquero and Sealock, 2004; Sigfusdottir et al., 2004).

The anger of females is more often accompanied by emotions like depression, guilt, fear, anxiety, and shame. The anger of men, on the other hand, is more often characterized by moral outrage. Several reasons have been offered for these differences. It is said that females more often blame themselves when they experience strains, worry that their anger might lead them to harm others and jeopardize valued relationships, and view their anger as inappropriate and a failure of self-control (these arguments are said to be more true of white than African-American females). Males, on the other hand, are quicker to blame others for their strains and to interpret the negative treatment they experience as a deliberate challenge or insult. They are less concerned about hurting others or disrupting relationships, and they often view anger as an affirmation of their masculinity. Such differences, of course, reflect differences in the socialization of males and females, as described above. Among other things, females are taught to be more concerned about others and to exercise greater self-control.

These gender differences in the experience of anger may help explain gender differences in crime, since the moral outrage of the angry male is more conducive to serious violent and property crime, while the depression and misgivings of the angry female may lead her to express anger in different ways. In particular, anger among females may be more conducive to self-destructive forms of deviance such as illegal drug use (see Kring, 2000).

Gender Differences in Coping Skills, Resources, and Conventional Social Supports Increase the Likelihood of Criminal Coping by Males. Males are more likely to be low in constraint and high in negative emotionality, which reduces their ability to cope with strains in a legal manner (see Chapter 4). For example, they are more likely to act without thinking and to lack the social skills necessary for legal coping. These traits also increase their disposition for criminal coping, creating an attraction to risky activities, among other things. Further, males are physically larger and stronger than females, which increases their ability to engage in criminal coping. (However, the "sexualization and commodification of the young, female body" makes it easier for females to engage in selected crimes, like prostitution [Gaarder and Belknap, 2002:485].) Finally, data suggest that males are lower in certain types of conventional social support, particularly emotional support, and that the provision of social support may have less impact on males (Agnew and Brezina, 1997; McCarthy et al., 2004; Robbers, 2004; Sigfusdottir et al., 2004; Tolan et al., 2002). This too may increase the likelihood of criminal coping.

Males Are Lower in Social Control. As indicated, males are lower in several types of social control. They are less well-supervised by parents, less strongly tied to the household, less likely to be sanctioned for aggressive behavior, more weakly tied to school, and less likely to condemn crime. The costs of criminal coping may therefore be lower for males.

Males Are More Likely to Associate With Other Criminals and Hold Beliefs Favorable to Crime. As indicated in Chapter 4, such association and beliefs reduce the ability to engage in legal coping, lower the costs of crime, and increase the disposition for crime.

Males Hold Gender-Related Beliefs and Identities That Are Conducive to Criminal Coping, While Females Hold Gender-Related Beliefs and Identities That Inhibit Other-Directed Crime. Due to gender differences in socialization and social position, males are more likely to believe that they are (or should be) tough, aggressive, independent, and competitive, while females are more likely to believe they are weak, submissive, dependent on others, and concerned about others. These beliefs and identities increase the disposition of males to engage in crime, but they reduce the disposition of females for other-directed crime, as such crime strongly violates their gender beliefs and identities (see Burt and Clay-Warner, 2004; Heimer and De Coster, 1999; Jensen, 2003; Mullins et al., 2004; Van Gundy, 2002).

In sum, GST has a good deal to say about the reasons why males are more likely than females to engage in crime, especially serious crime. Males are said to be more likely to experience those strains conducive to crime and to cope with strains in a criminal manner.

Why Do Some Females Engage in Crime?

While males more often engage in crime than females, many females do engage in crime, including some serious crime. GST explains such crime by arguing that some females experience strains conducive to crime, such as sexual abuse, intimate partner violence, and gender discrimination, and have characteristics that favor criminal coping. This explanation is similar to feminist explanations of female crime, which argue that female crime is rooted in the oppression of women. Like feminist theories, GST argues that oppressed individuals may turn to crime in an effort to reduce or escape from the strains they experience, seek revenge, or alleviate their negative emotions (see Broidy and Agnew, 1997; Chesney-Lind and Shelden, 2004; Gaarder and Belknap, 2002).

The Strains Experienced by Females

Females do sometimes experience strains conducive to crime. In fact, females are more likely than males to experience strains such as sexual abuse and gender discrimination. In this area, one major theory of serious female delinquency argues that such delinquency is often rooted in the *sexual abuse of females by family members* (Chesney-Lind, 1989; Chesney-Lind and Sheldon, 2004). There is often little that adolescent females can do to end this abuse through legal channels, so they frequently escape from it by running away from home (note that females have rates of running away similar to that of males). Their age and runaway status make it very difficult for them to obtain legitimate work, so they often have to turn to crimes like theft and prostitution to survive on the street. Further, they are frequently abused and exploited by the males they encounter on the street. The juvenile justice system often does little to help them, and in fact may return them to the families where they experienced abuse.

Considerable data support this argument, with sexual abuse being quite common in the histories of serious female offenders (e.g., Acoca, 1998; Daly, 1992; Gilfus, 1992). Gaarder and Belknap (2002), for example, examined the life histories of 22 serious female offenders and found that experiences like the following were common:

> Tammy, a white 19-year-old serving 4 to 15 years for attempted murder, had a long history of sexual and physical abuse. Tammy's parents divorced when she was 2, and she shuffled back and forth between their homes as she got older. Her mother was a drug addict and her father was an alcoholic who hit her frequently. Between the ages of 8 and 13, she was sexually molested by different men who hung around her mother's house. She said, "my mom knew, but she'd let it happen. Then she wouldn't have to have sex with them herself, for the drugs and stuff." At age 13, Tammy moved back to her father's house. It was there that she was sexually abused by one of her father's friends. Although she told her father what had happened, "he chose not to believe it, not to believe me. He'd call me names, saying that if it did happen, it was my fault, that I was a slut." (493)

In addition, females are frequently subject to sexual, physical, and emotional abuse by their current and former romantic partners. Gaarder and Belknap (2002) also found that such abuse was common among the female offenders they interviewed (also see Miller and White, 2003). To illustrate, they describe the relationship between a young woman and her abusive boyfriend:

One day in school the principal saw him shove me into the lockers. They called my mom and he ended up getting house arrest for two weeks. He still kept coming over, even on house arrest. He got a key to my house somehow. I would call the police when he showed up, but they couldn't do anything. By the time they got there, he was gone. I figured he's come back and do it [beat me] worse next time. (494)

Females are also more likely to experience *gender discrimination*, with some data suggesting that such discrimination increases the likelihood of female crime (Katz, 2000; Eitle, 2002). This discrimination may assume a range of forms. In the family, females (a) often perform low-skill, monotonous tasks that are not in keeping with their skills and qualifications; (b) routinely attend to the needs of their spouses and children but receive little attention to their own needs; and (c) do a disproportionate share of all housework, even if they are working full time outside the home. As an illustration, the Bureau of Labor Statistics recently interviewed 21,000 people, asking them how they had spent their previous day. Among those in households where both the man and woman worked, about 20 percent of the men reported doing some sort of housework, like cleaning or laundry, versus 55 percent of the women, and about 35 percent of the men said they cooked or washed dishes, versus 66 percent of the women (McNeil, 2004). At work, females are often employed in "pink-collar" jobs that are not commensurate with their skills and educational backgrounds. Further, they continue to receive lower pay than do men in similar positions. In interpersonal relations with males, females often give more than they receive. Finally, females find it difficult to engage in many behaviors that they may value, like going out alone at certain times or in certain places. While certain types of gender discrimination may reduce the likelihood of other-directed crime for many females, some females may cope with gender discrimination through crime—with crime being a way to flout or escape from gender barriers, seek revenge, or seek relief from the negative emotions caused by discrimination.

Eitle (2002) found support for this argument in an examination of young adult women. He found that those women who reported that they had experienced major instances of gender-based discrimination were more likely to engage in both crime and drug abuse. Major instances of discrimination based on gender included:

- being unfairly fired or denied a promotion
- not being hired for a job
- being unfairly treated by the police
- being unfairly discouraged by a teacher or advisor from pursuing a desired job or career
- for unfair reasons, having a landlord or realtor refuse to sell or rent a house or apartment
- for unfair reasons, having neighbors make life difficult

In addition to sexual abuse, partner abuse, and gender discrimination, females have become much more likely to experience *monetary strains*. While the economic situation for many women has improved, conditions have not changed as much as many people believe. There has been little change in the types of jobs most women hold or their compensation relative to men, with many women still confined to "pink-collar" jobs with low pay. Further, conditions have deteriorated for many women because of the "feminization of poverty." Increases in divorce and illegitimacy, the decline of low-skill jobs that pay a decent wage, and a decline in social services have dramatically increased the number of females who head households and live in poverty (Heimer, 2000). The monetary strain these women face is said to be a major source of female crime and to account for much of the increase in female crime in recent decades. Limited data support this position. Most serious female offenders tend to be poor and unmarried. The increase in female-headed households below the poverty line has paralleled the increase in female crime. And female offenders frequently state that they engaged in crime because of a desperate need for money (see Heimer, 2000, for an overview).

Finally, females may sometimes experience certain of the other strains conducive to crime, such as parental rejection, harsh discipline, negative secondary-school experiences, peer abuse, homelessness, marital problems, and criminal victimization. And certain of these strains, particularly marital problems, may be more likely to lead to crime among females. Simons and associates (2002), for example, found that having a poor-quality relationship with a romantic partner was more likely to lead to crime among females than males.

It is important to note that some females are more likely to experience these strains than others. In particular, lower-class females and the members of certain racial and ethnic groups, like African Americans and Latinos, are more likely to experience most of the strains conducive to crime (see Gaarder and Belknap, 2002). And it is partly for this reason that such females have higher rates of offending.

Certain Females Possess Characteristics That Increase the Likelihood of Criminal Coping

While females are less likely than males to possess many of those characteristics conducive to criminal coping, many females do possess such characteristics. And such females should be more likely to respond to the above strains with crime. Among other things, a criminal response should be more likely among females who are poor, are low in constraint and high in negative emotionality, are low in conventional social support, are low in social control, associate with criminal others, hold beliefs favorable to crime, and reject traditional gender beliefs (see Heimer, 2000).

How Does General Strain Theory Explain Why Lower-Class Individuals Have Higher Rates of Crime?

Individuals' social class is typically measured in terms of their income, education, occupational prestige, or some combination of these factors (or, in the case of juveniles, the income, education, and occupation of their parents or guardians). The more recent and best studies indicate that lower-class individuals are more likely than middle- and upper-class individuals to engage in crime, particularly serious crime. This is especially true of lower-class individuals who have been very poor for a long period of time (see Agnew, 2005a; Jarjoura et al., 2002). GST explains the relationship between social class and crime in pretty much the same way it explains the relationship between gender and crime. Lower-class individuals are more likely to experience strains conducive to crime and to cope with strains in a criminal manner.

Data suggest that lower-class individuals are more likely to experience the following strains conducive to crime (for overviews, see Agnew, 2005b; Agnew et al., 2000; Bradley and Corwyn, 2002; Brooks-Gunn and Duncan, 1997; Colvin, 2000; Jarjoura et al., 2002;

Taylor and Turner, 2002; Turner and Avison, 2003; Turner et al., 1995):

- A range of family problems, including parental rejection; erratic, excessive, and harsh supervision; child abuse and neglect; and marital problems such as conflict and abuse. Parents who are poor are more likely to experience a range of stressors, including financial problems, unemployment, work in "bad" jobs, housing problems, health problems, and residence in high-crime communities. These problems often make them depressed and irritable, which lead to parenting problems. Depressed and irritable parents have less interest in their children, and so they are more likely to poorly supervise them, neglect them, and reject them. Also, these parents are more easily upset and less able to cope effectively when upset. As a consequence, they are more likely to discipline their children in a harsh, erratic manner and abuse them. Likewise, married individuals who are poor are more likely to abuse and get into conflicts with one another.

- School problems, such as poor academic performance, low attachment to school, and negative relations with teachers. Poor parents are less able to equip their children with the skills and attitudes necessary to do well in school, including the intellectual skills and the self-control required to pay attention to teachers and complete schoolwork. Among other things, poor parents more often lack these skills themselves, they frequently lack the resources to provide an intellectually stimulating environment, and they are often preoccupied with a range of stressors. Poor parents are also less likely to become involved in school activities, monitor their children's school performance, and provide assistance when necessary. Further, poor parents are less able to send their children to high-quality schools. For all these reasons, the academic performance of poor children suffers, their dislike of school increases, and they get into conflicts with teachers.

- Abusive peer relations. Lower-class individuals are more likely to become part of delinquent peer groups and gangs, whose members more often abuse and get into conflicts with one another. Lower-class individuals are more involved in such groups partly because they are more likely to possess the traits of negative emotionality and low constraint (see below), which increases the appeal of such groups. They are also lower in social control; for example, they are less well-supervised by parents and less committed to school. This increases their freedom to associate with such groups. Further, they more often live in deprived communities, where such groups are more common. Finally, they see such groups as a way of coping with many of the strains they face. For example, such groups may help them secure money and enhance their status.

- Chronic unemployment and work in the secondary labor market. The relationship between social class, unemployment, and work in the secondary labor market is of course quite intimate. Individuals who are unemployed for long periods or who work in "bad jobs" are lower-class by definition, since they lack incomes, have low incomes, and/or work in low prestige jobs. One dimension of lower-class status, however, contributes to unemployment and the nature of one's work, with poorly educated individuals having more trouble obtaining work, particularly work in the primary labor market.

- Failure to achieve their monetary and status goals. This statement may seem self-evident, but a good number of researchers have argued that lower-class individuals are *not* more likely to experience goal blockage in these areas. Most notably, it has been claimed that lower-class individuals adapt to their deprived position by lowering their monetary goals (see Agnew, 1995d). So while lower-class individuals have less money, they also *want* less money. This is certainly the case for many lower-class individuals; they have learned to be content with their limited lot in life. It is also true that many higher-class individuals desire more money than they currently have. Robert Merton, the "father" of strain theory, described such a situation when he stated that "in the American Dream there is no final stopping point . . . at each income level Americans want about twenty-five percent more (but of course this 'just a bit more' continues to operate once it is obtained)" (Merton, 1968:190). But at the same time, the data suggest that lower-class individuals are more likely to be dissatisfied with their monetary situation than higher-class individuals (Agnew et al., 1996). And there is some reason to believe that lower-class individuals have more difficulty satisfying their status goals—that is, their desire to be viewed and treated with respect by others (Anderson, 1999).

- Criminal victimization. Lower-class individuals have a higher rate of criminal victimization for most types of crime, especially violent crimes (Catalano, 2004). They are also more likely to have their family members and friends victimized and to anticipate they will be victimized in the future. There are several reasons for this, including the fact that lower-class individuals more often live in deprived communities with high rates of crime.

- Residence in economically-deprived communities and homelessness. Not surprisingly, lower-class individuals are more likely to live in economically deprived communities and to be homeless (Bradley and Corwyn, 2002).

Lower-class individuals, then, are more likely to experience virtually all of those strains conducive to crime. Further, GST also argues that lower-class individuals are more likely to cope with these strains through crime. There are several reasons for this.

First, *lower-class individuals are less likely to possess the skills and resources necessary for legal coping.* They are more likely to be low in constraint and high in negative emotionality (see Agnew, 2005b). Among other things, their parents are less likely to teach them these traits and they are more likely to inherit these traits from their lower-class parents (individuals with these traits are less likely to get good jobs and so are more often in the lower class). Lower-class individuals are also less likely to possess other coping skills and resources, like social and problem-solving skills, a sense of self-efficacy, and, of course, money (Bradley and Corwyn, 2002; McLeod and Kessler, 1990; Mirowsky and Ross, 1989; Thoits, 1995).

Second, *the costs of crime are less for lower-class individuals because they are lower in social control.* Lower-class individuals are less likely to be caught and sanctioned for their criminal acts. They are less well-supervised by family members and more likely to live in deprived communities, where community residents are less likely to sanction one another for crime (see Chapter 7). Lower-class individuals have less to lose if they are caught. Their relations with family members are often strained and they do not have good jobs to lose. And lower-class individuals are less likely to believe that crime is wrong, partly because they have not been as well socialized by their parents.

Third, *lower-class individuals are more likely to be disposed to crime.* This disposition partly stems from the fact that lower-class individuals are more likely to be lower in constraint and higher in negative emotionality. It partly stems from exposure to parents who employ harsh or abusive disciplinary methods, thus modeling aggressive behaviors. And it stems from the greater involvement of lower-class individuals in delinquent groups, whose members model crime, reinforce crime, and teach beliefs favorable to crime.

These ideas have not yet received a good test. That is, no one has examined the extent to which these class differences in strains and in factors that influence criminal coping explain the greater involvement of lower-class individuals in serious crime.

How Does General Strain Theory Explain Race/Ethnic Differences in Crime?

This section uses GST to explain why African Americans have higher rates of crime, especially serious crime, than whites. I focus on African Americans and whites because we have the most data on these groups, but many of the arguments made would likely apply to other race/ethnic groups that have relatively high rates of offending, such as Latinos and Native Americans (see Agnew, 2005a; Hawkins et al., 2000).

Race Differences in Strains and Criminal Coping

The primary reason African Americans have higher rates of offending is because they are more likely to experience those strains conducive to crime, such as abuse, chronic unemployment, work in the secondary labor market, criminal victimization, and discrimination. They are also more likely to cope with such strains through crime.

The main reason for these race differences, in turn, is that African Americans are more likely to be poor and to live in high-poverty communities than whites. It is important to stress that most African

Americans are *not* poor, but due to the effects of past and present discrimination, African Americans are more likely to be poor than whites. In 2003, 24.4 percent of African Americans lived below the poverty line ($18,810 for a family of four), versus 8.2 percent of non-Hispanic whites. And as indicated above, poor individuals are more likely to experience strains conducive to crime, and to cope with such strains in a criminal manner. Further, poor African Americans are several times more likely than poor whites to live in *poor communities*—that is, communities where a high percentage of the other residents are poor. This is due to such things as the effects of housing discrimination and the tendency to locate public housing in African-American communities (see Agnew, 2005a; Wilson, 1987). As indicated in Chapter 7, the residents of poor communities are more likely to experience strains conducive to crime and cope with such strains in a criminal manner. Race-related differences in strains and criminal coping, then, are largely due to the fact that African Americans are more likely to be poor and live in poor communities.

If this argument is correct, we would expect that the relationship between race and crime would be considerably diminished if we took account of the social class of individuals and the class composition of their communities. For example, we would expect that the crime rate of poor African Americans living in poor communities would be comparable to that of poor whites living in poor communities. The few studies that have made such comparisons have found that taking account of *both* individual and community-level social class substantially reduces the relationship between race and crime (Benson and Fox, 2004; McNulty and Bellair, 2003; McNulty and Holloway, 2000; Peeples and Loeber, 1994).

Race-related differences in individual and community-level social class, however, do not fully explain the higher crime rate of African Americans. This is due to the fact that even after we take account of such differences, African Americans are still more likely to experience strains conducive to crime and to engage in criminal coping (see Harrell, 2000; Kaufman et al., 2005; Reskin and Padavic, 1999; Taylor and Turner, 2002; Turner and Avison, 2003). Most notably, African Americans at all class levels are more likely to experience discrimination than whites. They are more likely to be discriminated against in the school system. School officials, for example, expect less from them and are more likely to place them in lower tracks. They face discrimination by police and other justice officials.

In many cases, for example, the police are more likely to stop and question African Americans, and to arrest them. They face discrimination from employers. And they face discrimination from the broader community.

One study that involved interviews with students in a New York City High School describes certain of these discriminatory experiences:

> When African-American and Latino students were asked about their experiences with discrimination, they described hostile relationships with adults in positions of authority such as police officers, shopkeepers, and teachers in school. Many of the African American and Latino students reported being followed by shopkeepers in stores with friends and sometimes when they were with their parents. Stories were told repeatedly about being harassed by police officers while walking through their neighborhood, and hanging out with friends in and around school. . . . These stories were not isolated or singular events. They were experienced repeatedly over the years and in different locations. . . . The Latino and African-American students also perceived their teachers as implicitly or explicitly racist or discriminatory. . . . They described the teachers' low academic expectations and stereotypes about "bad kids" or kids who "start trouble." The teachers were generally, in the eyes of Latino and Black students, uncaring and ineffective. (Rosenbloom and Way, 2004:434, 435)

This discrimination is a major source of strain in and of itself. And recent data suggest that race-related discrimination increases negative emotions and the likelihood of crime (Eitle and Turner, 2003; Harrell, 2000; Martin et al., 2003; Simons et al., 2003). Further, this discrimination increases the likelihood that African Americans will experience other strains conducive to crime, like school problems, peer abuse, unemployment, and work in the secondary labor market. In addition, such discrimination increases the likelihood that African Americans will blame the strains they experience on the deliberate acts of others, thus increasing the likelihood they will view their strains as unjust.

There has not been much research on the extent to which GST can explain race-related differences in crime. Two studies, however, suggest that race-related differences in stressors, such as criminal victimization and witnessing violence, go a long way toward explaining the higher crime rate of African Americans (Eitle and Turner, 2003; Kaufman et al., 2005).

Summary

GST, then, can help explain group differences in crime rates, including gender, age (see Chapter 5), class, and race/ethnic differences. Such differences are partly due to the fact that certain groups are more likely to experience strains conducive to crime and to cope with strains through crime. I should emphasize, however, that GST does not provide a full explanation of group differences in crime rates. Most notably, it does not fully describe *why* certain groups are more likely to experience strains or possess those characteristics that promote criminal coping. For example, it does not explain why gender and race/ethnicity influence the way in which people are treated and their social position in our society. Macrolevel theories address these issues, including conflict theories, institutional anomie theory, feminist theories, and others (see Cullen and Agnew, 2003). A major challenge for researchers is to better integrate GST with such theories. Also, biological theories are of some relevance in explaining sex, age, and possibly class differences in the exposure and reaction to strain. More integrative work is also needed in this area (see Walsh, 2000, for an excellent discussion).

Review and Discussion Questions

1. At a general level, how does general strain theory explain group differences in crime rates?

2. How do biopsychological, social control, and social learning theories explain the higher rate of female offending?

3. How does GST explain the higher rate of female offending?

4. What types of strains conducive to crime are males more likely to experience? Why are males more likely to experience strains conducive to crime?

5. What types of strains are females more likely to experience? Which of these strains might inhibit crime and which are conducive to crime?

6. What are some of the negative consequences of strains other than crime?

7. Why are males more likely to cope with strains through other-directed crime? Related to this, how does the emotional reaction of males to strains differ from that of females?

8. How does GST explain female crime? Related to this, what strains play an important role in the generation of female crime?

9. Gender differences in offending are relatively small for minor property crime, family violence, and many types of illegal drug use. How might GST explain this?

10. How does GST explain social class differences in crime rates?

11. How does GST explain race/ethnic differences in crime rates? What role does discrimination play in race differences in crime rates? ✦

Chapter 7

How Does General Strain Theory Explain Community and Societal Differences in Offending?

Some communities have much higher crime rates than others. Consider, for example, the following description of a high-crime community in Denver, based on interviews with a sample of adolescents who lived there:

> Approximately one-fourth of the adolescents interviewed reported confronting violence regularly. While going to school, walking in their neighborhoods, and hanging out with friends, they expected to confront violence. Their expectations often came to brutal fruition, forcing them to negotiate frequent conflicts. Benny, a 14-year-old Latino living in Allenspark, illustrates the experiences within this group. . . . He complained that there was much more violence among youths in his new neighborhood and, although he did not mind the fistfights occurring in Allenspark (usually fights between Latino and Vietnamese American youths), he feared occasions when outsiders entered the neighborhood carrying weapons. . . . "The kids are the worst. There's gangs, like the NSMs [North Side Mafia] and the Untouchables and stuff. The westsiders [teens from the west side of Denver] will come over here and they'd start shooting." (Irwin, 2004:460)

Those communities with high crime rates tend to have certain characteristics. *The people living in them are poor, have high rates of residential mobility (they move a lot), and have high levels of family disruption (many are divorced or separated, many families are headed by single parents).* The effect of these characteristics on community crime rates is usually explained in terms of social disorganization theory. Social disorganization theorists draw heavily on social control theory, and they argue that the people in these communities are less willing and able to exercise effective control over one another. For example, they are less willing to sanction individuals who violate the law. Social learning theory has also been used to explain the effect of these characteristics on crime rates. Communities with these characteristics are said to be more likely to develop values conducive to crime. For example, some people in these communities come to justify or excuse theft and violence under certain conditions. Also, delinquent peer groups and gangs are more likely to form in these communities. I do not dispute these arguments, but in this chapter I argue that general strain theory (GST) can also help explain why crime rates are highest in communities with high levels of poverty, mobility, and family disruption ("deprived communities"). Not surprisingly, I argue that people in these communities experience more strains conducive to crime and are more likely to cope with strains through crime (this chapter draws heavily on Agnew, 1999).

I define communities quite broadly. They include areas of settlement as small as the "block" on which an individual lives and the neighborhood in which this block is located. They also include larger units, such as cities and standard metropolitan statistical areas (SMSAs), which are made up of cities and their surrounding suburbs. These larger units are often quite diverse in terms of such things as income level. An SMSA, for example, may contain some areas that are quite poor and some that are quite wealthy. Nevertheless, there are often gross differences between SMSAs in overall levels of income. Also, we can take account of the extent to which a factor like income varies in a community. Two SMSAs, for example, may have the same overall level of income, but there may be much income inequality in one of the SMSAs (many people are poor and many are rich) and little income inequality in the other (most people are middle class). As indicated below, high levels of income inequality may increase crime in certain cases.

While the discussion that follows focuses on communities, the final part of this chapter uses GST to explain why some societies have higher crime rates than others. There has been much less research on societal differences in crime than on community differences. This partly reflects the fact that definitions of crime and the accuracy of crime statistics often vary from society to society, making it difficult to compare levels of crime across societies. Nevertheless, some important research has been done in this area and, as argued below, GST can also help explain intersocietal variation in crime rates.

How Does General Strain Theory Explain Community Differences in Crime Rates?

Before describing how GST explains community differences in crime rates, I first want to present brief descriptions of how social disorganization and social learning theories explain such differences. As you will see, GST draws on these theories, especially when explaining why the residents of deprived communities are more likely to cope with strains through crime.

Social disorganization theorists argue that the residents of deprived communities are less able and willing to sanction other residents for crime, establish close ties to them, help them in their educational and employment pursuits, and teach them to condemn crime. To understand why this is the case, imagine that you are the resident of such a community. You are struggling with a range of financial and other problems (or strains), such as housing and health problems. You are trying to raise your children without the assistance of a spouse. And you do not know your neighbors well, because people frequently move into and out of the community. In fact, you do not like the neighborhood very much and hope to move out of it as soon as you are able. Given such circumstances, you probably do not have the time or the desire to engage in activities like monitoring other people in the community and sanctioning them if they misbehave. Studies provide some support for this argument, suggesting that factors like economic deprivation, residential mobility, and family disruption reduce the extent to which community residents intervene in neighborhood problems like crime, form close ties to one another, and assist one another. And this breakdown in social control contributes to higher rates of crime (see Agnew, 2005a; Cullen and Agnew, 2003; Sampson et al., 1997).

Social learning theorists argue that community characteristics like economic deprivation may lead some residents to develop beliefs favorable to crime. In particular, individuals who cannot achieve money through legal channels may come to justify or excuse illegal methods of making money, such as theft and drug selling. And individuals who cannot achieve the more general goal of status or respect through legal channels may attempt to achieve it through violence. That is, they may attempt to coerce or intimidate others into treating them with respect. Anderson (1999) illustrates these points, drawing on his observations of a poor, African-American, inner-city community:

> Many of the young blacks who have difficulty obtaining a job feel victimized by prejudice and discrimination. Such feelings of victimization may lead to a greater understanding, if not tolerance, of those who resort to selling drugs to "survive." In these circumstances the drug trade, so dangerous and problematic for local communities and societies, becomes normal happenstance. (Anderson, 1999:111)

> There is a general sense that very little respect is to be had, and therefore everyone competes to get what affirmation he can from what is available. The resulting craving for respect gives people thin skins and short fuses . . . there is an especially heightened concern about being disrespected. Many inner-city young men in particular crave respect to such a degree they will risk their lives to attain and maintain it . . . people often feel constrained not only to stand up and at least attempt to resist during an attack but also to "pay back"—to seek revenge—after a successful assault on their person. (Anderson, 1999:75–76)

Related to this, delinquent peer groups and gangs are more likely to develop in these communities. This occurs partly because social control is low, so residents are less able to stop such groups from forming or operating. Also, the high levels of strain in such communities motivate individuals to form such groups. Such groups are often viewed as a solution to strains. Gangs, for example, may be used to make money through illegal channels or enhance status (see Chapter 2). Delinquent peer groups and gangs, of course, foster the social learning of crime in several ways. They model crime, reinforce crime, and teach beliefs favorable to crime.

GST adds to these explanations, claiming that deprived communities also have higher crime rates because community residents are more likely to experience strains conducive to crime and cope with strains through crime. Part of the reason for this is that deprived communities are more likely to attract and retain strained individuals. For example, poor individuals are more likely to move into these communities because they cannot afford to live elsewhere and because community residents are less able to resist their immigration. Poor individuals are also less able to move out of such communities. GST, however, argues that deprived communities have higher crime rates not only because they are more likely to attract and retain strained individuals, but also because they cause strains and increase the likelihood of criminal coping.

In particular, as Ross (2000:177) has suggested, the types of neighborhoods that people live in have a large effect on the strains they experience. Some neighborhoods are "clean and safe; houses, apartments, and other buildings are well maintained; and residents are respectful of one another and each others' property." But in other neighborhoods, residents "report noise, litter, vandalism, graffiti, drug use, trouble with neighbors, and other incivilities." Likewise, neighborhood characteristics influence the likelihood that individuals will cope with their strains through crime.

Deprived Communities Cause Strains Conducive to Crime

The Inability To Achieve Monetary and Status Goals. The residents of deprived communities are more likely to experience certain types of goal blockage conducive to crime, even after we take account of their individual characteristics (e.g., education and personality traits). Most notably, it is more difficult for them to achieve their economic goals through legal channels. The residents have less access to stable, high-paying jobs, like manufacturing jobs. Such jobs are often located in suburban areas, so they are less accessible to the residents, many of whom lack cars. Relatively few individuals in the community have the types of job contacts or connections that might help others get jobs. There are fewer individuals in the community to teach and model the skills and attitudes necessary for successful job performance. And the schools in deprived communities are generally inferior to those elsewhere. As a consequence, the residents of such communities are more likely to engage in illegal methods of making money, such as theft, drug-selling, and prostitution. The frustration they feel also increases the likelihood they will engage in violence.

Closely related to the desire for money is the desire for status: "achieving respect in the eyes of one's fellows" (Cohen, 1955:65). Individuals may desire status in general as well as particular types of status, with the desire for "masculine status" being especially relevant to crime (see Majors and Billson, 1992; Messerschmidt, 1993). In the United States, status—including masculine status—is partly a function of income and occupation, factors which are influenced by community characteristics. Status is also a function of the income level and racial composition of the community in which one lives. As a consequence, individuals in poor, minority communities are often "looked down" upon and treated in a disrespectful manner by others. They may adapt by attempting to achieve status through illegal means. As described by Anderson (1999), they may adopt a tough demeanor, which includes the willingness to respond to even minor shows of disrespect with violence. They may take material possessions from others. And they may actively "campaign for respect" by verbally and physically abusing others (also see Bernard, 1990; Majors and Billson, 1992; Mullins et al., 2004).

High Levels of Income Inequality ('Poverty in the Midst of Plenty') May Further Increase the Likelihood of Crime. Several strain theorists have argued that economic deprivation may be especially likely to lead to crime when poor people are surrounded by wealthier people (poverty in the midst of plenty). Poor people in such circumstances may be more likely to feel that they deserve more for themselves, making their poverty all the more difficult to bear. Researchers have tested this idea by examining the relationship between income inequality and community crime rates. Some communities have little inequality, meaning that most people have similar incomes. Other communities have high levels of inequality, meaning that some people have much larger incomes than other people. Studies tend to suggest that high levels of income inequality increase the likelihood of crime, although not all studies find this (see Agnew, 1999). Part of the reason for these mixed results is that it is difficult to distinguish the effect of income inequality on crime from the effect of poverty, since most communities with high levels of income inequality also have high percentages of poor people (Land et al., 1990). Also, inequality may contribute to crime in some cases, but not others. For example, it has been argued that income inequality is more likely to lead to crime when it is linked to race, with African Americans having lower incomes than whites (Blau and Blau, 1982; Philips, 1997). When income inequality is linked to race, it is more likely to be seen as unfair or unjust (see Agnew, 1999:134–135 for a more general discussion of the conditions under which inequality is most likely to lead to crime).

Family, School, and Peer Problems. The employment problems faced by the residents of deprived communities contribute to a host of other problems, including family, school, and peer problems (e.g., Chapter 6; Ainsworth, 2002; Bellair et al., 2003; Benson et al., 2000; Conger et al., 1994; Rankin and Quane, 2002). Individuals with economic difficulties are more likely to get divorced or never marry. In fact, economic problems are perhaps the major cause of family disruption. Economic problems and family disruption, in turn, contribute to such family problems as parental conflict; parental rejection of children; the use of harsh, erratic disciplinary techniques; and child abuse and neglect. Likewise, economic problems and family disruption contribute to school problems, including poor academic performance, negative relations with teachers, and the experience of school as boring and a waste of time. Parents are less able to prepare their children for school, to monitor their children's school performance, and to assist their children when necessary. Also, the schools in deprived communities are inferior. They tend to receive less funding than the schools in more affluent areas and have less experienced teachers (Winter, 2004). Further, parental involvement is lower in such schools and such schools are populated by economically deprived children, many of whom are poorly prepared for schoolwork. Finally, delinquent peer groups and gangs are more common in deprived communities, which increases the likelihood of peer abuse.

Unemployment and Work in the Secondary Labor Market. For reasons indicated above, it is more difficult to get work in deprived communities, particularly work in the primary labor market. As a result, rates of unemployment are high and those who do work are usually employed in jobs with poor pay, few benefits, limited opportunities for advancement, and unpleasant working conditions.

Homelessness. Rates of homelessness are also higher in deprived communities, as a consequence of the above problems, such as unemployment and family disruption.

Experiences With Prejudice and Discrimination. The residents of deprived communities—especially those with high concentrations of African Americans and other minority groups—may be more likely to experience and perceive discrimination. The existence of such communities may increase the likelihood that others will form negative stereotypes of the residents who live there and treat them in a discriminatory manner. There is some evidence that this is the case with the police, for example (Miller, 1996). Also, the existence of such communities may lead residents to the obvious conclusion that race/ethnicity is strongly correlated with a host of social ills, thereby fostering impressions of discrimination.

Abusive Treatment Resulting From Frequent Interaction With Other Strained and Angry Individuals. Individuals in deprived communities are not only more likely to experience the above strains, they are also more likely to interact with other strained and angry individuals, which increases the likelihood they will be treated in an abusive manner. For example, Warner and Fowler (2003) found that the residents of deprived communities were much more likely to report that they or someone in their household had (a) received verbal threats or insults, (b) felt cheated by someone, and (c) been harassed by the police. Further, these strains influenced neighborhood levels of violence.

Residents are more likely to interact with other strained and angry individuals because there is a higher percentage of such individuals in deprived communities. Further, the characteristics of such communities foster frequent interaction between these people, particularly in poorly supervised settings like the street. This partly stems from the high rates of unemployment and family disruption in deprived communities, which create a large pool of unsupervised teenagers and unattached adults who "hang out" in the street. It partly stems from overcrowded living arrangements, which make street life more attractive. And it partly stems from the mixed-use nature of many deprived communities (businesses mixed in with residences), which provide opportunities for congregating outside the home. The end result is that large numbers of strained and angry people are in frequent contact with one another. And this increases the likelihood of abusive treatment, which in turn contributes to crime.

Brezina et al. (2001) found support for certain of these arguments in a study of high schools throughout the United States. In particular, they found that schools with a higher percentage of angry students had higher levels of student-to-student aggression, even after taking account of a range of other school characteristics. They also found that individual students in schools with a higher percentage of angry students were more likely to get into conflicts with other students, even after taking account of their own level of anger and other factors. As Brezina et al. (2001:375) state, "in such schools, students may have frequent contact with angry and potentially hostile peers and, consequently, high levels of exposure to the type of interactions that promote conflict and aggression."

Criminal Victimization. Deprived communities have higher rates of crime and criminal victimization for several reasons: levels of social control are lower in such communities, residents are more likely to learn to engage in crime, *and* residents are more likely to experience the above types of strains. It is important to emphasize, however, that the higher rates of crime in these communities function as a major type of strain in and of themselves, and thereby contribute to further crime. In particular, individuals in deprived communities are more likely to be criminally victimized and this victimization motivates further crime. Also, the residents are more likely to have their family members and friends victimized. And as Agnew (2002) demonstrates, the victimization of family members and friends is a potent type of strain that may increase the likelihood of crime, even after individuals' own victimization experiences and other factors are taken into account.

Further, the generally high rates of crime in deprived communities may contribute to other types of strains. Most notably, high rates of crime may cause businesses and more advantaged residents to flee the community, thereby further contributing to the economic problems of those residents who remain. High rates of crime also contribute to such strains as school problems. To illustrate, consider this account from a researcher who interviewed third- and sixth-grade students in a school located in a lower-income community:

> The violence they encountered in their community was these children's overriding concern. Such violence was not a

topic in the other two schools I observed, both of which are situated in middle- and upper-middle–class neighborhoods. The [students] initiated discussions about . . . the activities of neighborhood hustlers and gangs, the murdering or imprisonment of friends and relatives, the desire to leave the community to escape from danger, and in-school violence. . . . These children's comments made me aware that whatever it was that was going on in school, good or bad, was by far overshadowed by the violence in their community. The witnessing of murders; anxieties about having one's money or other valuables stolen; the fear of leaving the house even to go to the corner store; the need to keep bats and knives around the house for protection; feelings that one must almost board up one's doors at night to keep thieves away; the resignation that one's own life might be as short as that of friends and family members who have fallen victim to crime, drugs, or poverty; and the desire to move away to a more peaceful place—all these thoughts—indeed, concerns for basic safety—occupied the minds of the 8- to 13-year-old youngsters with whom I spoke. How much energy and attention could these inner-city youth have left for spelling, mathematics, and social studies. . . . Why was Robert sleeping in class? His uncle had been killed during the night and his mother's crying had kept him awake. Why was Tiera so sullen and unresponsive to her teacher? She was worried about the domestic violence occurring in her home. Why did Michael act up in the classroom? His uncle had been arrested the day before. . . . There is no doubt that the violence to which inner-city children are exposed affects their school performance. (Towns, 1998: 377, 378, 387, 388)

Summary. Living in a deprived community, then, increases the likelihood of experiencing several strains conducive to crime: the inability to achieve monetary and status goals; family, school, and peer problems; unemployment and work in the secondary labor market; homelessness; experiences with prejudice and discrimination; abusive treatment by others; and criminal victimization. GST argues that these strains, in turn, help explain the higher rates of crime in deprived communities. Unfortunately, there has not been much research on the extent to which this is the case. Two recent studies, however, do suggest that deprived communities have higher rates of crime partly because the residents of such communities experience more strains (Boardman et al., 2001; Warner and Fowler, 2003). Data also suggest that the residents of deprived communities are more likely to experience certain negative emotions, like depression, even after taking account of a range of individual characteristics (e.g., Latkin and Curry, 2003; Ross, 2000). As discussed in Chapter 2, strains are said to increase crime primarily through their effect on negative emotions.

People in Deprived Communities Are More Likely to Cope With Strains Through Crime

People in deprived communities are not only more likely to experience strains conducive to crime, they are also more likely to cope with strains through crime. There are several reasons for this.

Limited Coping Skills and Resources. The residents of deprived communities are less able to engage in legal coping due to their limited coping skills and resources, including their lack of money, more limited problem-solving skills, and higher levels of irritability. These limited skills and resources are partly a function of community characteristics. As indicated, it is more difficult for individuals in deprived communities to satisfy their monetary goals. There are fewer people to teach and model effective problem-solving skills in deprived communities (Anderson, 1990). And the many strains in deprived communities foster the trait of negative emotionality (see Chapter 2; Bernard, 1990).

Low Levels of Conventional Social Support. Also, the residents of deprived communities are less able to cope as a community. As indicated above, the residents are often consumed with their own problems, do not know their neighbors well, and hope to move out of the community as soon as they are able. These factors limit their ability and desire to unite with one another to solve community-wide problems. These factors also limit the amount of *social support* or assistance they provide one another. Data suggest that community differences in social support have an important effect on the ability of individuals to cope with strains and that such differences in support are linked to community differences in crime rates (Warner and Fowler, 2003).

Low Social Control. As indicated above, deprived communities are lower in social control. In particular, community residents are less likely to be closely monitored and sanctioned for criminal behavior, establish close ties to others, have an investment in conventional institutions, and learn to condemn crime. This too increases the likelihood of criminal coping, since the costs of crime are lower (although see Warner and Fowler, 2003).

More Likely to Associate With Other Criminals and Hold Beliefs Favorable to Crime. The fact that the residents of deprived communities are more likely to associate with other criminals and hold beliefs favorable to crime further increases the likelihood of criminal coping. In fact, a central component of those beliefs favorable to crime is that one is justified in responding to strains with crime. For example, one is justified in responding to economic problems with income-generating crimes or to disrespectful treatment with violence.

The Public Nature of Strains. As indicated, people in deprived communities spend a great deal of their time in public settings. The result is that their strains are more likely to be witnessed by or become known to others. As Hagan and Peterson (1995:27) state, the "press of people in dense underclass areas imposes upon residents a unique kind of community organization characterized by a high level of mutual surveillance. This restricts residents' privacy, making their activities, both legal and illegal, more frequently 'public' " (also see Stark, 1987). Because their strains are widely known, individuals are frequently reminded of the negative treatment they have experienced, which makes it more difficult for them to ignore or discount such treatment. Also, individuals feel under more pressure to respond to negative treatment with crime in order to "save face" and prevent further predation by others (see Anderson, 1999).

Summary. The residents of deprived communities are not only more likely to experience strains conducive to crime, they are also more likely to cope with strains through crime. This is because such residents have more limited coping skills and resources, have lower levels of conventional social support, are lower in social control, are more likely to associate with criminal others and hold beliefs favorable to crime, and are more likely to have their strains become known to others.

How Does General Strain Theory Explain Societal Differences in Crime Rates?

GST was developed with the United States in mind, but the theory can be used to explain crime in other societies. In fact, the theory has been successfully applied to the explanation of crime in China (Bao et al., 2004), the Philippines (Maxwell, 2001), Korea (Morash and

Moon, 2005a), and Israel (Landau, 1998). It should be noted, however, that societies may differ somewhat in the events and conditions which function as major strains and in the factors that influence the impact of strains on crime (more below). GST can also be used to explain differences in crime rates *across* societies, including developed societies like the United States, Japan, and Western Europe; developing societies, which are in the process of becoming industrialized; and undeveloped or preindustrial societies. As is the case with communities, crime rates should be highest in those societies that experience more strains conducive to crime and that score higher on those factors that increase the likelihood of criminal coping.

There has not been much research on the explanation of cross-national differences in crime due to the difficulty of collecting good data in the area. Most of the research that has been done examines developed societies and selected developing societies, where decent data are more readily available. This research focuses on the crime of homicide, since homicide is more likely to be similarly defined across societies, reported to the police, and recorded in crime statistics than other crimes (see LaFree, 1999; Neapolitan, 1997; see van Wilsem et al., 2003, for cross-national research on other crimes using victimization data). And this research focuses on just a few of the potential causes of crime. In particular, cross-national data on most of the strains conducive to crime are not available. Likewise, data on most of the factors said to influence the effect of strains on crime are not available.

Nevertheless, the cross-national research on crime is generally supportive of GST. Measures of economic strain are usually found to be the strongest predictors of cross-national variations in crime rates. In particular, crime rates are generally higher in societies where levels of economic inequality are high (e.g., LaFree, 1999; Messner, 2003; Neapolitan, 1997, 1998; Pratt and Godsey, 2003; van Wilsem et al., 2003; also see Roberts and LaFree, 2004). Also, some data suggest that at least certain types of homicide are higher in societies characterized by high rates of family disruption, the negative treatment of women, high rates of battle deaths, histories of colonialization and conquest, and ongoing oppression (e.g., Gartner, 1990; Neapolitan, 1997). Further, several studies indicate that the effect of economic strains on crime is much stronger in societies that provide low levels of social support, including welfare assistance, unemployment insurance, workers' compensation, social security, and health benefits (e.g.,

Messner, 2003; Messner and Rosenfeld, 1997; Pratt and Godsey, 2003; Savolainen, 2000).

A Complication in Applying GST to the Explanation of Societal Differences in Crime Rates

It is, however, important to note that applying GST to the explanation of societal differences in crime rates is not as straightforward as it might seem. In particular, *there may be some variation across societies in those strains that are conducive to crime.* That is, an event or condition which functions as a strain conducive to crime in one society may not do so in another. Let me provide an example.

Suppose you had a meager income and few material possessions. You lived in a primitive shelter that lacked all the "basic" conveniences, such as a toilet, running water, electricity, a refrigerator, and a stove, and you had to survive by hunting and gathering what food you could find. I suspect that you would be quite dissatisfied with your circumstances. That is, your level of material deprivation would qualify as a major strain. Further, the frustration resulting from this strain might well drive you to crime. However, the Kung Bushmen of the Kalahari desert live in precisely these conditions—yet most accounts describe them as a peaceful, gentle people (Fabbro, 1978). There are several reasons for their peaceful disposition, perhaps the most important of which is that they do not view their "deprivation" in the same way that you might. In particular, it is not a major strain conducive to crime for them. (The Kung Bushmen are also said to be quite unlikely to respond to strains with violence. Among other things, they were raised to avoid violence whenever possible and to employ certain nonviolent mechanisms for resolving disputes [Fabbro, 1978; Ury, 1995].)

If GST is to adequately explain societal differences in crime rates, then, it must take account of the fact certain events and conditions may function as strains conducive to crime in some societies, but not in others. This point becomes all the more important when we are examining a broad range of societies, including undeveloped ones.

Factors Affecting Whether Events and Conditions Function as Strains Conducive to Crime

What determines whether certain events and conditions function as strains conducive to crime in a given society? That is, what determines whether these events and conditions (a) are seen as severe or high in magnitude, (b) are seen as unjust, (c) are associated with low social control, and (d) create some pressure or incentive for criminal coping? It is not possible to provide a complete answer in this short book, but I do want to describe certain of the factors that may be relevant.

The Event or Condition Is an 'Extreme Stressor.' One such factor is whether the event or condition is an "extreme stressor" or "traumatic event." Extreme stressors and traumatic events are so severe that "all usual activities are disrupted and all of the individual's goals are in jeopardy" (Dohrenwend, 2000:8; see Chapter 3). Examples include serious physical assaults and sexual assaults. Extreme stressors are likely to be viewed as severe strains by people in all or most societies given their far-ranging effects. They are also likely to be seen as unjust *if they are believed to be the result of voluntarily and deliberate acts by others* (see Agnew, 2001). There are no or very few justifications for the deliberate infliction of such stressors. Further, the experience of such stressors dramatically reduces individuals' levels of social control, since these stressors threaten virtually all areas of life. Individuals experiencing such stressors, then, have little to lose by engaging in crime. Finally, these stressors frequently create some pressure or incentive for criminal coping. In particular, they often provide models for crime and foster beliefs favorable to crime.

There Is Much Inequality in the Experience of the Event/Condition. But what about those events and conditions that are not extreme stressors? What factors determine whether they will function as strains conducive to crime? One such factor involves the social comparison process. As several strain theorists have argued (e.g., Agnew, 1992; Cohen, 1955; Passas, 1997), people frequently evaluate their own situation by comparing themselves to others. For example, you determine whether you are "poor" partly by comparing your economic situation to that of the people around you. If other people have more money than you, you are likely to conclude that you are poor. If they have the same amount or less money than you, you are likely to conclude that you are *not* poor. Likewise, the social comparison process plays a role in determining whether you believe you are being treated in a just or fair manner. Suppose, for example, you are trying to decide whether your salary is fair. You compare your salary to that of similar others; for example, others with the same experience and skills who work in similar jobs. If you are earning less than these others, you are likely to conclude that you are being treated unfairly by your employer (see Agnew, 1992, 2001).

The research on those factors influencing societal differences in crime illustrates the importance of the social comparison process. This research finds that poverty or economic deprivation, in and of itself, is not that strongly related to crime rates (e.g., Messner, 2003; Neapolitan, 1997). What is strongly related to crime is the level of economic inequality in a society, with high levels of inequality contributing to high crime rates. Related to this, crime rates appear to be increasing most rapidly in developing countries; that is, countries that were once very poor but are starting to make some economic progress (Deng and Cordilia, 1999; LaFree and Drass, 2002). These findings are easily explained in terms of the social comparison process.

When income inequality is high, poor people are exposed to wealthier people. As a consequence, poor people are made aware of the material benefits they lack, making their poverty seem all the more severe. Also, their poverty may seem unjust, because they see that a better life is possible in their society. In this area, data suggest that crime rates are especially high in societies where economic inequality is the result of discrimination against racial, ethnic, or religious groups (Messner, 1989; Messner and Rosenfeld, 1997; Neapolitan, 1997). Further, high levels of economic inequality may reduce social control, since they may alienate poor people from others in the society. The same logic can be used to explain the rapid rise in crime in many developing countries. As countries start to develop, some people achieve substantial wealth while many others remain poor.

These points were vividly illustrated in a series of recent newspaper articles about China. One article described the construction of a 50 million dollar French chateau in the countryside outside Beijing (Kahn, 2004a). The chateau is surrounded by a manicured sculpture garden and a broad moat, and is protected by uniformed guards. Eight hundred "now landless peasants . . . used to grow wheat on its expansive lawns." One of these peasants commented "it was once our land and now we have to apply to work there. . . . To look at the place brings tears to my eyes." According to this article, the rapid economic growth in China has produced "tens of thousands of multimillionaires," but large numbers of people remain quite poor. As a consequence, "a wide income gap, like that in Britain and the US at the end of the 19th century," has emerged. A follow-up article describes how this growing gap between the "haves" and the "have nots" is contributing to increased crime (Kahn, 2004b; also see Bao and Haas, 2005).

So certain events and conditions, like economic deprivation, are more likely to function as strains conducive to crime when there is great inequality in the experience of these events/conditions. This inequality frequently leads deprived individuals to compare their situation to that of more advantaged individuals, thereby fostering the belief that their deprivation is both severe and unjust and reducing their level of social control. Deprived individuals, then, may strike out at others in their frustration and seek to obtain the privileges that are denied them through illegal means.

I should note, however, that the social comparison process is somewhat more complicated than just described (see Agnew, 1999, 2001; Passas, 1997). Deprived individuals do not always compare themselves to advantaged individuals and, even if they do, they do not always conclude that their deprivation is unjust. This is illustrated by data suggesting that inequality is associated with higher homicide rates in developed and developing societies, but is not in undeveloped societies (Rosenfeld and Messner, 1991). One explanation for this is that inequality, especially inequality based on ascribed characteristics like race, is more likely to be viewed as unjust in developed and developing societies. In particular, it is said that "one of the most striking—indeed defining—characteristics of modern industrial societies is the widespread belief that social rewards should be allocated according to individual talents" (Rosenfeld and Messner, 1991:65). But this belief is not shared in many undeveloped societies, so inequality in such societies may be less likely to be viewed as unjust. This point highlights a third factor that influences whether an event or condition comes to function as a strain conducive to crime in a given society.

The Cultural Values or Beliefs of the Society Have a Large Impact on Whether Events and Conditions Function as Strains Conducive to Crime. In particular, the cultural values and beliefs of a society may define particular events and conditions in ways that increase the likelihood they will be seen as severe and unjust, will be associated with low social control, and will prompt a criminal response (see Linsky et al., 1995; Pearlin, 1989). So in certain societies, economic inequalities based on race or other ascribed characteristics may be defined as unjust, while in other societies they may not. To give another illustration of the importance of cultural values and beliefs, consider a recent study that used GST to explain the increased rates of juvenile delinquency in China in recent decades.

According to Bao and Haas (2005), these increased rates are partly due to the fact that people in China, especially parents in urban areas, have come to place an extremely high value on academic success. This high value is partly rooted in the traditional emphasis placed on education by the Chinese. It is also rooted in certain of the social changes that China has experienced in recent years. In the words of Bao and Haas (2005, 10–11):

> In the new market-oriented economy, education and skills are even more crucial to obtaining well-paid and secure jobs, while the inadequately educated and unskilled have a greater chance of becoming poor. Almost all high school graduates take the tough Entrance Examination to get into college . . . [but] less than 5% of all students reach universities or colleges. Parents start preparing their children for this intense competition at a young age and play a prominent role in ensuring their children's school success. To help with schoolwork, parents are likely to tutor their children, check homework, assign additional work, and serve as strict time-keepers. In fact, Chinese parents tend to make such assistance the focus of parenting, and parents' approval is often the primary motivation for students to do well in school. Thus, children's academic achievement is seen as a reflection of successful parenting and childrearing. Children's success in school brings honor to the family, while failure brings embarrassment to the parents. The emphasis on academic success has become heavier in recent years as a result of the one-child policy [enforced in urban areas in the 1980s], which makes the only child, whether male or female, the unique focus of parental ambitions and desires. Because the family is the main "welfare agency" and the single child will be the only caretaker for the parents in their old age, a youth's academic performance becomes a major family concern.

So there has been an increased emphasis on academic success in China in recent decades. As a consequence, academic failure has come to be viewed as a severe strain and to have far-ranging consequences. The juveniles who experience academic failure are quite upset. Their parents, teachers, and peers are greatly disappointed in them, and sometimes come to treat them in a harsh, even abusive manner. And they face bleak job prospects. As a result of such reactions, the failed juveniles often feel they have been unjustly treated by others. Also, the failed juveniles experience a dramatic reduction in social control, since relations with parents and teachers are disrupted and their "stake in conformity" is reduced. Further, the abusive behavior of others toward the failed juveniles provides both a model and justification for crime.

Morash and Moon (2005a) describe a similar situation in Korea:

> In South Korea, the continuum of the most to the least noxious stimuli may not be similar to the continuum in the US, because in Korea, adolescents spend most of the day with tutors and teachers, and achievement in academics is singularly valued. . . . There is a singular emphasis on passing examinations in order to be accepted at a small number of top universities. . . . [Also] traditional Confucian values, which emphasize the importance of acquiring high levels of education and academic achievement, continue to have tremendous influence in Korean society. . . . High school students, especially juniors and seniors, spend most of their time studying in school (usually more than fourteen hours a day), and they give up their social lives to devote every minute to gaining a good college entrance examination score. . . . Both teachers and parents make every imaginable effort to prepare students for the college entrance examinations. . . . Frequently, emotional or physical violence is imposed by teachers or parents on students whose academic performance falls short.

To give yet another example of the importance of values, Maxwell (2001) found that parental disciplinary practices such as spanking, slapping, hitting, and beating children with a belt did not increase crime among Filipino youth. She speculates that the "cultural acceptance of spanking and other physical forms of punishment in the Philippines" may have accounted for this (Maxwell, 2001:287).

So the cultural values and beliefs of a society, along with the underlying structural arrangements that support such values and beliefs, can also help us understand why certain events and conditions function as strains conducive to crime in some societies but not others.

Factors That Influence the Effect of Strains on Crime

The residents of various societies not only differ in the likelihood they will experience strains conducive to crime, but also in the likelihood that they will cope with strains through crime. There has not been much research in this area, except for that examining whether levels of social support across societies influence the effect of economic strains on crime. Nevertheless, data suggest that the residents of various societies differ in terms of such factors as their coping skills and resources, social control, association with criminal others, beliefs regarding crime, and opportunities for crime (Gartner, 1990; LaFree, 1999; Neapolitan, 1997; Pampel and Gartner, 1995; van Wilsem et al., 2003). As suggested in previous chapters, there is reason to believe that such differences may affect the reaction to strain.

Summary

GST is quite compatible with the cross-national data on crime, with this data indicating that economic strain is a major cause of societal differences in crime rates. This is particularly true when such strain results from racial, ethic, or religious discrimination. Also, such strain has an especially large effect on crime when societies provide their residents with little social support, such as welfare assistance and unemployment compensation. Further, more limited data suggest that other strains, like war and oppression, may increase the likelihood of crime. It was noted, however, that there is some variation across societies in those events and conditions that function as strains conducive to crime, particularly when undeveloped societies are considered. And there was some discussion of those factors that influence whether events and conditions function as strains conducive to crime, although more work is needed in this area.

While GST helps explain why some societies have higher crime rates than others, GST does *not* explain *why* some societies are more likely than others to experience strains conducive to crime or to score high on those factors that increase the likelihood of criminal coping. For example, GST does not explain why some societies have higher levels of economic inequality than others. Many macro-level theories of crime, however, do address these issues, including conflict theories, institutional anomie theory, feminist theories, cultural deviance theories, modernization theories, and dependency theories (see Cullen and Agnew, 2003; LaFree and Drass, 2002; Messner, 2003; Messner and Rosenfeld, 2001; Neapolitan, 1997). Future research should attempt to integrate GST with these theories.

Review and Discussion Questions

1. What are the characteristics of communities with high rates of crime?

2. How do social disorganization and social learning theorists explain why deprived communities have higher crime rates?

3. How does general strain theory explain why deprived communities have higher crime rates? Related to this, why do high levels of economic inequality increase crime? Why are the residents of deprived communities more likely to interact with strained, angry individuals? And why do high rates of criminal victimization increase the likelihood of further crime in the community?

4. Why are the residents of deprived communities more likely to cope with strains in a criminal manner?

5. What factors influence societal levels of crime?

6. What factors influence whether particular events and conditions are seen as strains in a given society? Related to this, why is economic inequality—but not economic deprivation—related to societal crime rates?

7. What factors influence the likelihood that individuals will cope with strains in a criminal manner? ✦

Chapter 8

What Recommendations Does General Strain Theory Make for Reducing Crime?

Current efforts to control crime focus on "getting tough" with offenders; that is, increasing the likelihood that offenders will be punished and increasing the severity of their punishment. These get-tough efforts are reflected in a range of recent laws that increase the penalties for certain crimes, including the "three strikes and you're out" laws, which typically impose long prison sentences on individuals upon their third conviction for a serious offense. They are also reflected in efforts to limit the discretion of judges, making it more difficult for them to impose "lenient" punishments. And at the juvenile level, they are reflected in efforts to make it easier to try juveniles who commit certain serious offenses in adult court, where they are generally subject to more severe punishments. As a result of such efforts, the rate of imprisonment in the United States has increased five-fold since the early 1970s, with the United States now having the highest rate of imprisonment in the world.

Evidence on the effectiveness of these get-tough approaches is mixed. Punishing individuals for their offenses or punishing them more severely does not seem to deter them from further crime. In fact, it may sometimes increase the likelihood of further crime. As argued below, one reason for this is that punishments often function as strains conducive to crime. That is, punishments are often experienced as severe and unjust, lead to reductions in social control, and foster the social learning of crime. Punishing some offenders for their crimes may have a *modest* deterrent effect on *other* individuals who are not punished. And locking offenders up for long periods does prevent some crime, because offenders cannot commit crimes on the street when they are imprisoned. However, this "incapacitation effect" is not as large as many of its proponents have argued, and it comes at a high financial and social cost (see Agnew, 2005a; Cullen, 1995).

GST suggests a rather different approach to controlling crime. We should reduce crime by reducing (a) individuals' exposure to strains conducive to crime, and (b) the likelihood that individuals will cope with strains through crime. This is not to say that we should stop punishing offenders. Such punishment is important because, among other things, it reduces the likelihood of criminal coping. But we can alter the way in which we punish so that our punishments are less likely to function as strains conducive to crime. For example, we can take steps to increase the likelihood that punishments will be seen as just. GST, however, places most emphasis on the use of prevention and rehabilitation programs that reduce exposure to strains and criminal coping. Prevention programs focus on individuals who have not yet engaged in crime, while rehabilitation programs focus on offenders. (The same programs, however, are often used for both prevention and rehabilitation purposes.)

A more detailed discussion of GST's recommendations for controlling crime follows. It is not possible in this short book to describe all of the programs which might reduce exposure to the 13 strains conducive to crime listed in Chapter 3, nor is it possible to describe all of the programs which address those factors which influence the likelihood of criminal coping (see Chapter 4). I do, however, provide examples of programs that have shown some success in reducing the exposure to strains and criminal coping. None of these programs is explicitly based on GST, but all address the causes of crime identified in GST (and they frequently address the causes of crime identified by other theories as well). My description of these programs is derived from several sources, most notably Agnew (1995c, 2005a), Blueprints for Violence Prevention (http://www/colorado.edu/cspv/blueprints/), the Coordinating Council on Juvenile Justice and Delinquency Prevention (1996), Cullen and Gendreau (2000), Currie (1998), Howell (2003), McCord et al. (2001), Sampson (2002), Sherman et al. (2002), Thornton et al. (2002), and the U.S. Department of Health and Human Services (2001).

Reducing Exposure to Strains Conducive to Crime

There are five strategies for reducing the exposure of individuals to strains conducive to crime. The first four strategies focus on "objective strains," that is, those events and conditions which are disliked by most people in a given group. I argue that we should attempt to eliminate such strains, alter the characteristics of such strains so they are less conducive to crime, remove individuals from such strains, and increase the ability of individuals to avoid such strains. The fifth strategy dos not attempt to reduce the individual's exposure to objective strains, rather it attempts to alter the perceptions and goals of individuals so that strainful events and conditions are *subjectively evaluated* as less severe and more just.

Attempt to Eliminate Those Strains Conducive to Crime

The ideal strategy for reducing crime is to eliminate those strains conducive to crime. For example, we might convince or force parents to stop punishing their children in a harsh manner, teachers to stop belittling their students, peers to stop abusing one another, and people to stop discriminating against one another. We might also transform deprived communities so that they no longer increase exposure to strains conducive to crime. And we might create a sufficient number of decent jobs so that work in the secondary labor market and chronic unemployment disappear. These may sound like utopian proposals, but a number of programs have shown some success in reducing certain of the strains conducive to crime. Two such programs are briefly described below: parent-training programs that attempt to reduce a range of family-related strains and anti-bullying programs that attempt to reduce peer abuse. Programs focusing on other strains conducive to crime, like negative secondary-school experiences, marital problems, work in the secondary labor market, and residence in deprived communities, are described in the references cited above.

Parent-Training Programs. The family is a major source of strains conducive to crime, with parental rejection; erratic, excessive, and/or harsh discipline; and child abuse and neglect contributing to crime. A number of parent-training programs attempt to reduce such strains (as well as increase control and foster the social learning of conformity). Some of these programs are offered to families at risk for poor parenting, such as teenage parents or families where there is evidence of family violence. Other programs target the families of delinquents or juveniles at risk for delinquency. The best programs are intensive; that is, they last for several months or longer and involve frequent contact between the program staff and family members. They also employ a variety of instructional methods. For example, family members may be given materials to read, given instruction by the staff, exposed to role-playing situations where good parenting techniques are demonstrated, asked to participate in role-playing situations, and given assignments where they apply what they have learned in the "real world." They receive frequent feedback and reinforcement when appropriate. Such programs have shown some success at reducing delinquency, and *one* of the reasons for this may be that they reduce several strains conducive to delinquency.

Such programs typically teach parents how to effectively discipline their children. In particular, parents are taught how to set reasonable rules for their children, monitor their children's behavior, consistently sanction their children in an appropriate manner, and reinforce prosocial behavior. Parents are encouraged to make more use of positive reinforcers, such as praise, rewards, privileges, and attention, and to make less use of punishers, such as criticism, yelling, and hitting. The preferred strategies of punishment involve time outs (for children), loss of privileges, the imposition of chores, clear expressions of disapproval, and reasoning. Older juveniles may be given some say in developing the rules that govern their behavior and determining the sanctions for rule violations. In particular, parents and juveniles may negotiate a behavioral contract, specifying the rules that juveniles must follow and the consequences for following and breaking rules.

Parent-training programs also teach family members how to better resolve conflicts that arise, with part of this instruction focusing on the development of better communication skills. They encourage family members to spend more time together in pleasurable activities, and they may attempt to alter the expectations that parents have for their children. The unrealistic expectations of parents sometimes contribute to abuse and other problems. Further, certain of these programs may attempt to reduce the strains that parents are experiencing, because these strains are a major cause of poor parenting. For example, they may assist parents with financial, housing, health, family violence, and other problems.

Parent-training programs have the effect of strengthening the bond between parents and children, thereby reducing the likelihood of parental rejection. They do this by improving disciplinary practices, reducing family conflict, and encouraging family members to engage in pleasurable activities together. Further, such programs reduce the frequency of both abuse and harsh, erratic, and excessive discipline. In addition, such programs may directly and indirectly reduce other strains conducive to crime. Juveniles in such programs may be better able to achieve their desire for autonomy, because parental discipline is more reasonable and juveniles are frequently given some say over the rules they must follow and the sanctions they receive. And juveniles who are strongly bonded to and well-supervised by parents are less likely to associate with delinquent peers, which reduces the likelihood of peer abuse.

Anti-Bullying Programs. Peer abuse is a major type of strain for juveniles and many adults. One study asked a sample of college students about the sources of their happiness and unhappiness during childhood and adolescence (Ambert, 1994). Peer abuse emerged as the main source of unhappiness, far surpassing parents in importance. Much peer abuse occurs in school, and this abuse frequently takes the form of "bullying." According to Olweus (1991:413), "a person is being bullied when he or she is exposed, repeatedly and over time, to negative actions on the part of one or more other persons." Negative actions are defined as those intentional actions that inflict or attempt to inflict injury or discomfort on another. Such actions include both physical and verbal abuse (e.g., hitting, pushing, name calling, threatening, malicious teasing, spreading nasty rumors). Consider the following newspaper account:

> For two years, Johnny, a quiet 13-year-old, was a human plaything for some of his classmates. The teenagers badgered Johnny for money, forced him to swallow weeds and drink milk mixed with detergent, beat him up in the rest room, tied a string around his neck, and led him around like a "pet." When Johnny's torturers were asked about the bullying, they said they pursued their victim because "it was fun." (Blueprints for Violence Prevention, 2004a:2)

Data suggest that about 15 to 20 percent of students are subject to bullying at school each year. Teachers, however, often do little to stop bullying and many parents are unaware of the problem. The

Bullying Prevention Program, however, has shown some success at reducing this type of strain (Blueprints for Violence Prevention, 2004a).

The Bullying Prevention Program begins with a school survey designed to estimate the extent and nature of bullying. Parents, teachers, and students are then made aware of the bullying problem in their school. A Bullying Prevention Coordinating Committee is formed to plan a response. The response typically includes the following: teachers hold meetings with their students to discuss bullying and its harmful consequences. The teachers then establish clear rules against bullying; more closely monitor students so as to better detect bullying; use nonhostile, nonphysical sanctions against bullies; and support and protect victims. School officials make sure that the "hot spots" where bullying is most likely to occur, such as playgrounds, cafeterias, and rest rooms, are better monitored. The students themselves may engage in activities—like role playing and discussions—that focus on the harm caused by bullying and strategies to combat it. And efforts are made to enlist the support of parents and actively involve them in efforts to reduce bullying.

Alter Strains So as to Make Them Less Conducive to Crime

Sometimes it is not possible to eliminate or substantially reduce those strains conducive to crime. It may, however, be possible to alter the nature of these strains so that they are less conducive to crime; that is, alter the strains so they are less likely to be seen as severe, to be seen as unjust, to result in reduced social control, and to foster the social learning of crime. For example, teachers will probably continue to give out low grades, the justice system will probably continue to sanction individuals in disliked ways, and many individuals will probably continue to work in the secondary labor market. But we can alter such strains so as to make them less conducive to crime. For example, we can raise the minimum wage and provide benefits like health insurance to all workers. Such steps would make work in the secondary labor market seem less severe and unjust, and would increase the social control of workers by strengthening their investment in their jobs. Two additional examples of how we might alter strains so as to make them less conducive to crime are provided below.

School Programs. Several school strains are conducive to crime, including low grades, negative relations with teachers, and the experience of school as boring and a waste of time. We can eliminate these strains for some students, but it is unlikely that we can eliminate them for all students without radically restructuring our educational system. Some students, in particular, will continue to receive low grades, have conflicts with teachers, and find school boring. Nevertheless, we can alter these strains in ways that make them less conducive to crime. The following steps have been employed in various school-based programs and all show some promise in reducing delinquency.

Many school-based programs change the way that teachers instruct students and manage their classrooms. One program that has had some success in reducing delinquency employs the strategies of interactive teaching, proactive learning, and cooperative learning groups. Interactive teaching provides students with specific objectives they must master, employs objective grading, and bases grades on mastery of material and improvement over past performance—not on comparisons with other students. Teachers using proactive classroom management are taught to clearly state rules for classroom behavior, recognize and reward attempts to cooperate, make frequent use of encouragement and praise, and attempt to minimize the impact of disruptions. Cooperative learning groups involve small, heterogenous groups of students who help one another master classroom materials and who receive recognition as a team for their accomplishments (see Catalano et al., 1998).

Still other programs try to change the nature of the school environment. Teams including students, teachers, administrators, and parents may be formed to evaluate a school and plan and implement school-wide improvements. Among other things, school-pride campaigns may be launched, involving pep rallies and school clean-up programs. Students may be enlisted to help develop school disciplinary rules, publicize these rules, and help ensure that they are enforced in a fair manner. And efforts may be made to increase the involvement and success experiences of high-risk students, usually through an expansion of extracurricular activities and through special academic and counseling programs such as career exploration programs and job-seeking skills programs.

These efforts may eliminate school strain for some students, helping them achieve good grades, get along better with teachers, and enjoy school. But I believe these efforts are also of value to other students. Those students who continue to receive low grades are likely to view these grades as less severe and more fair, since alternative opportunities for success have been provided, instruction is better, and grading is done in a more objective manner. Further, such students are less likely to experience a reduction in control or to associate with delinquent peers, because they are better integrated into the school through cooperative learning groups, extracurricular activities, and job-related programs. Similar arguments can be made for those students who get into conflicts with teachers or find school boring.

The Restorative Justice Approach. Arrest and sanction by the criminal justice system function as a strain conducive to crime for many individuals. Such individuals are treated rudely by criminal justice officials, given little opportunity to present their side of the case, and subject to severe sanctions like imprisonment (see Acoca, 1998; Colvin, 2000). Further, they find that others continue to view and treat them as dangerous criminals upon their release. Conventional others do not want to associate with them and employers will not hire them, which increases their strain and reduces their level of social control. They end up associating with other criminals as a result, which further increases their strain and fosters the social learning of crime. It is no surprise, then, that many of these individuals increase their levels of offending. These arguments, of course, are at the heart of labeling theories of crime (see Cullen and Agnew, 2003).

It is quite unlikely that we will stop sanctioning offenders or that offenders will ever be fully satisfied with the sanctions they receive. But we can alter the arrest and sanctioning process so that it is less conducive to crime. One way to do this is have the police treat suspected offenders in a more respectful manner, avoiding insults and excessive aggressiveness and taking the time to listen to the offenders' side of the story. Limited data suggest that offenders are less likely to reoffend when treated in this way by police. And Sherman (2002) provides several suggestions for ways in which we might foster respectful behavior by the police, including better methods of monitoring police behavior.

We can also alter the court process and the sanctions we impose, with the restorative justice approach providing a useful model (Bazemore, 2000; Braithwaite, 2002). Under this approach, there is a "conference" or meeting involving offenders, victims, family members of the offenders and victims, and selected community residents. Offenders learn firsthand of the harm that they have caused, and have the opportunity to explain why they committed the offenses. For example, the offenders and family members might describe problems in the offenders' lives. Then everyone, including the offenders, helps develop a plan to repair the harm that was done, often through restitution to the victims and community service. The offenders are forgiven when the harm is repaired, and community members take steps to reintegrate offenders into the community, often through mentoring offenders, involving them in volunteer activities, and helping them obtain work.

The restorative justice approach frequently results in the imposition of less severe sanctions, with an effort being made to avoid the use of imprisonment. The sanctions that are administered are more likely to be seen as just, because offenders better appreciate the harm they have caused, have an opportunity to present their side of the story, and have some say in determining the sanctions they receive. And offenders are less likely to experience a reduction in social control or associate with criminal others, because they are forgiven for their crimes and efforts are made to reintegrate them into conventional society. Data suggest that the restorative justice approach holds some promise for reducing at least certain types of crime (Braithwaite, 2002; Hayes and Daly, 2003).

Remove Individuals From Strains Conducive to Crime

Sometimes it is not possible to eliminate or alter strains conducive to crime. For example, certain parents may refuse to participate in parent-training programs or they may continue to treat their children in a harsh manner, despite their participation in such programs. To give another example, it is quite difficult to transform deprived communities in ways that substantially reduce the experience of strains conducive to crime, although efforts continue (Sampson, 2002). In such cases, it may be necessary to remove individuals from the strainful environment. Such action is often taken as a last resort. It may mean removing children from their parents. Also, removing selected individuals from their schools or communities may make conditions worse for those who are left behind. Further, there is the chance that the new environment may be just as aversive as the old, as witnessed in several well-publicized cases where children placed in foster care were abused by their caretakers. Nevertheless, carefully designed programs may allow for the removal of individuals from highly strainful environments and their placement in less strainful environments. Two examples follow.

Group Homes. Group homes are small residential facilities generally housing four to 12 juveniles. They are frequently used for delinquent and other children who have been mistreated or neglected in their regular homes. The juveniles in group homes often attend local schools and have some free time in the community. Group homes employing the "Teaching-Family" approach are directed by married couples called "teaching parents," who do much to reduce those family-related strains conducive to crime (Braukmann and Wolf, 1987). In particular, the teaching parents attempt to create a pleasant, nonaversive environment for the juveniles. They spend enjoyable time with the juveniles, regularly express interest in them, and attempt to help them deal with their problems. The juveniles also have some voice in how the home is run. There is group decision making on a wide range of issues, and democratically elected peer managers play a major role in the discipline process. Further, there is an attempt to explain the rationale behind all rules. Such homes provide a much less strainful environment than the homes in which many juveniles reside, and some evidence suggests that the Teaching-Family approach is effective in controlling disruptive behavior. In addition to group homes, juveniles may be placed in foster care. Some evidence suggests that certain foster-care programs may also be effective in reducing delinquency (see Blueprints for Violence Prevention, 2004b).

The Moving to Opportunity Program. This program focused on families with children who lived in very poor communities. Certain of these families were provided with rent subsidies, and in some cases it was stipulated that the families could only use the subsidies in areas with low rates of poverty. A good number of these families moved to less deprived communities. The children in these families had fewer subsequent behavioral problems than the children in comparable families who were not given rent subsidies (McCord et al., 2001). So while it may not be easy to transform deprived communities, it is possible to help at least some individuals escape from these communities.

Equip Individuals With the Traits and Skills to Avoid Strains Conducive to Crime

Individuals often play some role in bringing about the strains they experience. In particular, individuals with certain characteristics are more likely to (a) provoke others into treating them in a negative manner; (b) select themselves into strainful environments, like delinquent peer groups and bad jobs; and (c) fail to achieve their goals. For example, irritable individuals may provoke negative reactions from others, including family members, peers, and teachers. And individuals with low motivation and poor job skills may select themselves into jobs in the secondary labor market. While there may be some value in attempting to eliminate, alter, or remove such individuals from the strains they experience, it is also important to equip such individuals with the traits and skills necessary to avoid strains. Otherwise, such individuals are likely to encounter new strains in the future. Several programs have achieved some success in this area, with three examples below.

Social Skills Training. Social skills programs teach juveniles how to better achieve certain of their goals and how to interact with others in ways that do not provoke negative reactions. Certain of the skills taught are very specific, such as increasing the frequency of eye contact and reducing fidgeting movements; others are quite complex, such as improving negotiation skills with adults and resisting peer pressure. As an illustration, the social skills training component of Aggression Replacement Training focuses on 50 skills (see Goldstein et al., 1989). These skills are divided into six broad groups: (a) beginning social skills (e.g., listening, starting a conversation), (b) advanced social skills (e.g., asking for help, apologizing), (c) skills for dealing with feelings (e.g., dealing with someone else's anger), (d) skill alternatives to aggression (asking permission, responding to testing), (e) skills for dealing with stress (making a complaint, responding to failure), and (f) planning skills (e.g., deciding on something to do). Juveniles are not taught all 50 skills, only those skills in which they are deficient. Five or six juveniles with similar skill deficiencies are placed in the same training group. Each week the group and its trainers decide on what skill will be taught, with each skill being divided into several steps. The philosophy behind social skills training is perhaps best expressed by Michaelson (1987:294), who says juveniles "are encouraged to express themselves, but in ways that do not violate other peoples' rights or feelings and to engage in self-control procedures as a means of deflecting and redirecting anger, hostility, and aggressive behavior."

Preschool Enrichment. Certain preschool enrichment programs have shown success in equipping juveniles with the skills and attitudes necessary to do well in school. Most such programs focus on preschool children in disadvantaged areas, and they attempt to promote the social and intellectual development of these children as well as increase their parents' involvement in the educational process. The best preschool programs being early in life, last two years or more, have low student-to-teacher ratios, and employ carefully designed curricula. In addition, teachers meet regularly with the parents to discuss ways that the parents can foster their children's social and intellectual development. Many Head Start programs throughout the country meet these criteria.

Vocational Training. Vocational training programs teach individuals job skills and help them find employment. Many such programs are not effective in reducing crime, but certain well-designed programs have shown some success. Such programs are intensive and long-term, they help individuals deal with the other problems they may be facing, and they provide incentives for participation. The federal government's Job Corps program is an example.

Alter the Perceptions/Goals of Individuals to Reduce Subjective Strains

The above strategies focus on reducing individuals' exposure to objective strains by eliminating such strains, altering them, removing individuals from them, or equipping individuals with the traits and skills to avoid them. A final strategy for reducing exposure to strains involves altering individuals' perceptions or goals in ways that reduce *subjective* strains. For example, some juveniles may believe that the rules and sanctions imposed by their parents are severe and unjust. Rather than changing such rules and sanctions, one might attempt to convince these juveniles that the rules and sanctions are in fact comparable to those imposed by other parents, and that there is a good rationale behind them. Or certain males may be upset because they believe that they are not being treated as "real men;" for example, they may believe that their spouses are not sufficiently subservient to them. Rather than changing the behavior of their spouses, we might attempt to alter their views about what it means to be a "real man."

This strategy, however, must be used with great caution. Many individuals are experiencing strains that most people would define as severe and unjust (objective strains). We do not necessarily want to convince these people to define such strains as minor. Some individuals, however, are not experiencing objective strains, but are nevertheless high in subjective strain. This may occur because such individuals misperceive their situation. For example, they may mistakenly believe they are being punished more severely than similar others or punished for no good reason. This may also occur because such individuals are pursuing unreasonable goals. For example, they may have grandiose dreams of making much money in a short period of time or they may believe that all women should treat them as superior. Efforts to alter perceptions and goals are more justified in such circumstances.

The BrainPower Program. Data indicate that highly aggressive individuals are more likely to incorrectly attribute hostile intentions to the acts of others (de Castro et al., 2002). For example, if they are bumped while walking down the hall at school or someone spills something on them on in the cafeteria, they are more likely to assume that the bump or spill was deliberate. This attributional bias contributes to their aggression because, as indicated in Chapter 3, strains are more likely to cause crime when they are seen as unjust (or as *deliberate* violations of justice rules). The tendency of aggressive individuals to attribute hostile intentions to others is at least partly due to the fact that they are more likely to quickly evaluate situations and ignore relevant social cues.

The BrainPower Program teaches juveniles to better evaluate situations and, in doing so, it reduces their tendency to attribute hostile intentions to the acts of others. So rather than viewing the bump as a deliberate effort to harm, they learn to view it as accidental. Participants in the program receive 12 lessons designed to teach them how to (a) better "search for, interpret, and properly categorize the verbal, physical, and behavioral cues exhibited by others in social situations;" (b) increase their tendency to first attribute ambiguous negative events to accidental causes; and (c) respond to ambiguous events in a nonaggressive manner (Hudley et al., 1998:274, 275). Limited data suggest that the program reduces the tendency of aggressive juveniles to make hostile attributions and act aggressively (Hudley et al., 1998; Thornton et al., 2002). Several other programs contain components that attempt to reduce hostile attributions, and they too have shown signs of success (Conduct Problems Prevention Research Group, 2002).

Altering Goals. I am not aware of any crime-control programs that attempt to alter the goals that individuals pursue in an effort to reduce strains, but such programs are certainly possible. Many males, for example, pursue masculinity goals that are often difficult for them to achieve through legal channels. Among other things, such males believe that, as men, they must refrain from showing emotion, treat women as subordinate, have very active sex lives, be physically strong, and excel in all competitive endeavors. Data suggest that the failure to accomplish these objectives (or "accomplish masculinity" in the words of Messerschmidt [1993]) is major strain for many men, one that contributes to crime (e.g., Jakupcak, 2003; Messerschmidt, 1993; Mullins et al., 2004). And there has been some discussion of how to alter masculinity goals in ways that reduce the likelihood of crime. For example, proposals have been made to alter school curriculums so that they help challenge traditional conceptions of what it means to be a man (e.g., Kenway and Fitzclarence, 1997).

Summary

Several strategies were suggested for reducing the exposure of individuals to strains conducive to crime. Examples of programs that employ these strategies were presented, and such programs show some promise in reducing both exposure to strains and crime. It is important to note, however, that these programs usually attempt to address other causes of crime besides strains. Parent-training programs, for example, increase the level of social control to which juveniles are subject and reduce the social learning for crime. It is not entirely clear, then, to what extent these programs reduce crime because they reduce exposure to strains or because they affect other causes of crime. I suspect these programs are successful because they affect several of the causes of crime, including those identified in GST. And research, in fact, suggests that the best way to reduce crime is to address all or most of the major causes of crime.

Reducing the Likelihood That Individuals Will Cope With Strains Through Crime

As suggested above, there is much we can do to reduce individuals' exposure to strains conducive to crime. But it is quite unlikely that we can eliminate all such exposure. For example, while there are steps we can take to reduce peer abuse, peer abuse will likely continue at some level. Given this fact, GST also recommends that we take steps to reduce the likelihood that individuals will cope with the strains they experience in a criminal manner. That is, we should develop programs that focus on those factors that influence the likelihood of criminal coping, as listed in Chapter 4. Such programs might improve coping skills and resources, increase social support, increase social control, reduce association with delinquent peers, foster beliefs opposed to crime, and reduce exposure to situations conducive to crime. A number of programs have already shown some success in these areas. The discussion below provides a few brief examples.

Improving Coping Skills and Resources

Several programs attempt to equip individuals with the skills and resources that will allow them to legally cope with the strains they face. These include social-skills programs of the type described above. These programs not only teach individuals to act in ways that do not antagonize or provoke others, but also how to respond to strains in a noncriminal manner. Many programs, for example, contain units on how to respond to teasing, deal with teachers' criticisms, behave during police encounters, and keep out of fights. A central goal of many of these programs is to teach juveniles to be assertive, but *not* aggressive.

Problem-solving skills and anger management programs also attempt to equip individuals with the skills to engage in legal coping. Problem-solving programs teach individuals to pause before they act, carefully evaluate their situation, think about how they might respond, consider the possible consequences of different responses, and enact the chosen response. In other words, individuals are taught to think before they act. Anger management training is sometimes used in conjunction with such programs. Individuals are taught how to better control their anger and respond to problems in more adaptive ways. In particular, individuals are taught to recognize those things that make them angry, to be aware of the early warning signs of anger, and to take steps to control their anger, like deep breathing, muscle relaxation, and imaging peaceful scenes. It should be noted that problem-solving skills and anger management programs target certain of the specific traits that characterize people who are low in constraint and high in negative emotionality—traits like impulsivity and quickness to anger. Such programs have shown some success in reducing offending when properly implemented.

Increasing Social Support

Many individuals lack conventional social supports; that is, conventional others who can help them cope in a legal manner by providing advice, emotional support, and direct assistance. A range of programs attempt to increase social support, including programs that teach family members and teachers to provide more support to juveniles. Many of these programs focus on delinquents or juveniles at high risk for delinquency. One program, for example, focuses on juveniles making the transition from correctional institutions to public schools. And certain of these programs focus on individuals who are experiencing strains or are at high risk for strains, such as unemployed individuals.

Big Brothers/Big Sisters. The Big Brothers/Big Sisters Program is a mentoring program focusing on children from single-parent families (Blueprints for Violence Prevention, 2004c). The adult volunteers for the program are carefully screened and receive training in areas like youth development and relationship-building skills. Special care is taken in matching volunteers with children. Each volunteer or mentor spends an average of three to five hours a week with their child over the course of a year or longer. The mentor tries to form a "caring and supportive" relationship with the child, and the mentor and a case manager develop an individualized "case plan" for the child. The plan identifies goals for the child, like regular school attendance and developing certain skills. The mentor helps the child achieve these goals, with the case manager providing assistance and monitoring the relationship. The Big Brothers/Big Sisters program has shown some success in reducing delinquency, although it should be noted that *less structured* mentoring programs have not been effective in reducing delinquency.

Government Assistance Programs. Adults are also in need of social support, and one major source of such support is government agencies. Such agencies sometimes provide support to those facing strains conducive to crime, particularly economic strains such as unemployment and work in the secondary labor market. In particular, the government may provide welfare assistance, unemployment insurance, and health care. Such support reduces the likelihood that economic strains will lead to crime (DeFronzo, 1997; Hannon and DeFronzo, 1998; Pratt and Godsey, 2003).

Increasing Social Control

A range of programs attempt to increase individuals' levels of social control. Certain of these programs have already been described, such as the parent training, school-based, and vocational programs listed above. In addition to reducing exposure to strains, these programs usually try to increase direct control or the extent to which juveniles are monitored and consistently sanctioned for rule violations. They also try to increase the individuals' bonds to conventional others, such as parents and teachers, and investment in conventional activities, such as school and work. And they sometimes try to foster the belief that crime is wrong (Agnew, 2005a).

Reducing Criminal Beliefs and Association With Delinquent Peers

A number of programs have tried to remove juveniles from delinquent groups or change such groups so that they are less disposed to delinquency. Such efforts, however, have not fared well. Perhaps the most successful programs at reducing peer delinquency are those which attempt to influence individual traits, family factors, and school factors. Individuals are much less likely to get involved with delinquent peers if they are high in constraint and low in negative emotionality, are strongly bonded to and well supervised by parents, and are doing well in school. Several programs have also tried to teach juveniles moral beliefs opposed to crime or particular types of crime, like illegal drug use. Certain of these programs have achieved some success, particularly those programs that employ peer educators, actively involve juveniles in the instructional process, teach skills to resist social pressure for crime, and then get groups of juveniles—like classroom groups—to take a public stand against crime.

Reducing Exposure to Situations Conducive to Crime

Several programs have tried to reduce the likelihood that individuals will be exposed to situations conducive to crime, such as situations where the costs of crime are low and the benefits are high. One example is supervised recreational programs, many of which are run after school, when the likelihood of juvenile violence is highest. Such programs attempt to monitor youth who might otherwise be unsupervised (thus increasing the costs of crime). They may also attempt to establish a positive bond between the adults who run the program and the juveniles in it. Data suggest that certain of these programs are effective in reducing crime, particularly those programs that provide high levels of supervision and make an effort to aggressively recruit and retain juveniles in the community.

Summary

GST, then, recommends that we reduce crime by reducing exposure to strains conducive to crime and the likelihood that individuals will respond to strains with crime. In particular, we can reduce exposure to strains conducive to crime by:

- eliminating strains conducive to crime

- altering strains so as to make them less conducive to crime

- removing individuals from strains conducive to crime

- equipping individuals with the traits and skills that will allow them to avoid such strains

- altering the perceptions and goals of individuals so they are less likely to view *certain* strains as severe and unjust

And we might reduce the likelihood that individuals will respond to strains with crime by:

- improving their coping skills and resources

- increasing their level of conventional social support

- increasing their level of social control

- reducing their association with delinquent peers and beliefs favorable to crime

- reducing their exposure to situations conducive to crime

A number of programs that accomplish these goals were described and certain new programs were suggested. We can employ these programs as part of a *prevention* strategy; that is, we might offer these programs to individuals at risk for crime. Individuals, in particular, might be screened and offered those programs that they need. Individuals experiencing family problems, for example, might be provided with parent training. And in certain cases, it might be useful to offer these programs to broad groups of people, particularly when it can be done at a reasonable cost and there is reason to believe that most such individuals will benefit from the programs. For example, social- and problem-solving–skills training might be offered to all high-school students. Offering programs to broad groups has the advantage of reducing any stigma associated with participation in the program.

Such programs can also be employed as part of a *rehabilitation* strategy, with criminals being offered those programs they need. In addition, criminals on probation or parole might be regularly monitored to determine whether they are experiencing any strains conducive to crime. Steps can then be taken to reduce their exposure to such strains before crime results.

Review and Discussion Questions

1. What are the two major recommendations that general strain theory makes for reducing crime?

2. Use GST to evaluate the wisdom of "get-tough" approaches to controlling crime, which increase the certainty and especially the severity of punishment.

3. How does prevention differ from rehabilitation?

4. Briefly describe the five major ways to reducing individuals' exposure to strains conducive to crime. Discuss how any three of the specific programs described above (e.g., parenting training programs, anti-bully programs) attempt to reduce exposure to strains. Describe the restorative justice approach, and indicate why it is compatible with GST.

5. Briefly describe the major ways of reducing the likelihood that individuals will cope with strains through crime. Discuss how any three of the specific programs described above (e.g., Big Brothers/Big Sisters) attempt to reduce the likelihood of criminal coping. ✦

Chapter 9

An Overview of General Strain Theory

This last chapter is in three parts. I first draw on the previous chapters to describe the central propositions of general strain theory (GST). I then summarize the empirical support for GST, noting areas where further research is needed. Finally, I discuss the possibility of combining GST with other major crime theories so as to construct a general or integrated theory of crime.

The Central Propositions of General Strain Theory

1. Strains refer to events and conditions that are disliked by individuals. There are three major types of strains. Individuals may (a) lose something they value, (b) be treated in an aversive or negative manner by others, and (c) be unable to achieve their goals. It is also useful to distinguish between "objective" and "subjective" strains. Objective strains refer to events and conditions that are disliked by most people or at least most people in a given group. "Subjective" strains refer to events and conditions that are disliked by the individuals experiencing them. Individuals sometimes differ in their subjective evaluation of the same events and conditions, so there is only partial overlap between objective and subjective strains. Subjective strains should have a stronger impact on crime (Chapter 1).

2. Strains increase the likelihood of *particular* crimes primarily through their impact on a range of negative emotional *states*. While anger is a key negative emotion in GST, particularly with respect to violent crime, other negative emotions are also important. Negative emotions create pressure for corrective action, with crime being one possible response. Individuals may engage in crime to reduce or es-

cape from their strains (e.g., steal the money they need, run away from abusive parents), seek revenge against the source of their strains or related targets (e.g., assault the peers who harass them), or alleviate their negative emotions (e.g., take illegal drugs to feel better). Negative emotions may also reduce the ability to engage in legal coping, reduce the perceived costs of crime, and increase the disposition for crime. Different strains may lead to different emotions, and different emotions may be conducive to different types of crime. For example, anger may be most conducive to violent crime, while frustration and envy may be most conducive to property crime. In addition, strains may lead to temporary reductions in social control and temporarily foster the social learning of crime (e.g., the belief that crime is justified). Further, *chronic or repeated strains* may create a predisposition for or general willingness to engage in crime by contributing to negative emotional *traits,* reducing social control, fostering beliefs favorable to crime, increasing association with delinquent peers, and contributing to traits conducive to crime, like low constraint and negative emotionality (Chapter 2).

3. Those strains most likely to cause crime (a) are seen as high in magnitude, (b) are seen as unjust, (c) are associated with low control, and (d) create some pressure or incentive to engage in criminal coping (Chapter 3; Agnew, 2001). In Western industrialized societies, such strains include:

- parental rejection

- supervision/discipline that is erratic, excessive, and/or harsh

- child abuse and neglect

- negative secondary-school experiences (e.g., low grades, negative relations with teachers, the experience of school as boring and a waste of time)

- abusive peer relations (e.g., insults, threats, physical assaults)

- work in the secondary labor market (i.e., "bad jobs")

- chronic unemployment

- marital problems

- the failure to achieve selected goals, including thrills/excitement, high levels of autonomy, masculine status, and the desire for much money in a short period of time

- criminal victimization

- residence in economically deprived communities

- homelessness

- discrimination based on characteristics like race/ethnicity and gender

Both "experienced" strains and *certain types* of vicarious and anticipated strains may result in crime, although experienced strains generally have larger effects on crime (Chapter 1; Agnew, 2002).

4. The likelihood that individuals will react to strains and negative emotions with crime depends on a range of factors that influence the individual's (a) ability to engage in legal coping, (b) costs of crime, and (c) disposition for crime (Chapter 4). Those factors that increase the likelihood of criminal coping include:

- poor conventional coping skills and resources, including poor problem-solving and social skills, personality traits like negative emotionality and low constraint, low socioeconomic status, and low self-efficacy

- criminal skills and resources, such as "criminal self-efficacy," and, for violent crime, large physical size and strength

- low levels of conventional social support

- low levels of social control, including low direct control, weak bonds to conventional others, little investment in conventional institutions, and the failure to condemn crime

- association with criminal others and beliefs favorable to crime

- exposure to situations where the costs of crime are low and the benefits are high

5. While GST focuses on the explanation of individual differences in offending, it can also shed light on patterns of offending over the life course, group differences in crime, and community and societal differences in crime. Such patterns and differences can be partly explained in terms of differences in the exposure to strains

conducive to crime and in the possession of those factors that influence the likelihood of criminal coping (Chapters 5–7). For example, gender differences in crime are partly due to the fact that males are more often exposed to strains conducive to crime and are more likely to cope with strains through crime.

6. Crime can be reduced by reducing individuals' exposure to strains conducive to crime and their likelihood of responding to strains with crime. Strategies for reducing the exposure to strains include (a) eliminating strains conducive to crime, (b) altering strains so as to make them less conducive to crime, (c) removing individuals from strains conducive to crime, (d) equipping individuals with the traits and skills to avoid strains conducive to crime; and (e) altering the perceptions/goals of individuals to reduce subjective strains. Strategies for reducing the likelihood that individuals will respond to strains with crime include (a) improving conventional coping skills and resources, (b) increasing social support, (c) increasing social control, (d) reducing association with delinquent peers and beliefs favorable to crime, and (e) reducing exposure to situations conducive to crime.

The Empirical Support for General Strain Theory and Areas Where Further Research Is Needed

I believe that GST has amassed sufficient empirical support to qualify it as one of the leading explanations of crime, with this support being briefly summarized below. At the same time, there are important gaps in the research on GST and areas where support for the theory is mixed. These gaps and areas of mixed support are also briefly described, along with suggestions for further research on the theory.

The Effect of Strains on Crime

Data suggest that most of those strains said to be conducive to crime are in fact associated with crime, with certain of these strains being among the strongest correlates of crime. In particular, data suggest that parental rejection, harsh/erratic discipline, criminal victimization, and homelessness (at least among youth) have relatively strong associations with crime. Data also suggest that child abuse and neglect, negative school experiences, chronic unemployment, and residence in deprived communities are important causes of crime. Certain of the research on these strains is longitudinal and takes account of a wide range of additional causes of crime, increasing our confidence that these strains actually have a *causal* effect on crime. More longitudinal research that takes account of a broad range of variables is needed, however. Other of the strains conducive to crime have not been well investigated, including peer abuse, work in the secondary labor market, marital problems, the failure to achieve goals such as autonomy and masculine status, and experiences with prejudice and discrimination. A *few* studies suggest that these strains may also be important correlates of crime, but the results of such studies should be verified with additional research.

Further, researchers should not only focus on those strains predicted to increase crime, but should also test GST's predictions that certain strains do *not* increase the likelihood of crime—for example, excessive demands associated with conventional pursuits that are well-rewarded (e.g., the long working hours associated with many professional and managerial jobs) (see Chapter 3). Researchers should also examine GST's predictions about *why* certain strains do or do not increase the likelihood of crime. For example, they should measure the perceived magnitude and injustice of strains and determine whether those strains seen as high in magnitude and unjust are more likely to cause crime (see Baron and Hartnagel [2002] and Paternoster and Mazerolle [1994] for examples). In addition, researchers should test GST's prediction that the strains conducive to crime interact with one another in their effect on crime, such that individuals are much more likely to turn to crime when they experience several strains close together in time.

All of the above research should also take account of the fact that the impact of strains on crime may be partly indirect, through the effect of strains on social control, social learning, and personality variables (see Chapter 2). And all of this research should attempt to better measure strains, avoiding simplistic measures that provide little information on the magnitude and nature of strains (Chapter 3).

The Reasons Why Strains Affect Crime

One of the core propositions of GST is that strains lead to particular crimes primarily through their effect on negative emotional *states*, such as anger, frustration, malicious envy, depression, and fear. Surprisingly, only a few studies have examined this proposition (see Chapter 2). These studies suggest that strains do increase state anger and that such anger explains much of the effect of strains on crime. More research is clearly needed in this area, however, including research that examines emotions other than anger. Such research should also examine whether particular types of strains are more likely to result in certain emotions. Peer abuse, for example, may be especially likely to result in anger, while the inability to achieve monetary goals may be more likely to result in frustration. And such research should examine whether different emotions are conducive to different types of crime. In addition, researchers should examine the extent to which strains affect crime by temporarily reducing social control and fostering the social learning of crime.

Further, researchers should examine the extent to which chronic or repeated strains create a predisposition for crime. Research suggests that strains increase levels of trait anger or the tendency to become easily upset and experience intense anger when upset. Some data suggest that strains may contribute to other emotional traits, such as trait depression, although more research is needed here. Research is also needed on the extent to which strains contribute to the traits of low constraint and negative emotionality, reduce social control, and foster the social learning of crime—including association with criminal others and the adoption of beliefs favorable to crime. As indicated in Chapter 2, a few studies provide tentative support for these arguments.

Factors Influencing the Likelihood of Criminal Coping

GST predicts that a range of factors influence or condition the effect of strains on crime, but the research in this area has produced mixed results. For example, while some studies have found that strains are more likely to lead to crime among those who associate with delinquent peers, other studies have not (see Chapter 4). I think there are several reasons for these mixed results, the most important being the difficulty of detecting conditioning effects with survey data (McClelland and Judd, 1993). Researchers, then, should explore conditioning effects using other methods, like experimental studies, including studies evaluating rehabilitation and prevention programs, vignette studies, and observational studies. Many rehabilitation and prevention programs focus on individuals under great strain; for example, individuals who are failing at school or who live in high-poverty communities. Such programs then manipulate certain of the factors that condition the effect of strains on crime, like coping skills or level of social support (see Agnew, 2005a). Evaluations of such programs may provide much information on conditioning effects. Vignette studies typically describe strainful events to respondents and then ask them to estimate the likelihood they would respond to such events with crime (e.g., Capowich et al., 2001). Researchers might select respondents who differ on key conditioning variables and determine if such differences influence their anticipated responses to strain. Alternatively, researchers might manipulate key conditioning variables when constructing the vignettes (e.g., tell some respondents that the probability of being sanctioned for a criminal response is 10 percent and others that it is 50 percent). Observational studies may also provide information on conditioning factors. Anderson (1999), for example, found evidence that the children of "decent" families were less likely than the children of "street families" to respond to provocations with violence. There are, then, some ways around the methodological limitations of survey research, although these alternative methods sometimes have problems of their own.

The mixed evidence on conditioning effects may also stem from a tendency to examine conditioning variables in isolation from one another. For example, a researcher might examine whether problem-solving skills condition the effect of strains on crime, with a range of other conditioning variables held constant. But whether problem-solving skills influence the effect of strains on crime likely depends on the level of other conditioning variables. To illustrate, individuals with poor problem-solving skills may *not* respond to strains with crime if their level of social control or conventional social support is high. Given this argument, it may be best for researchers to consider the individuals' *overall standing* on all of those factors that increase the likelihood of responding to strains with crime. Criminal coping should be most likely among those who score high on all or most of these factors.

Explaining Patterns of Offending Over the Life Course, Group Differences in Crime, and Community and Societal Differences in Crime

Most of the research on GST has focused on explaining individual differences in offending, with this research focusing on broad samples of individuals or individuals in particular subgroups, like police officers and adjudicated delinquents. Only a few studies have applied GST to the explanation of group or community differences in offending, with most of these studies focusing on gender differences in offending. These studies typically attempt to determine whether gender differences in offending are due to gender differences in the extent of strains, the types of strains experienced, and/or the tendency to respond to strains with crime. These studies, however, fail to examine most of the strains conducive to crime, reflecting the fact that currently available surveys fail to measure many strains. Research opportunities in this area, then, are "wide open."

As indicated in Chapters 5–7, while GST can help explain group differences in crime, it cannot explain *why* some groups are more likely than others to experience strains conducive to crime or to possess those factors that increase the likelihood of criminal coping. For example, GST can help explain gender differences in crime by arguing that males are more likely than females to experience strains conducive to crime (like criminal victimization). But GST cannot explain why males are more likely to experience such strains. Explanations of this type are the province of biological and macrolevel theories, like feminist, conflict, social disorganization, and institutional anomie theories (see Cullen and Agnew, 2003; Walsh, 2000). Future research should attempt to better integrate GST with such theories.

Summary

In sum, data suggest that many of the strains conducive to crime listed in Chapter 3 do in fact increase the likelihood of crime, with certain of these strains being among the most important causes of crime. Further, more limited data suggest that these strains increase the likelihood of crime for reasons indicated by GST, including their impact on negative emotional states and traits. Most of the core propositions of GST, then, have some support. At the same time, many of the other propositions of GST are in need of further research.

The Relationship Between GST and the Other Major Theories of Crime

As indicated in Chapter 1, GST is distinguished from the other major theories of crime in two ways. It focuses explicitly on *negative relationships with others*: relationships in which others take individuals' valued possessions, treat them in an aversive manner, or prevent them from achieving their goals. Biopsychological theories focus on individual traits rather than relationships with others (although such traits may contribute to negative relationships). Control theories focus on the *absence of positive relationships* with others. And social learning theories focus on *positive relationships with deviant others*. Further, GST argues that individuals are *pressured into crime* by these negative relationships or strains, particularly by the negative emotions that result from these strains. By contrast, control theories argue that individuals are *freed to engage in crime*, while social learning theorists argue that individuals *come to view crime as a desirable or at least justifiable form of behavior under certain circumstances*.

At the same time, GST is intimately related to the other leading theories of crime. As argued at several points in this book, strains may contribute to personality traits conducive to crime, reduce social control, and foster the social learning of crime (see Chapter 2). Conversely, individuals' exposure to strains is influenced by their personality traits, level of control, and factors associated with the social learning of crime (see especially Chapters 5–7). Further, the factors associated with all of these theories interact with one another in their effect on crime. In particular, the effect of strains on crime is influenced or conditioned by personality traits, level of social control, and those factors that foster the social learning of crime—like association with delinquent peers (see especially Chapter 4). Likewise, the effect of these later factors on crime is influenced by exposure to strains. Those low in social control, for example, are more likely to engage in crime if they are experiencing strains.

Finally, at a more *concrete* level, many of the specific factors that cause crime—like child abuse, work in the secondary labor market, and residence in deprived communities—index or reflect levels of strain, control, *and* the social learning for crime. That is, the concrete measures of strain, control, and social learning overlap with one another to some extent. Harsh discipline, for example, can be taken as a measure of strain, low social control (poor discipline), and the social learning of crime (exposure to aggressive models). I elaborate on this theme in a recent book (Agnew, 2005b; also see Agnew, 1993; 1995a).

GST, then, is distinct from, but intimately related to the other leading theories of crime. Given this fact, one might wonder about the possibility of developing a general or integrated theory of crime.

At one level, we might argue that strain, social control, social learning, and personality variables mutually affect one another and interact with one another in their affect on crime. At a more concrete level, such an integration might assume the form described in my recent book, *Why Do Criminal's Offend? A General Theory of Crime* (Agnew, 2005b). This book examines the effect of several broad sets of factors on crime: the individual traits of low constraint and negative emotionality, poor parenting practices, negative school experiences, delinquent peer association and peer abuse, marital problems, and unemployment/bad jobs. Each of these factors is said to index or reflect high levels of strain, low control, and the social learning of crime (or, in the case of low constraint and negative emotionality, personality traits conducive to crime). And these factors mutually influence one another and interact in their effect on crime.

At the present time, I think it is useful to pursue both the development of individual theories, like GST, *and* integrated or general theories of crime. Each of the major theories is in need of further refinement and testing, particularly GST. And such refinement will contribute to the development of integrated theories, since integrated theories can be no better than their component parts. But it is also useful to explore the ways in which the different theories are related to one another and work together to affect crime. And such exploration can contribute to the development of the individual theories, by making one more aware of the larger context in which these theories operate.

In any event, it should be kept in mind that GST is a work in progress. While the core propositions of the theory have substantial support, there are some areas of mixed support where further research is needed. Most notably, more research is needed on GST's predictions about those factors that condition or influence the effect of strains on crime. In addition, several important predictions of the theory have not yet been the subject of much research. For example, we need more research on the effect of certain strains on crime and on the extent to which emotional states explain the effect of strains on crime. Further, there are many new topics to which GST can be applied, particularly the explanation of group differences in crime. The research in all of these areas should lead to the further refinement of GST and, hopefully, should help solidify GST's status as one of the leading theories of crime and delinquency.

Review and Discussion Questions

1. What are the core propositions or arguments of general strain theory?

2. Describe the empirical evidence on GST, noting areas where further research is needed.

3. Why do I argue that criminologists should attempt to integrate GST with macrolevel theories of crime?

4. How is GST distinct from biopsychological, social control, and social learning theories? How is GST related to these theories? How might these theories be combined to construct an integrated or general theory of crime? ✦

References

Acoca, Leslie. 1998. "Outside/inside: The violation of American girls at home, on the streets, and in the juvenile justice system." *Crime & Delinquency* 44:561–589.

Agnew, Robert. 1984. "Goal achievement and delinquency." *Sociology and Social Research* 68:435–451.

———. 1985. "A revised strain theory of delinquency." *Social Forces* 64:151–167.

———. 1989. "A longitudinal test of the revised strain theory." *Journal of Quantitative Criminology* 5:373–387.

———. 1990a. "The origins of delinquent events: An examination of offender accounts." *Journal of Research in Crime and Delinquency* 27:267–294.

———. 1990b. "Adolescent resources and delinquency." *Criminology* 28:535–566.

———. 1992. "Foundation for a general strain theory of crime and delinquency." *Criminology* 30:47–87.

———. 1993. "Why do they do it? An examination of the intervening mechanisms between 'social control' variables and delinquency." *Journal of Research of Crime and Delinquency* 30:245–266.

———. 1995a. "Testing the leading crime theories: An alternative strategy focusing on motivational processes." *Journal of Research in Crime and Delinquency* 32:363–398.

———. 1995b. "The contribution of social-psychological strain theory to the explanation of crime and delinquency." In *The Legacy of Anomie Theory, Advances in Criminological Theory*, Vol. 6, eds. Freda Adler and William S. Laufer. New Brunswick, NJ: Transaction.

———. 1995c. "Controlling delinquency: Recommendations from general strain theory." In *Crime and Public Policy*, ed. Hugh Barlow. Boulder, CO: Westview.

———. 1995d. "Strain and subcultural theories of crime." In *Criminology: A Contemporary Handbook,* ed. Joseph F. Sheley. Belmont, CA: Wadsworth.

———. 1997. "Stability and change in crime over the life course : A strain theory explanation." In *Developmental Theories of Crime and Delinquency, Advances in Criminological Theory,* Vol. 7, ed. Terence P. Thornberry. New Brunswick, NJ: Transaction.

———. 1999. "A general strain theory of community differences in crime rates." *Journal of Research in Crime and Delinquency* 36:123–155.

———. 2001. "Building on the foundation of general strain theory: Specifying the types of strain most likely to lead to crime and delinquency." *Journal of Research in Crime and Delinquency* 38:319–361.

———. 2002. "Experienced, vicarious, and anticipated strain: An exploratory study focusing on physical victimization and delinquency." *Justice Quarterly* 19:603–632.

———. 2003. "An integrated theory of the adolescent peak in offending." *Youth & Society* 34:263–299.

———. 2004. "A general strain theory approach to violence." In *Violence: From Theory to Research,* eds. Maraget A. Zahn, Henry H. Brownstein, and Shelly L. Jackson. Cincinnati: Anderson and LexisNexis.

———. 2005a. *Juvenile Delinquency: Causes and Control.* Los Angeles: Roxbury.

———. 2005b. *Why Do Criminals Offend? A General Theory of Crime and Delinquency.* Los Angeles: Roxbury.

———. 2006a. "Storylines as a new set of factors in the causes of crime research." *Journal of Research in Crime and Delinquency,* forthcoming.

———. 2006b. "General strain theory: Current status and directions for further research." In *Taking Stock: The Status of Criminological Theory, Advances in Criminological Theory,* eds. Francis T. Cullen, John Paul Wright, and Michelle Coleman. New Brunswick, NJ: Transaction.

Agnew, Robert, and Timothy Brezina. 1997. "Relational problems with peers, gender, and delinquency." *Youth and Society* 29:84–111.

Agnew, Robert, Timothy Brezina, John Paul Wright, and Francis T. Cullen. 2002. "Strain, personality traits, and delinquency: Extending general strain theory." *Criminology* 40:43–72.

Agnew, Robert, Francis T. Cullen, Velmer S. Burton Jr., T. David Evans, and R. Gregory Dunaway. 1996. "A new test of classic strain theory." *Justice Quarterly* 13:681–704.

Agnew, Robert, and Ardith A.R. Peters. 1986. "The techniques of neutral-ization: An analysis of predisposing and situational factors." *Criminal Justice and Behavior* 13:81–97.

Agnew, Robert, and David M. Petersen. 1989. "Leisure and delinquency." *Social Problems* 36:332–350.

Agnew, Robert, Cesar Rebellon, and Sherod Thaxton. 2000. "A general strain theory approach to families." In *Families, Crime and Criminal Justice,* eds. Greer Litton Fox and Michael L. Benson. New York: JAI.

Agnew, Robert, and Helene Raskin White. 1992. "An empirical test of General Strain Theory." *Criminology* 30:475–499.

Ainsworth, James W. 2002. "Why does it take a village? The mediation of neighborhood effects on educational achievement." *Social Forces* 81:117–152.

Akers, Ronald L. 1998. *Social Learning and Social Structure: A General Theory of Crime and Deviance.* Boston: Northeastern University Press.

Ambert, Anne-Marie. 1994. "A qualitative study of peer abuse and its effects: Theoretical and empirical implications." *Journal of Marriage and the Family* 56:119–130.

Anderson, Elijah. 1990. *Streetwise: Race, Class and Change in an Urban Community.* Chicago: University of Chicago Press.

———. 1994. "Code of the streets." *Atlantic Monthly* 273:81–94.

———. 1999. *Code of the Street.* New York: W. W. Norton.

Aseltine, Robert H., Jr., and Susan L. Gore. 2000. "The variable effects of stress on alcohol use from adolescence to early adulthood." *Substance Use & Misuse* 35:643–668.

Aseltine, Robert H., Jr., Susan Gore, and Jennifer Gordon. 2000. "Life stress, anger and anxiety, and delinquency: An empirical test of general strain theory." *Journal of Health and Social Behavior* 41:256–275.

Averill, James, R. 1982. *Anger and Aggression.* New York: Springer-Verlag.

———. 2001. "Studies on anger and aggression: Implications for theories of emotion." In *Emotions in Social Psychology,* ed. W. George Parrott. Philadelphia: Taylor & Francis.

Bandura, Albert. 1997. *Self-Efficacy: The Exercise of Control.* New York: W.H. Freeman.

Bao, Wan-Ning, and Ain Haas. 2005. "Social change and life strain among Chinese urban adolescents." Unpublished paper, Indiana University–Purdue University at Indianapolis.

Bao, Wan-Ning, Ain Haas, and Yijun Pi. 2004. "Life strain, negative emotions, and delinquency: An empirical test of general strain theory in

208 ✦ *Pressured Into Crime*

the People's Republic of China." *International Journal of Offender Therapy and Comparative Criminology* 48:281–297.

Baron, Stephen W. 2004. "General strain theory, street youth and crime: A test of Agnew's revised theory." *Criminology* 24:457–483.

Baron, Stephen W., and Timothy F. Hartnagel. 1997. "Attributions, affect, and crime: Street youths' reactions to unemployment." *Criminology* 35:409–434.

———. 2002. "Street youth and labor market strain." *Journal of Criminal Justice* 30:519–533.

Baron, Stephen W., David R. Forde, and Leslie W. Kennedy. 2001. "Rough justice: Street youth and violence." *Journal of Interpersonal Violence* 16:662–678.

Bazemore, Gordon. 2000. "Community justice and a vision of collective efficacy: The case of restorative conferencing." In *Policies, Processes, and Decisions of the Criminal Justice System, Criminal Justice 2000*, Vol. 3, ed. Julie Horney. Washington, DC: National Institute of Justice.

Bellair, Paul E., Vincent J. Roscigno, and Thomas McNulty. 2003. "Linking local labor market opportunity to violent adolescent delinquency." *Journal of Research in Crime and Delinquency* 40:6–33.

Benson, Michael L. 2004. "Denying the guilty mind: Accounting for involvement in white-collar crime." In *About Criminals*, ed. Mark Pogrebin. Thousand Oaks, CA: Sage.

Benson, Michael L., and Greer Litton Fox. 2004. *When Violence Hits Home*, NIJ Research in Brief. Washington, DC: National Institute of Justice.

Benson, Michael L., Greer Litton Fox, Alfred DeMaris, and Judy Van Wyk. 2000. "Violence in families: The intersection of race, poverty, and community context." In *Families, Crime, and Criminal Justice*, eds. Greer Litton Fox and Michael L. Benson. New York: JAI.

Bernard, Thomas J. 1990. "Angry aggression among the 'truly disadvantaged.' " *Criminology* 28:73–96.

Billson, Janet Mancini. 1996. *Pathways to Manhood: Young Black Males Struggle for Identity*. New Brunswick, NJ: Transaction.

Black, Donald. 1983. "Crime as social control." *American Sociological Review* 48:34–45.

Blau, Judith R., and Peter M. Blau. 1982. "The cost of inequality: Metropolitan structure and violent crime." *American Sociological Review* 47:114–129.

Blazak, Randy. 2001. "White boys to terrorist men." *American Behavioral Scientist* 44:982–1000.

Blueprints for Violence Prevention. 2004a. *Bullying Prevention Program.* http://www/colorado.edu/cspv/blueprints/mode/programs/.

———. 2004b. *Multidimensional Treatment Foster Care (MTFC).* http://www/colorado.edu/cspv/blueprints/mode/programs/.

———. 2004c. *Big Brothers Big Sisters of America (BBBS).* http://www/colorado.edu/cspv/blueprints/mode/programs/.

Boardman, Jason D., Brian Karl Finch, and Christopher G. Ellison. 2001. "Neighborhood disadvantage, stress, and drug use among adults." *Journal of Health and Social Behavior* 42:151–165.

Box, Steven. 1987. *Recession, Crime, and Punishment.* Basingstoke, UK: Macmillan.

Bradley, Robert H., and Robert F. Corwyn. 2002. "Socioeconomic status and child development." *Annual Review of Psychology* 53:371–99.

Braithwaite, John. 2002. *Restorative Justice and Responsive Regulation.* Oxford: Oxford University Press.

Braukmann, Curtis J., and Montrose M. Wolf. 1987. "Behaviorally-based group homes for juvenile offenders." In *Behavioral Approaches to Crime and Delinquency*, eds. Edward K. Morris and Curtis J. Braukmann. New York: Plenum.

Brezina, Timothy. 1996. "Adapting to strain: An examination of delinquent coping responses." *Journal of Research in Crime and Delinquency* 34:39–60.

———. 1998. "Adolescent maltreatment and delinquency: The question of intervening processes." *Journal of Research in Crime and Delinquency* 35:71–99.

———. 1999. "Teenage violence toward parents as an adaptation of family strain." *Youth & Society* 30:416–444.

———. 2000. "Delinquent problem-solving: An interpretative framework for criminological theory and research." *Journal of Research in Crime and Delinquency* 37:3–30.

Brezina, Timothy, Alex R. Piquero, and Paul Mazerolle. 2001. "Student anger and aggressive behavior in school: An initial test of Agnew's macro-level strain theory." *Journal of Research in Crime and Delinquency* 38:362–386.

Broidy, Lisa M. 2001. "A test of general strain theory." *Criminology* 39:9–33.

Broidy, Lisa M., and Robert Agnew. 1997. "Gender and crime: A general strain theory perspective." *Journal of Research in Crime and Delinquency* 34:275–306.

Brooks-Gunn, Jeanee, and Greg J. Duncan. 1997. "The effects of poverty on children." *The Future of Children* 7:55–71.

Brown, Tony W., David R. Williams, James S. Jackson, Harold W. Neighbors, Myriam Torres, Sherill L. Sellers, and Kendrick T. Brown. 1999. "Being black and feeling blue: The mental health consequences of racial inequality." *Race and Society* 2:117–131.

Bryant, Clifton D. 2001. *The Encyclopedia of Criminology and Deviant Behavior.* Philadelphia: Brunner Routledge.

Burt, Callie Harbin, and Jody Clay-Warner. 2004. "Not just 'rogue males:' Gender identity in general strain theory." Paper presented at the annual meeting of the American Society of Criminology, Nashville.

Burton, Velmer S., Jr., Francis T. Cullen, T. David Evans, Leanne F. Alarid, and R. Gregory Dunaway. 1998. "Gender, self-control, and crime." *Journal of Research in Crime and Delinquency* 35:123–147.

Campbell, Anne. 1990. "Female participation in gangs." In *Gangs in America,* ed. C. Ronald Huff. Newbury Park, CA: Sage.

Canary, Daniel J., and Beth A. Semic. 1999. "Anger." In *Encyclopedia of Human Emotions,* eds. David Levinson, James J. Ponzetti, and Peter F. Jorgensen. New York: Macmillan.

Capowich, George P., Paul Mazerolle, and Alex R Piquero. 2001. "General strain theory, situational anger, and social networks: An assessment of conditional influences." *Journal of Criminal Justice* 29:445–461.

Carey, Benedict. 2004. "Payback time: Why revenge tastes so sweet." *New York Times,* July 27, D1, 6.

Caspi, Avshalom. 1998. "Personality development across the life course." In *Handbook of Child Psychology,* Vol. 3, ed. Nancy Eisenberg. New York:Wiley.

Caspi, Avshalom, Darly J. Bem, and Glen H. Elder Jr. 1989. "Continuities and consequences of interactional styles across the life course." *Journal of Personality* 57:375–406.

Caspi, Avshalom, D. Lynam, Terrie E. Moffitt, and Phil A. Silva. 1993. "Unraveling girls' delinquency: Biological, dispositional, and contextual contributions to adolescent misbehavior." *Developmental Psychology* 29:19–30.

Caspi, Avshalom, Terrie E. Moffitt, Phil A. Silva, Magda Stouthamer-Loeber, Robert F. Krueger, and Pamela S. Schmutte. 1994. "Are some people crime-prone? Replications of the personality-crime relationship across countries, genders, race, and methods." *Criminology* 32:163–196.

Catalano, Richard F., Michael W. Arthur, J. David Hawkins, Lisa Berglund, and Jeffrey J. Olson. 1998. "Comprehensive community and school-based interventions to prevent antisocial behavior." In *Serious and Violent Juvenile Offenders,* eds. Rolf Loeber and David P. Farrington. Thousand Oaks, CA: Sage.

Catalano, Shannon M. 2004. *Criminal Victimization, 2003.* Washington, DC: Bureau of Justice Statistics.

Cerbone, Felicia Gray, and Cindy L. Larison. 2000. "A bibliographic essay: The relationship between stress and substance use." *Substance Use & Misuse* 35:757–786.

Cernkovich, Stephen A., Peggy G. Giordano, and Jennifer L. Rudolph. 2000. "Race, crime, and the American dream." *Journal of Research in Crime and Delinquency* 37:131–170.

Chesney-Lind, Meda. 1989. "Girls' crime and woman's place: Toward a feminist model of female delinquency." *Crime and Delinquency* 35:5–29.

Chesney-Lind, Meda, and Randall G. Sheldon. 2004. *Girls, Delinquency, and Juvenile Justice.* Belmont, CA: Thomson/Wadsworth.

Clarke, Ronald V., and Derek B. Cornish. 1985. "Modeling offenders' decisions: A framework for research and policy." *Crime and Justice* 6:147–183.

Cloward, Richard, and Lloyd Ohlin. 1960. *Delinquency and Opportunity.* Glencoe, IL: Free Press.

Cohen, Albert K. 1955. *Delinquent Boys.* Glencoe, IL: Free Press.

Cohen, Sheldon, Ronald C. Kessler, and Lynn Underwood Gates. 1995. *Measuring Stress.* New York: Oxford University Press.

Colvin, Mark. 2000. *Crime & Coercion.* New York: St. Martin's Press.

Compas, Bruce E., Jennifer K. Connor-Smith, Heidi Saltzman, Alexandra Harding, and Martha E. Wadsworth. 2001. "Coping with stress during childhood and adolescence: Problems, progress, and potential in theory and research." *Psychological Bulletin* 127:87–127.

Conduct Problems Prevention Research Group. 2002. "Using the Fast Track randomized prevention trial to test the early-starter model of the development of serious conduct problems." *Development and Psychopathology* 14:925–943.

Conger, Rand D., Xiaojia Ge, Glen Elder, Jr., Frederick O. Lorenz, and Ronald L. Simons. 1994. "Economic stress, coercive family process, and developmental problems of adolescents." *Child Development* 65:541–561.

Coordinating Council on Juvenile Justice and Delinquency Prevention. 1996. *Combating Violence and Delinquency.* Washing, DC: U.S. Department of Justice.

Cromwell, Paul, ed. 2003. *In Their Own Words: Criminals on Crime.* Los Angeles: Roxbury.

Cromwell, Paul, Lee Parker, and Shawna Parker. 2003. "The five-finger discount." In *In Their Own Words: Criminals on Crime*, ed. Paul Cromwell. Los Angeles: Roxbury.

Crutchfield, Robert D., and Susan R. Pitchford. 1997. "Work and crime: The effects of labor stratification." *Social Forces* 76:93–118.

Cullen, Francis T. 1984. *Rethinking Crime and Deviance Theory*. Totowa, NJ: Rowman and Allanheld.

———. 1994. "Social support as an organizing concept for criminology." *Justice Quarterly* 11:527–559.

———. 1995. "Assessing the penal harm movement." *Journal of Research in Crime and Delinquency* 32:338–358.

Cullen, Francis T., and Robert Agnew. 2003. *Criminological Theory: Past to Present*. Los Angeles: Roxbury.

Cullen, Francis T., and Paul Gendreau. 2000. "Assessing correctional rehabilitation: Policy, practice, and prospects." In *Policies, Processes, and Decisions of the Criminal Justice System, Criminal Justice 2000*, ed. Julie Horney. Washington, DC: National Institute of Justice.

Currie, Elliott. 1998. *Crime and Punishment in America*. New York: Owl Books.

Curry, David G., and Scott H. Decker. 2003. *Confronting Gangs*. Los Angeles: Roxbury.

Daly, Kathleen. 1992. "Women's pathways to felony court: Feminist theories of lawbreaking and problems of representation." *Review of Law and Women's Studies* 2:11–52.

de Castro, Bram Orobio, Nico W. Slot, Joop D. Bosch, Willem Koops, and Jan W. Veerman. 2002. "Hostile attributions of intent and aggressive behavior: A meta-analysis." *Child Development* 73:916–934.

Decker, Scott H., and Barrik Van Winkle. 1996. *Life in the Gang*. Cambridge, England: Cambridge University Press.

De Coster, Stacy, and Lisa Kort-Butler. 2004. "How general is general strain theory? Assessing the specific domains of strains and delinquent responses." Paper presented at the annual meeting of the American Society of Criminology, Nashville.

DeFronzo, James. 1997. "Welfare and homicide." *Journal of Research in Crime and Delinquency* 34:395–406.

Deng, Xiaogang, and Ann Cordilia. 1999. "To get rich is glorious: Rising expectations, declining control, and escalating crime in contemporary China." *International Journal of Offender Therapy and Comparative Criminology* 43:211–229.

Dodge, Kenneth. 1986. *Social Competence in Children.* Chicago: University of Chicago Press.

Dohrenwend, Bruce P. 1998. *Adversity, Stress, and Psychopathology.* New York: Oxford University Press.

———. 2000. "The role of adversity and stress in psychopathology: Some evidence and its implications for theory and research." *Journal of Health and Social Behavior* 41:1–19.

Dornfeld, Maude and Candance Kruttschnitt. 1992. "Do the stereotypes fit? Mapping gender-specific outcomes and risk factors." *Criminology* 30:397–419.

Dutton, Donald G., Cynthia van Ginkel, and Andrew Starzomski. 1995. "The role of shame and guilt in the intergenerational transmission of abusiveness." *Violence and Victims* 10:121–131.

Eitle, David J. 2002. "Exploring a source of deviance-producing strain for females: Perceived discrimination and general strain theory." *Journal of Criminal Justice* 30:429–442.

Eitle, David J., Steven Gunkel, and Karen Van Gundy. 2004. "Cumulative exposure to stressful life events and male gang membership." *Journal of Criminal Justice* 32:95–111.

Eitle, David J., and R. Jay Turner. 2002. "Exposure to community violence and young adult crime: The effects of witnessing violence, traumatic victimization, and other stressful life events." *Journal of Research in Crime and Delinquency* 39:214–237.

———. 2003. "Stress exposure, race, and young adult crime." *Sociological Quarterly* 44:243–269.

Elliott, Delbert S., David Huizinga, and Susan S. Ageton. 1985. *Explaining Delinquency and Drug Use.* Beverly Hills, CA: Sage.

Elliott, Delbert S., and Harwin Voss. 1974. *Delinquency and Dropout.* Lexington, MA: Lexington.

Esbensen, Finn-Aage, Elizabeth Piper Deschenes, and L. Thomas Winfree, Jr. 1999. "Differences between gang girls and gang boys." *Youth and Society* 31:27–53.

Fabbro, David. 1978. "Peaceful societies: An introduction." *Journal of Peace Research* 15:67–83.

Farrington, David F. 1992. "Explaining the beginning, progress, and ending of antisocial behavior from birth to adulthood." In *Facts, Frameworks, and Forecasts,* ed. Joan McCord. New Brunswick, NJ: Transaction.

————. 2005. *Integrated Developmental & Life-Course Theories of Offending, Advances in Criminological Theory*, Vol. 14. New Brunswick, NJ: Transaction.

Felson, Marcus. 2002. *Crime and Everyday Life*. Thousand Oaks, CA: Sage.

Felson, Richard. 1996. "Big people hit little people: Sex differences in physical power and interpersonal violence." *Criminology* 34:433–452.

Fishbein, Diana. 2001. *Biobehavioral Perspectives in Criminology*. Belmont, CA: Wadsworth.

Fleming, Zachary. 2003. "The thrill of it all: Youthful offenders and auto theft." In *In Their Own Words: Criminals on Crime*, ed. Paul Cromwell. Los Angeles: Roxbury.

Fox, Greer Linton, and Dudley Chancey. 1998. "Sources of economic distress." *Journal of Family Issues* 19:725–749.

Gaarder, Emily, and Joanne Belknap. 2002. "Tenuous borders: Girls transferred to adult court." *Criminology* 40:481–518.

Gartner, Rosemary. 1990. "The victims of homicide: A temporal and cross-national comparison." *American Sociological Review* 55:92–106.

Gettleman, Jeffrey. 2004. "Anti-U.S. outrage sends Iraqis into militancy." *Atlanta Journal-Constitution*, April 11, A14.

Gibson, Chris L., Marc L. Swatt, and Jason R. Jolicoeur. 2001. "Assessing the generality of general strain theory: The relationship among occupational stress experienced by male police officers and domestic forms of violence." *Journal of Crime and Justice* 24:29–57.

Gilfus, Mary E. 1992. "From victims to survivors to offenders: Women's routes of entry and immersion into street crime." *Women and Criminal Justice* 4:63–89.

Giordano, Peggy C., Stephen A. Cernkovich, and M.D. Pugh. 1986. "Friendships and delinquency." *American Journal of Sociology* 91:1170–1202.

Goldstein, Arnold P., Leonard Krasner, and Sol L. Garfield. 1989. *Reducing Delinquency: Intervention in the Community*. New York: Pergamon.

Gottfredson, Michael R., and Travis Hirschi. 1990. *A General Theory of Crime*. Stanford, CA: Stanford University Press.

Greenberg, David. 1985. "Age, crime, and social explanation." *American Journal of Sociology* 91:1–27.

Greenberg, David F. 1977. "Delinquency and the age structure of society." *Contemporary Crisis* 1:189–223.

Guerrero, Laura K. 1994. " 'I'm so mad I could scream': The effects of anger expression on relational satisfaction and communication competence." *The Southern Communication Journal* 59:125–141.

Hagan, John, and Bill McCarthy. 1997. *Mean Streets.* Cambridge, England: Cambridge University Press.

Hagan, John, and Ruth D. Peterson, eds. 1995. *Criminal Inequality in America: Patterns and Consequences.* Stanford, CA: Stanford University Press.

Hale, Robert. 2004. "Motives of reward among men who rape." In *About Criminals,* ed. Mark Pogrebin. Thousand Oaks, CA: Sage.

Hannon, Lance, and James DeFronzo. 1988. "Welfare and property crime." *Justice Quarterly* 15:273–288.

Harmon, Amy. 2004. "Internet gives teenage bullies weapons to wound from afar." *New York Times,* August 26, A1, 26.

Harnish, Jennifer D., Robert H. Aseltine, Jr., and Susan Gore. 2000. "Resolution of stressful experiences as an indicator of coping effectiveness in young adults: An event history analysis." *Journal of Health and Social Behavior* 41:121–136.

Harrell, Shelly P. 2000. "A multidimensional conceptualization of racism-related stress: Implications for the well-being of people of color." *American Journal of Orthopsychiatry* 70:42–57.

Hawkins, Darnell F., John H. Laub, Janet L. Lauritsen, and Lynn Cothern. 2000. *Race, Ethnicity, and Serious Violent Juvenile Offending.* Washington, DC: Office of Juvenile Justice and Delinquency Prevention.

Hay, Carter. 2003. "Family strain, gender, and delinquency." *Sociological Perspectives* 46:107–136.

Hayes, Hennessey, and Kathleen Daly. 2003. "Youth justice conferencing and reoffending." *Justice Quarterly* 20:725–764.

Heimer, Karen. 2000. "Changes in the gender gap in crime and women's economic marginalization." In *The Nature of Crime: Continuity and Change, Criminal Justice 2000,* Vol. 1, eds. Eric Jefferis and Richard Titus. Washington, DC: National Institute of Justice.

Heimer, Karen, and Stacy De Coster. 1999. "The gendering of violent delinquency." *Criminology* 37:277–318.

Herbert, Tracy B., and Sheldon Cohen. 1996. "Measurement issues in research on psychosocial stress." In *Psychosocial Stress,* ed. Howard B. Kaplan. San Diego, CA: Academic Press.

Hewitt, John D., and Robert M. Regoli. 2002. "Holding serious juvenile offenders responsible: Implications from differential oppression theory." *Free Inquiry in Creative Sociology* 30:1–8.

Hill, Karl G., James C. Howell, J. David Hawkins, and Sara R. Battin-Pearson. 1999. "Childhood risk factors for adolescent gang membership." *Journal of Research in Crime and Delinquency* 36:300–322.

Hirschi, Travis. 1969. *Causes of Delinquency.* Berkeley: University of California Press.

Hoffmann, John P. 2000. "Introduction to the special issue on stress and substance use." *Substance Use & Misuse* 35:635–641.

———. 2003. "A contextual analysis of differential association, social control, and strain theories of delinquency." *Social Forces* 81:753–85.

Hoffmann, John P., and Felicia G. Cerbone. 1999. "Stressful life events and delinquency escalation in early adolescence." *Criminology* 37:343–374.

Hoffmann, John P., Felicia Gray Cerbone, and Susan S. Su. 2000. "A growth curve analysis of stress and adolescent drug use." *Substance Use & Misuse* 35:687–716.

Hoffmann, John P., and Alan S. Miller. 1998. "A latent variable analysis of General Strain Theory." *Journal of Quantitative Criminology* 14:83–110.

Hoffmann, John P., and Susan S. Su. 1997. "The conditional effects of stress on delinquency and drug use: A strain theory assessment of sex differences." *Journal of Research in Crime and Delinquency* 34:46–78.

Hollist, Dusten. 2004. "Adolescent maltreatment, negative emotion, personal and social resources, and delinquency." Paper presented at the annual meeting of the American Society of Criminology, Nashville.

Horney, Julie, D. Wayne Osgood, and Ineke Haen Marshall. 1995. "Criminal careers in the short-term: Intra-individual variability in crime and its relation to local life circumstances." *American Sociological Review* 60:655–673.

Howell, James C. 2003. *Preventing and Reducing Juvenile Delinquency.* Thousand Oaks, CA: Sage.

Hudley, Cynthia, Brenda Britsch, William D. Wakefield, Tara Smith, Marllene Demorat, and Su-Je Cho. 1998. "An attribution retraining program to reduce aggression in elementary school students." *Psychology in the Schools* 35:271–282.

Inciardi, James A., Ruth Horowitz, and Anne E. Pottieger. 1993. *Street Kids, Street Drugs, Street Crime.* Belmont, CA: Wadsworth.

Ireland, Timothy O., Carolyn A. Smith, and Terence P. Thornberry. 2002. "Developmental issues in the impact of child maltreatment on later delinquency and drug use." *Criminology* 40:359–400.

Irwin, Katherine. 2004. "The violence of adolescent life." *Youth & Society* 35:452–479.

Jakupcak, Matthew. 2003. "Masculine gender role stress and men's fear of emotions as predictors of self-reported aggression and violence." *Violence and Victims* 18:533–541.

Jang, Sung Joon, and Byron R. Johnson. 2003. "Strain, negative emotions, and deviant coping among African Americans: A test of general strain theory." *Journal of Quantitative Criminology* 19:79–105.

———. 2005. "Gender, religiosity, and reactions to strain among African Americans." *Sociological Quarterly* 46:323–357.

Jarjoura, G. Roger, Ruth A. Triplett, and Gregory P. Brinker. 2002. "Growing up poor: Examining the link between persistent childhood poverty and delinquency." *Journal of Quantitative Criminology* 18:159–187.

Jensen, Gary F. 1995. "Salvaging structure through strain: A theoretical and empirical critique." In *The Legacy of Anomie Theory, Advances in Criminological Theory*, Vol. 6, eds. Freda Adler and William S. Laufer. New Brunswick, NJ: Transaction.

———. 2003. "Gender variation in delinquency: Self-images, beliefs, and peers as mediating mechanisms." In *Social Learning Theory and the Explanation of Crime*, eds. Ronald L. Akers and Gary F. Jensen. New Brunswick, NJ: Transaction.

Kahn, Joseph. 2004a. "China's elite learn to flaunt it while the new landless weep." *New York Times*, December 25, A1, C4.

———. 2004b. "China's 'haves' stir the 'have nots' to violence." *New York Times*, December 31, A1, A16.

Kaplan, Howard B. 1996. "Psychosocial stress from the perspective of self theory." In *Psychosocial Stress*, ed. Howard B. Kaplan. San Diego, CA: Academic Press.

Katz, Jack. 1988. *Seductions of Crime*. New York: Basic Books.

Katz, Rebecca. 2000. "Explaining girls' and women's crime and desistance in the context of their victimization experiences." *Violence Against Women* 6:633–660.

Kaufman, Joanne M., Cesar Rebellon, Sherod Thaxton, and Robert Agnew. 2005. "A general strain theory of the race-crime relationship." In *General Strain Theory: Essential Readings*, eds. Paul Mazerolle and Robert Agnew. Los Angeles: Wadsworth.

Kenway, Jane, and Lindsay Fitzclarence. 1997. "Masculinity, violence and schooling: Challenging 'poisonous pedagogies.' " *Gender & Education* 9:117–133.

Kimmel, Michael S. 2002. " 'Gender symmetry' in domestic violence: A substantive and methodological research review." *Violence Against Women* 8:1332–1363.

Konty, Mark. 2005. "Microanomie: The cognitive foundations of the relationship between anomie and deviance." *Criminology* 43:107–132.

Kornhauser, Ruth Rosner. 1978. *Social Sources of Delinquency.* Chicago: University of Chicago Press.

Kring, Ann M. 2000. "Gender and anger." In *Gender and Emotion: Social Psychological Perspectives,* ed. Agneta H. Fischer. Cambridge: Cambridge University Press.

LaFree, Gary. 1999. "A summary and review of cross-national comparative studies of homicide." In *Homicide: A Sourcebook of Social Research,* eds. M. Dawyne Smith and Maraget A. Zahn. Thousand Oaks, CA: Sage.

LaFree, Gary, and Kriss A. Drass. 2002. "Counting crime booms among nations: Evidence for homicide victimization rates, 1956 to 1998." *Criminology* 40:769–800.

LaGrange, Teresa, and Robert A. Silverman. 1999. "Low self-control and opportunity: Testing the general theory of crime as an explanation for gender differences in delinquency." *Criminology* 37:41–72.

Land, Kenneth C., Patricia McCall, and Lawrence E. Cohen. 1990. "Structural covariates of homicide rates: Are they invariate across time and social space?" *American Journal of Sociology* 95:922–963.

Landau, Simha F. 1997. "Crime patterns and their relation to subjective social stress and support indicators: The role of gender." *Journal of Quantitative Criminology* 13:29–56.

———. 1998. "Crime, subjective social stress and support indicators, and ethnic origin: The Israeli experience." *Justice Quarterly* 15:243–272.

Langton, Lynn, and Nicole Leeper Piquero. 2004. "Can general strain theory explain white-collar crime? A preliminary investigation." Paper presented at the annual meeting of the American Society of Criminology, Nashville.

Lanza-Kaduce, Lonn, and Marcia J. Radosevich. 1987. "Negative reactions to processing and substance use among young incarcerated males." *Deviant Behavior* 8:137–148.

Larson, R., and M. Ham. 1993. "Stress and 'stress and storm' in early adolescence: The relationship of negative events with dysphoric affect." *Developmental Psychology* 29:130–140.

Larson, R., and C. Lampman-Petraitis. 1989. "Daily emotional states as reported by children and adolescents." *Child Development* 60:1250–1260.

Larson, R.W., M.H. Richards, G. Moneta, G. Holmbeck, and E. Duckett. 1996. "Changes in adolescents' daily interactions with their families from ages 10 to 18: Disengagement and transformation." *Developmental Psychology* 32:744–754.

Latkin, Carl A., and Aaron D. Curry. 2003. "Stressful neighborhoods and depression: A prospective study of the impact of neighborhood disorder." *Journal of Health and Social Behavior* 44:34–44.

Lauritsen, Janet L., John H. Laub, and Robert J. Sampson. 1992. "Conventional and delinquent activities: Implications for the prevention of violent victimization among adolescents." *Violence and Victims* 7:91–108.

Lauritsen, Janet L., Robert J. Sampson, and John H. Laub. 1991. "The link between offending and victimization among adolescents." *Criminology* 29:265–292.

Lazarus, Richard S. 1999. *Stress and Emotion: A New Synthesis.* New York: Springer.

Leblanc, Lauraine. 2000. *Pretty in Punk: Resistance in a Boy's Subculture.* New Brunswick, NJ: Rutgers University Press.

Leiber, Michael L., Margaret Farnworth, Katherine M. Jamieson, and Mahesh K. Nalla. 1994. "Bridging the gap in criminology: Liberation and gender-specific strain effects on delinquency." *Sociological Inquiry* 64:56–68.

Lempers, Jacques D., Dania Clark-Lempers, and Ronald L. Simons. 1989. "Economic hardship, parenting, and distress in adolescence." *Child Development* 60:25–39.

Levinson, David, James J. Ponzetti, Jr., and Peter F. Jorgensen, eds. 1999. *Encyclopedia of Human Emotions.* New York: Macmillan Reference.

Lewis, Michael, and Jeanette M. Haviland-Jones, eds. 2000. *Handbook of Emotions.* New York: Guilford Press.

Linksy, Arnold S., Ronet Bachman, and Murray A. Straus. 1995. *Stress, Culture, and Aggression.* New Haven, CT: Yale University Press.

Lockwood, Daniel. 1997. "Violence Among Middle School and High School Students: Analysis and Implications for Prevention." Washington, DC: National Institute of Justice.

Loeber, Rolf, Matthew Drinkwater, Yanming Yin, Stewart J. Anderson, Laura C. Schmidt, and Anne Crawford. 2000. "Stability of family interactions from ages 6 to 18." *Journal of Abnormal Psychology* 28:353–369.

Majors, Richard, and Janet Mancini Billson. 1992. *Cool Pose.* New York: Lexington Books.

Manasse, Michelle. 2002. "Gender, Crime, and Depression." Paper presented at the annual meeting of the American Society of Criminology, Chicago.

Martin, Jack K., Steven A. Tuch, and Paul M. Rodman. 2003. "Problem drinking patterns among African Americans: The impacts of reports of discrimination, perceptions of prejudice, and 'risky' coping strategies." *Journal of Health and Social Behavior* 44:408–425.

Marwell, Gerald. 1966. "Adolescent powerlessness and delinquent behavior." *Social Problems* 14:35–47.

Mattlin, Jay A., Elaine Wethington, and Ronald C. Kessler. 1990. "Situational determinants of coping and coping effectiveness." *Journal of Health and Social Behavior* 31:103–122.

Matza, David, and Gresham Sykes. 1961. "Juvenile delinquency and subterranean beliefs." *American Sociological Review* 26:713–719.

Maxwell, Shelia Royo. 2001. "A focus on familial strain: Antisocial behavior and delinquency in Filipino society." *Sociological Inquiry* 71:265–292.

Mayne, Tracy J., and George A. Bonanno, eds. 2001. *Emotions: Current Issues and Future Directions.* New York: Guilford.

Mazerolle, Paul. 1998. "Gender, general strain, and delinquency: An empirical examination." *Justice Quarterly* 15:65–91.

Mazerolle, Paul, Velmer S. Burton, Jr., Francis T. Cullen, T. David Evans, and Gary L. Payne. 2000. "Strain, anger, and delinquent adaptations: Specifying general strain theory." *Journal of Criminal Justice* 28:89–101.

Mazerolle, Paul, and Jeff Maahs. 2000. "General strain and delinquency: An alternative examination of conditioning influences." *Justice Quarterly* 17:323–343.

Mazerolle, Paul, and Alex Piquero. 1997. "Violent responses to strain: An examination of conditioning influences." *Violence and Victims* 12:323–343.

———. 1998. "Linking exposure to strain with anger: An investigation of deviant adaptations." *Journal of Criminal Justice* 26:195–211.

Mazerolle, Paul, Alex R. Piquero, and George E. Capowich. 2003. "Examining the links between strain, situational and dispositional anger, and crime." *Youth & Society* 35:131–157.

McCarthy, Bill, Diane Felmlee, and John Hagan. 2004. "Girl friends are better: Gender, friends, and crime among school and street youth." *Criminology* 42:805–835.

McClelland, Gary H., and Charles M. Judd. 1993. "Statistical difficulties of detecting interactions and moderator effects." *Psychological Bulletin* 114:376–390.

McCord, Joan, Cathy Spatz Widom, and Nancy A. Crowell, eds. 2001. *Juvenile Crime Juvenile Justice.* Washington, DC: National Academy Press.

McLeod, Jane D., and Ronald C. Kessler. 1990. "Socioeconomic status differences in vulnerability to undesirable life events." *Journal of Health and Social Behavior* 31:162–172.

McNeil, Donald G., Jr. 2004. "Real men don't clean bathrooms." *New York Times,* September 19, Section 4, 3.

McNulty, Thomas L., and Paul E. Bellair. 2003. "Explaining racial and ethnic differences in serious adolescent violent behavior." *Criminology* 41:709–746.

McNulty, Thomas L., and Steven R. Holloway. 2000. "Race, crime, and public housing in Atlanta: Testing a conditional effect hypothesis." *Social Forces* 79:707–729.

Melton, Heather C., and Joanne Belknap. 2003. "He hits, she hits: Assessing gender differences and similarities in officially reported intimate partner violence." *Criminal Justice & Behavior* 30:328–348.

Merton, Robert K. 1938. "Social structure and anomie." *American Sociological Review* 3:672–682.

———. 1968. *Social Theory and Social Structure.* New York: Free Press.

Messerschmidt, James W. 1993. *Masculinities and Crime.* Lanham, MD: Rowman and Littlefield.

Messner, Steven F. 1989. "Economic discrimination and societal homicide rates: Further evidence of the cost of inequality." *American Sociological Review* 54:597–611.

———. 2003. "Understanding cross-national variation in criminal violence." In *International Handbook of Violence Research,* eds. W. Heitmeyer and J. Hagan. New York: Kluwer Academic.

Messner, Steven F., and Richard Rosenfeld. 1997. "Political restraint of the market and levels of criminal homicide: A cross-national application of institutional-anomie theory." *Social Forces* 75:1393–1416.

———. 2001. *Crime and the American Dream.* Belmont, CA: Wadsworth.

Michaelson, Larry. 1987. "Cognitive-behavioral strategies in the prevention and treatment of antisocial disorders in children and adolescents." In *Prevention of Delinquent Behavior,* eds. John D. Burchard and Sara N. Burchard. Newbury Park, CA: Sage.

Miethe, Terance D., and Richard C. McCorkle. 2001. *Crime Profiles.* Los Angeles: Roxbury.

Miller, Jerome G. 1996. *Search and Destroy: African-American Males in the Criminal Justice System.* Cambridge: Cambridge University Press.

Miller, Jody. 2001. *One of the Guys: Girls, Gangs, and Gender.* New York: Oxford University Press.

Miller, Jody, and Norman A. White. 2003. "Gender and adolescent relationship violence: A contextual examination." *Criminology* 41:1207–1248.

Miller, Joshua D., and Donal Lynam. 2001. "Structural models of personality and their relation to antisocial behavior: A meta-analytic review." *Criminology* 39:765–798.

Mirowsky, John, and Catherine E. Ross. 1989. *Social Causes of Psychological Distress*. New York: Aldine de Gruyter.

Moffitt, Terrie E. 1993. "Adolescence-limited and life-course persistent antisocial behavior: A developmental taxonomy." *Psychological Review* 100:674–701.

Moffitt, Terrie E., Avshalom Caspi, Michael Rutter, and Phil A. Silva. 2001. *Sex Differences in Antisocial Behavior*. Cambridge, England: Cambridge University Press.

Morash, Merry, and Byong Ook Moon. 2005a. "Adaptation of theory for alternative cultural contexts: Agnew's general strain theory in South Korea." *Journal of International and Comparative Criminal Justice* (forthcoming).

———. 2005b. "Gender differences in the effects of strain on three types of delinquency: A test of theory outside of the United States." Unpublished manuscript.

Morgan, Rick L., and David Heise. 1988. "Structure of emotions." *Social Psychology Quarterly* 51:19–31.

Morris, William N., and Nora P. Reilly. 1987. "Toward the self-regulation of mood: Theory and research." *Motivation and Emotion* 11:215–245.

Mullins, Christopher, Richard Wright, and Bruce Jacobs. 2004. "Gender, streetlife, and criminal retaliation." *Criminology* 42:911–940.

Murnen, Sarah K., Carrie Wright, and Gretchen Kaluzny. 2002. "If 'boys will be boys,' then girls will be victims? A meta-analytic review of the research that relates masculine ideology to sexual aggression." *Sex Roles* 46:359–375.

Neapolitan, Jerome L. 1997. *Cross-National Crime*. Westport, CT: Greenwood Press.

———. 1998. "Cross-national variation in homicides: Is race a factor?" *Criminology* 36:139–156.

Neergaard, Lauran. 2004. "Brain scan shows revenge has its thrills." *New York Times*, August 27, A11.

Nyborg, Vanessa M., and John F. Curry. 2003. "The impact of perceived racism: Psychological symptoms among African American boys." *Journal of Clinical Child & Adolescent Psychology* 32:258–266.

Olweus, Dan. 1991. "Bully/victim problems among schoolchildren: Basic facts and effects of a school-based intervention program." In *The Development and Treatment of Childhood Aggression*, eds. Debra J. Pepler and Kenneth H. Rubin. Hillsdale, NJ: Lawrence Erlbaum.

Osgood, D. Wayne, Janet K. Wilson, Patrick M. O'Malley, Jerald G. Bachman, and Lloyd D. Johnston. 1996. "Routine activities and individual deviant behavior." *American Sociological Review* 61:635–655.

Padilla, Felix M. 2003. "Becoming a gang member." In *In Their Own Words: Criminals on Crime*, ed. Paul Cromwell. Los Angeles: Roxbury.

Pampel, Fred C., and Rosemary Gartner. 1995. "Age structure, sociopolitical institutions, and national homicide rates." *European Sociological Review* 11:243–260.

Parrott, W. Gerrod. 2001. *Emotions in Social Psychology*. Philadelphia: Taylor & Francis.

Passas, Nikos. 1997. "Anomie, reference groups and relative deprivation." In *The Future of Anomie Theory*, eds. Nikos Passas and Robert Agnew. Boston: Northeastern University Press.

Paternoster, Raymond, and Paul Mazerolle. 1994. "General Strain Theory and delinquency: A replication and extension." *Journal of Research in Crime and Delinquency* 31:235–263.

Patterson, Gerald R., Barbara D. DeBaryshe, and Elizabeth Ramsey. 1992. "A developmental perspective on antisocial behavior." *American Psychologist* 44:329–335.

Pearlin, Leonard I. 1989. "The sociological study of stress." *Journal of Health and Social Behavior* 30:241–256.

Peeples, Faith, and Rolf Loeber. 1994. "Do individual factors and neighborhood context explain ethnic differences in juvenile delinquency?" *Journal of Quantitative Criminology* 10:141–157.

Peirce, Robert S., Michael R. Frone, Marcia Russell, and M. Lynne Cooper. 1994. "Relationship of financial strain and psychological resources to alcohol use and abuse: The mediating role of negative affect and drinking motives." *Journal of Health and Social Behavior* 35:291–308.

Philips, Julie A. 1997. "Variation in African-American homicide rates: An assessment of potential explanations." *Criminology* 35:527–559.

Piquero, Alex R., and Timothy Brezina. 2001. "Testing Moffitt's account of adolescence-limited delinquency." *Criminology* 39:353–370.

Piquero, Alex R., Zenta Gomez-Smith, and Lynn Langton. 2004. "Discerning unfairness where others may not: Low self-control and unfair sanction perceptions." *Criminology* 42:699–733.

Piquero, Nicole Leeper, and Miriam D. Sealock. 2000. "Generalizing general strain theory: An examination of an offending population." *Justice Quarterly* 17:449–484.

———. 2004. "Gender and general strain theory: A preliminary test of Broidy and Agnew's gender/GST hypotheses." *Justice Quarterly* 21:125–158.

Power, Mick, and Tim Dalgleish. 1997. *Cognition and Emotion.* East Sussex, UK: Psychology Press.

Pratt, Travis C., and Francis T. Cullen. 2000. "The empirical status of Gottfredson and Hirschi's general theory of crime." *Criminology* 38:931–964.

Pratt, Travis C., and Timothy W. Godsey. 2003. "Social support, inequality, and homicide: A cross-national test of an integrated theoretical model." *Criminology* 41:611–643.

Quicker, John. 1974. "The effect of goal discrepancy on delinquency." *Social Problems* 22:76–86.

Raine, Adrian. 1993. *The Psychopathology of Crime.* San Diego, CA: Academic Press.

———. 2002. "The biological bases of crime." In *Crime,* eds. James Q. Wilson and Joan Petersilia. Oakland, CA: ICS Press.

Rankin, Bruce H., and James M. Quane. 2002. "Social contexts and urban adolescent outcomes: The interrelated effects of neighborhoods, families, and peers on African-American youth." *Social Problems* 49:79–100.

Reskin, Barbara F., and Irene Padavic. 1999. "Sex, race, and ethnic inequality in the United State workplace." In *Handbook of the Sociology of Gender,* ed. Janet Saltzman Chafetz. New York: Kluwer Academic.

Robbers, Monica L.P. 2004. "Revisiting the moderating effect of social support on strain: A gendered test." *Sociological Inquiry* 74:546–569.

Roberts, Aki, and Gary LaFree. 2004. "Explaining Japan's postwar violent crime trends." *Criminology* 42:179–209.

Rosenbloom, Susan Rakosi, and Niobe Way. 2004. "Experiences of discrimination among African American, Asian American, and Latino Adolescents in an urban high school." *Youth & Society* 35:420–451.

Rosenfeld, Richard, and Steven F. Messner. 1991. "The social sources of homicide in different types of societies." *Sociological Forum* 6:51–70.

Ross, Catherine E. 2000. "Neighborhood disadvantage and adult depression." *Journal of Health and Social Behavior* 41:177–187.

Rowe, David C. 2002. *Biology and Crime.* Los Angeles: Roxbury.

Rutter, Michael. 1985. "Family and school influences on behavioural development." *Journal of Child Psychology and Psychiatry* 26:349–368.

Rutter, Michael, Henri Giller, and Ann Hagell. 1998. *Antisocial Behavior by Young People*. Cambridge, England: Cambridge University Press.

Sampson, Robert J. 2002. "The community." In *Crime,* eds. James Q. Wilson and Joan Petersilia. Oakland, CA: ICS Press.

Sampson, Robert J., and John H. Laub. 1993. *Crime in the Making*. Cambridge, MA: Harvard University Press.

Sampson, Robert J., and Janet Lauritsen. 1993. "Violent victimization and offending: Individual-, situational-, and community-level risk factors." In *Understanding and Preventing Violence,* Vol. 3, ed. A. J. Reiss Jr. Washington, DC: National Research Council.

Sampson, Robert J., Stephen W. Raudenbush, and Felton Earls. 1997. "Neighborhoods and violent crime: A multilevel study of collective efficacy." *Science* 277:918–924.

Saunders, Daniel G. 2002. "Are physical assaults by wives and girlfriends a major social problem?" *Violence Against Women* 8:1424–1448.

Savolainen, Jukka. 2000. "Inequality, welfare state, and homicide: Further support for the institutional anomie theory." *Criminology* 38:1021–1042.

Schreck, Christopher J., Bonnie S. Fisher, and J. Mitchell Miller. 2004. "The social context of violent victimization: A study of the delinquent peer effect." *Justice Quarterly* 21:23–47.

Shaffer, Jennifer N. 2003. *The Victim-Offender Overlap: Specifying the Role of Peer Groups*. Doctoral Dissertation, The Pennsylvania State University.

Sharp, Susan F., Toni L. Terling-Watt, Leslie A. Atkins, Jay Trace Gilliam, and Anna Sanders. 2001. "Purging behavior in a sample of college females: A research note on general strain theory." *Deviant Behavior* 22:171–188.

Shaver, Philip, Judith Schwartz, Donald Kirson, and Cary O'Connor. 2001. "Emotion knowledge: Further exploration of a prototype approach." In *Emotions in Social Psychology: Essential Readings,* ed. Gerrod Parrott. New York: Psychology Press.

Sherman, Lawrence W. 1993. "Defiance, deterrence, and irrelevance: A theory of the criminal sanction." *Journal of Research in Crime and Delinquency* 30:445–473.

———. 2000. "The defiant imagination: Consilience and the science of sanctions." Albert M. Greenfield Memorial Lecture, University of Pennsylvania, February.

———. 2002. "Fair and effective policing." In *Crime,* eds. James Q. Wilson and Joan Petersilia. Oakland, CA: ICS Press.

Sherman, Lawrence W., David P. Farrington, Brandon C. Welsh, and Doris Layton MacKenzie, eds. 2002. *Evidence-Based Crime Prevention.* London: Routledge.

Shoemaker, Donald J. 2000. *Theories of Delinquency.* New York: Oxford University Press.

Sigfusdottir, Inga-Dora, George Farkas, and Eric Silver. 2004. "The role of depressed mood and anger in the relationship between family conflict and delinquent behavior." *Journal of Youth and Adolescence* 33:509–522.

Simoni-Wastila, Linda, Grant Ritter, and Gail Strickler. 2004. "Gender and other factors associated with the nonmedical use of abusable prescription drugs." *Substance Use & Misuse* 39:1–23.

Simons, Ronald L., Yi-Fu Chen, and Leslie G. Gordon. 2003. "Incidents of discrimination and risk for delinquency: A longitudinal study of African American adolescents." Paper presented at the annual meeting of the American Society of Criminology, Chicago.

Simons, Ronald L., Yi-Fu Chen, Eric A. Stewart, and Gene H. Brody. 2003. "Incidents of discrimination and risk for delinquency: A longitudinal test of strain theory with an African American sample." *Justice Quarterly* 20:827–854.

Simons, Ronald L., Eric Stewart, Leslie C. Gordon, Rand D. Conger, and Glen H. Elder Jr. 2002. "A test of life-course explanations for stability and change in antisocial behavior from adolescence to young adulthood." *Criminology* 40:401–434.

Smith, Carolyn, and Terence P. Thornberry. 1995. "The relationship between childhood maltreatment and adolescent involvement in delinquency." *Criminology* 33:451–481.

Solomon, Robert C., ed. 2003. *What Is an Emotion? Classic and Contemporary Readings.* New York: Oxford.

Spielberger, C.D., G. Jacobs, S. Russell, and R.S. Crane. 1983. "Assessment of anger: The state-trait anger scale." In *Advances in Personality Assessment,* Vol. 2, eds. James N. Butcher and Charles D. Spielberger. Hillsdale, NJ: Lawrence Erlbaum.

Spielberger, C.D., E.C. Reheiser, and S.J. Sydeman. 1995. "Measuring the experience, expression, and control of anger." In *Anger Disorders: Definition, Diagnosis, and Treatment,* ed. H. Kassonove. Washington, DC: Taylor & Francis.

Stark, Rodney. 1987. "Deviant places: A theory of the ecology of crime." *Criminology* 25:893–909.

Steffensmeier, Darrell. 1983. "Organization properties and sex-segregation in the underworld: Building a sociological theory of sex differences in crime." *Social Forces* 61:1010–1132.

Taylor, John, and R. Jay Turner. 2002. "Perceived discrimination, social stress, and depression in the transition to adulthood: Racial contrasts." *Social Psychology Quarterly* 65:213–225.

Tedeschi, James T., and Richard B. Felson. 1994. *Violence, Aggression, and Coercive Actions.* Washington, DC: American Psychological Association.

Thaxton, Sherod, and Robert Agnew. 2004. "The nonlinear effects of parental and teacher attachment on delinquency: Disentangling strain from social control explanations." *Justice Quarterly* 21:763–792.

Thoits, Peggy A. 1995. "Stress, coping, and social support processes: Where are we? What next?" *Journal of Health and Social Behavior* (Extra Issue):53–79.

Thornberry, Terence P. 1987. "Toward an interactional theory of delinquency." *Criminology* 25:863–891.

———, ed. 1997. *Developmental Theories of Crime and Delinquency, Advances in Criminological Theory,* Vol. 7. New Brunswick, NJ: Transaction.

Thornberry, Terence P., Timothy O. Ireland, and Carolyn A. Smith. 2001. "The importance of timing: The varying impact of childhood and adolescent maltreatment on multiple problem outcomes." *Development and Psychopathology* 13:957–979.

Thornberry, Terence P., and Marvin D. Krohn. 2001. "The development of delinquency: An interactionist perspective." In *Handbook of Youth and Justice,* ed. Susan O. White. New York: Kluwer Academic.

Thornton, Timothy N., Carole A. Craft, Linda L. Dahlberg, Barbara S. Lynch, and Katie Baer. 2002. *Best Practices of Youth Violence Prevention.* Atlanta, GA: Centers for Disease Control and Prevention.

Tittle, Charles R. 1995. *Control Balance: Toward a General Theory of Deviance.* Boulder, CO: Westview.

Tolan, Patrick H., Deborah Gorman-Smith, David Henry, Kyu-suk Chung, and Marcy Hunt. 2002. "The relation of patterns of coping of inner-city youth to psychopathology symptoms." *Journal of Research on Adolescence* 12:423–449.

Topalli, Volkon, and Richard Wright. 2004. "Dubs and dees, beats and rims: Carjackers and urban violence." In *About Criminals,* ed. Mark Pogrebin. Thousand Oaks, CA: Sage.

Towns, Donna Penn. 1998. " 'Rewind the world!': An ethnographic study of inner-city African American children's perceptions of violence." *Journal of Negro Education* 65:375–389.

Tunnell, Kenneth D. 1992. *Choosing Crime.* Chicago: Nelson-Hall.

Turner, R. Jay, and William R. Avison. 2003. "Status variations in stress exposure: Implications for the interpretation of research on race, socioeconomic status, and gender." *Journal of Health and Social Behavior* 44:488–505.

Turner, R. Jay, Blair Wheaton, and Donald A. Lloyd. 1995. "The epidemiology of social stress." *American Sociological Review* 60:104–125.

Tyler, Tom. 1990. *Why People Obey the Law*. New Haven, CT: Yale University Press.

Uggen, Christopher. 2000. "Work as a turning point in the life course of criminals: A duration model of age, employment, and recidivism." *American Sociological Review* 67:529–546.

Umberson, Debra, Kristi Williams, and Kristin Anderson. 2002. "Violent behavior: A measure of emotional upset?" *Journal of Health and Social Behavior* 43:189–206.

Ury, William L. 1995. "Conflict resolution among the Bushmen: Lessons in dispute resolution." *Negotiation Journal* 11:379–389.

U.S. Department of Health and Human Services. 2001. *Youth Violence: A Report of the Surgeon General of the United States*. Washington, DC: U.S. Department of Health and Human Services.

Van Gundy, Karen. 2002. "Gender, the assertion of autonomy, and the stress process in young adulthood." *Social Psychology Quarterly* 65:346–363.

van Wilsem, Johan, Nan Dirk de Graaf, and Karin Wittebrood. 2003. "Cross-national differences in victimization: Disentangling the impact of composition and context." *European Sociological Review* 19:125–142.

Vowell, Paul R., and David C. May. 2000. "Another look at classic strain theory: Poverty status, perceived blocked opportunity, and gang membership as predictors of adolescent violent behavior." *Sociological Inquiry* 70:42–60.

Voydanoff, Patricia, and Brenda W. Donnelly. 1998. "Parents' risk and protective factors as predictors of parental well-being and behavior." *Journal of Marriage and the Family* 60:344–355.

Wallace, John M., Jr., Jerald G. Bachman, Patrick M. O'Malley, John E. Schulenberg, Shauna M. Cooper, and Lloyd D. Johnston. 2003. "Gender and ethnic differences in smoking, drinking and illicit drug use among American 8th, 10th and 12th grade students, 1976–2000." *Addiction* 98:225–234.

Wallace, Lisa Hutchinson, Justin W. Patchin, and Jeff D. May. 2005. "Reactions of victimized youths: Strain as an explanation of school delinquency." *Western Criminology Review* 6:104–116.

Walsh, Anthony. 2000. "Behavior genetics and anomie/strain theory." *Criminology* 38:1075–1108.

———. 2002. *Biosocial Criminology.* Cincinnati, OH: Anderson.

Warner, Barbara D., and Shannon K. Fowler. 2003. "Strain and violence: Testing a general strain theory model of community violence." *Journal of Criminal Justice* 31:511–521.

Warr, Mark. 1993. "Age, peers, and delinquency." *Criminology* 31:17–40.

———. 2002. *Companions in Crime.* Cambridge, England: Cambridge University Press.

Weisburd, David, and Elin Waring. 2001. *White-Collar Crime and Criminal Careers.* Cambridge, England: Cambridge University Press.

Wethington, Elaine. 2000. "Contagion of stress." *Advances in Group Processes* 17:229–253.

Wethington, Elaine, George W. Brown, and Ronald Kessler, C. 1995. "Interview measurement of stressful life events." In *Measuring Stress,* eds. Sheldon Cohen, Ronald C. Kessler, and Lynn Underwood Gordon. New York: Oxford University Press.

Wheaton, Blair. 1990. "Life transitions, role histories, and mental health." *American Sociological Review* 55:209–224.

———. 1996. "The domains and boundaries of stress concepts." In *Psychosocial Stress,* ed. Howard B. Kaplan. San Diego, CA: Academic Press.

Wheaton, Blair, Patricia Roszell, and Kimberlee Hall. 1997. "The impact of twenty childhood and adult traumatic stressors on the risk of psychiatric disorder." In *Stress and Adversity Over the Life Course,* eds. Ian H. Gotlib and Blair Wheaton. Cambridge, England: Cambridge University Press.

White, Helene Raskin, Erich W. Labouvie, and Marsha E. Bates. 1985. "The relationship between sensation seeking and delinquency: A longitudinal analysis." *Journal of Research in Crime and Delinquency* 22:197–211.

Wilkinson, Deanna L. 2002. "Decision making in violent events among adolescent males: An examination of sparks and other motivational factors." In *Rational Choice and Criminal Behavior,* eds. Alex R. Piquero and Stephen G. Tibbetts. New York: Routledge.

Wilson, James Q., and Richard Herrnstein. 1985. *Crime and Human Nature.* New York: Simon and Schuster.

Wilson, William Julius. 1987. *The Truly Disadvantaged.* Chicago: University of Chicago Press.

Winter, Greg. 2004. "Financial gap is widening for rich and poor schools." *New York Times,* October 6, A15.

Wright, Bradley R. Entner, Avshalom Caspi, Terrie E. Moffitt, and Phil A. Silva. 1999. "Low self-control, social bonds, and crime: Social causation, social selection, or both?" *Criminology* 37:479–514.

Wright, John Paul, and Francis T. Cullen. 2001. "Parental efficacy and delinquent behavior: Do control and support matter?" *Criminology* 39:707–736.

Wright, Richard T., and Scott H. Decker. 1997. *Armed Robbers in Action.* Boston: Northeastern University Press. F

Author Index

Cohen, Lawrence E., 157
Cohen, Sheldon, 51, 83
Colvin, Mark, 9, 21, 25, 41, 42, 55, 71, 72, 73, 78, 82, 112, 142, 180
Compas, Bruce E., 89, 91
Conduct Problems Prevention Research Group, 185
Conger, Rand D., 48, 80, 141, 157, 182
Connor-Smith, Jennifer K., 89, 91
Cooper, M. Lynne, 35
Cooper, Shauna M., 77, 135
Coordinating Council on Juvenile Justice and Delinquency Prevention, 174
Cordilia, Ann, 166
Cornish, Derek B., 30
Corwyn, Robert F., 142, 145
Cothern, Lynn, 146
Craft, Carole A., 174, 185
Crane, R.S., 30, 32, 39
Crawford, Anne, 36
Cromwell, Paul, 1, 98
Crowell, Nancy A., 174, 182
Crutchfield, Robert D., 72
Cullen, Francis T., 19, 20, 21, 22, 24, 30, 71, 72, 82, 94, 97, 99, 100, 101, 119, 120, 129, 149, 154, 171, 174, 180, 200
Currie, Elliott, 174
Curry, Aaron D., 161
Curry, David G., 45
Curry, John F., 55

D

Dahlberg, Linda L., 174, 185
Dalgleish, Tim, 35
Daly, Kathleen, 81, 139
DeBaryshe, Barbara D., 122
de Castro, Bram Orobio, 185
Decker, Scott H., 1, 2, 11, 17, 31, 45, 98
De Coster, Stacy, 15, 34, 78, 80, 82, 129, 130, 138
DeFronzo, James, 189
de Graaf, Nan Dirk, 163, 170
DeMaris, Alfred, 157
Demorat, Marllene, 185
Deng, Xiaogang, 166
Deschenes, Elizabeth Piper, 44
Dodge, Kenneth, 93
Dohrenwend, Bruce P., 9, 60, 83, 165
Donnelly, Brenda W., 80
Dornfeld, Maude, 135
Drass, Kriss A., 166, 171
Drinkwater, Matthew, 36
Duckett, E., 109
Dunaway, R. Gregory, 73, 80, 82, 129, 145
Duncan, Greg J., 142
Dutton, Donald G., 35

E

Earls, Felton, 154
Eitle, David J., 10, 11, 46, 55, 74, 82, 96, 99, 101, 102, 134, 140, 148, 149
Elder, Glen H., Jr, 48, 80, 121, 141, 157, 182
Elliott, Delbert S., 8, 42, 43, 44, 47
Ellison, Christopher G., 161
Esbensen, Finn-Aage, 44
Evans, T. David, 21, 71, 73, 80, 82, 95, 100, 101, 129, 145

F

Fabbro, David, 164
Farkas, George, 34, 35, 82, 135, 136, 137
Farnworth, Margaret, 132
Farrington, David F., 37, 120, 174
Felmlee, Diane, 131, 137
Felson, Marcus, 30, 31, 119
Felson, Richard, 97
Finch, Brian Karl, 161
Fishbein, Diana, 21
Fisher, Bonnie S., 25, 112
Fitzclarence, Lindsay, 186
Fleming, Zachary, 1
Forde, David R., 12
Fowler, Shannon K., 82, 161, 162
Fox, Greer Litton, 80, 147, 157
Frone, Michael R., 35

G

Gaarder, Emily, 134, 137, 138, 139, 141
Garfield, Sol L., 183
Gartner, Rosemary, 163, 170
Gates, Lynn Underwood, 51
Ge, Xiaojia, 80, 157
Gendreau, Paul, 174
Gettleman, Jeffrey, 16
Gibson, Chris L., 41, 82
Gilfus, Mary E., 139
Giller, Henri, 21, 99
Gilliam, Jay Trace, 10, 41, 135
Giordano, Peggy C., 73, 80, 112
Godsey, Timothy W., 82, 163, 164, 189
Goldstein, Arnold P., 183
Gomez-Smith, Zenta, 21, 95, 112
Gordon, Jennifer, 7, 35, 41, 54, 82, 100, 101, 131
Gordon, Leslie G., 35, 74
Gore, Susan L., 7, 15, 35, 41, 54, 82, 89, 91, 100, 101, 131
Gorman-Smith, Deborah, 89, 91, 137
Gottfredson, Michael R., 20,
Greenberg, David, 115
Greenberg, David F., 8, 78, 114, 115
Guerrero, Laura K., 88
Gunkel, Steven, 46, 82

Majors, Richard, 156
Manasse, Michelle, 136,
Marshall, Ineke Haen, 37
Martin, Jack K., 148
Marwell, Gerald, 118
Mattlin, Jay A., 91
Matza, David, 73
Maxwell, Shelia Royo, 11 ,43, 46, 71, 82, 162, 169
May, David C., 46, 132
May, Jeff D., 41, 55, 72, 74, 82, 134
Mayne, Tracy J., 32
Mazerolle, Paul, 5, 6, 21, 31, 34, 39, 41, 43, 46, 71, 80, 82, 83, 93, 95, 96, 99, 102, 100, 101, 102, 104, 159, 197, 199
McCall, Patricia, 157
McCarthy, Bill, 1, 55, 73, 74, 131, 132, 137
McClelland, Gary H., 93, 198
McCord, Joan, 174, 182
McCorkle, Richard C., 16
McLeod, Jane D., 145
McNeil, Donald G., Jr., 140
McNulty, Thomas, 147, 157
Melton, Heather C., 133, 134
Merton, Robert K., 7, 42, 43, 56, 144
Messerschmidt, James W., 8, 9, 73, 78, 115, 132, 156, 186
Messner, Steven F., 164, 166, 167, 171
Michaelson, Larry, 183
Miethe, Terance D., 16
Miller, Alan S., 43, 82, 96, 101
Miller, Jerome G., 158
Miller, J. Mitchell, 25, 112
Miller, Jody, 14, 44, 45, 134, 139
Miller, Joshua D., 20
Mirowsky, John, 133, 135, 136, 145
Moffitt, Terrie E., 8, 20, 42, 45, 73, 78, 107, 114, 117, 120, 121, 129
Moneta, G., 109
Moon, Byong Ook, 72, 82, 100, 101, 102, 136, 163, 169
Morash, Merry, 72, 82, 100, 101, 102, 136, 163, 169
Morgan, Rick L., 32
Morris, William N., 48, 88
Mullins, Christopher, 8, 11, 14, 73, 91, 132, 134, 138, 156, 186
Murnen, Sarah K., 130

N

Nalla, Mahesh K., 132
Neapolitan, Jerome L., 163, 166, 170, 171
Neergaard, Lauran, 14, 47, 91
Neighbors, Harold W., 74
Nyborg, Vanessa M., 55

O

O'Connor, Cary, 32
Ohlin, Lloyd, 6, 42, 43, 44, 56, 97
Olson, Jeffrey J., 2, 179
Olweus, Dan, 177
O'Malley, Patrick M., 77, 78, 135
Osgood, D. Wayne, 37, 78

P

Padavic, Irene, 147
Padilla, Felix M., 2
Pampel, Fred C., 170
Parker, Lee, 1
Parker, Shawna, 1
Parrott, W. Gerrod, 32, 33
Passas, Nikos, 165, 167
Patchin, Justin W., 41, 55, 72, 74, 82, 134
Paternoster, Raymond, 5, 43, 46, 82, 83, 95, 96, 99, 101, 102, 197
Patterson, Gerald R., 122
Payne, Gary L., 21, 71, 82, 95, 100, 101
Pearlin, Leonard I., 80, 89, 167
Peeples, Faith, 147
Peirce, Robert S., 35
Peters, Ardith A.R., 47, 62, 102
Petersen, David M., 78
Petersen, Ruth, D., 162
Philips, Julie A., 157
Pi, Yujin, 34, 35, 41, 82, 162
Piquero, Alex R., 6, 21, 31, 34, 39, 41, 80, 62, 82, 95, 100, 101, 112, 115, 159, 199
Piquero, Nicole Leeper, 16, 35, 41, 72, 82, 135, 136
Pitchford, Susan R., 72
Ponzetti, James J., Jr., 32
Pottieger, Anne E., 15
Power, Mick, 35
Pratt, Travis C., 20, 82, 163, 164, 189
Pugh, M.D., 112

Q

Quane, James M., 157
Quicker, John, 8

R

Radosevich, Marcia J., 71, 76
Raine, Adrian, 21
Ramsey, Elizabeth, 122
Rankin, Bruce H., 157
Raudenbush, Stephen W., 154
Rebellon, Cesar, 42, 82, 100, 112, 142, 147, 149
Regoli, Robert M., 78
Reheiser, E.C. 32
Reilly, Nora P., 48, 88
Reskin, Barbara F., 147
Richards, M.H., 109

Subject Index